SKOLT SAAMI DANCE

SERIES: DANCE IN THE 21ST CENTURY

Dance in the 21st Century features books by leading scholars offering concise and accessibly written introductions to contemporary dance styles circulating in the world today that reflect the critical insights of dance studies in the twenty-first century. Together, they offer introductory texts on dance practices that resist over-simplification and focus on complexity. Varied approaches of discovery allow readers to look into differences, including historicity, intersectionality, and transcultural dimensions of dance practices. A major goal of this series is to increase the accessibility of decolonizing and anti-racist epistemologies in the global contemporary dance landscape. These include critiques of outdated binaries such as "dance history" and "world dance," as well as problematic orientalist, nationalist, and elitist conceptions of dance that often persist in public discourses, structures of higher education and funding schemes, and cultural programming for dance around the world. By making these critical approaches available to wider audiences, this series forwards a socially engaged public humanities agenda and aims to spark contemporary dialogue among stakeholders in dance communities.

SERIES EDITORS:

Emily Wilcox

Thomas F. DeFrantz

Hanna Järvinen

SKOLT SAAMI DANCE

The Transformative Journey of Tradition, Resilience, and the Arctic Quadrille

Petri Hoppu and Marko Jouste

methuen | drama
LONDON • NEW YORK • OXFORD • NEW DELHI • SYDNEY

METHUEN DRAMA
Bloomsbury Publishing Plc, 50 Bedford Square, London, WC1B 3DP, UK
Bloomsbury Publishing Inc, 1385 Broadway, New York, NY 10018, USA
Bloomsbury Publishing Ireland, 29 Earlsfort Terrace, Dublin 2, D02 AY28, Ireland

BLOOMSBURY, METHUEN DRAMA and the Methuen Drama logo are trademarks of
Bloomsbury Publishing Plc

First published in Great Britain 2026

Copyright © Petri Hoppu and Marko Jouste, 2026

Petri Hoppu and Marko Jouste have asserted their right under the Copyright,
Designs and Patents Act, 1988, to be identified as Authors of this work.

Photograph © People's Artist of Uzbekistan, Kizlarkhon Dusmukhamedova

All rights reserved. No part of this publication may be: i) reproduced or transmitted in any form, electronic or mechanical, including photocopying, recording or by means of any information storage or retrieval system without prior permission in writing from the publishers; or ii) used or reproduced in any way for the training, development or operation of artificial intelligence (AI) technologies, including generative AI technologies. The rights holders expressly reserve this publication from the text and data mining exception as per Article 4(3) of the Digital Single Market Directive (EU) 2019/790.

Bloomsbury Publishing Plc does not have any control over, or responsibility for, any third-party websites referred to or in this book. All internet addresses given in this book were correct at the time of going to press. The author and publisher regret any inconvenience caused if addresses have changed or sites have ceased to exist, but can accept no responsibility for any such changes.

A catalogue record for this book is available from the British Library.

A catalog record for this book is available from the Library of Congress.

ISBN: HB: 978-1-3502-4942-4
PB: 978-1-3502-4941-7
ePDF: 978-1-3502-4943-1
eBook: 978-1-3502-4944-8

Series: Dance in the 21st Century

Typeset by Newgen KnowledgeWorks Pvt. Ltd., Chennai, India
Printed and bound in Great Britain

For product safety related questions contact productsafety@bloomsbury.com.

To find out more about our authors and books visit www.bloomsbury.com
and sign up for our newsletters.

CONTENTS

List of Figures and Music Examples viii
Foreword xiii
Acknowledgments xiv

1 Introduction 1
   What Are the Dance Activities That the Contemporary Skolt
      Saami Regard as Their Own? 2
   What Discourses Concern Dance in the Skolt Saami
      Community? 3
   What Is the Role and Significance of Dance in Keeping
      and Preserving the Skolt Saami Embodied Culture,
      Communities, and Society? 4

**PART ONE CONTEXTUALIZING SKOLT SAAMI
                STUDIES**

2 Saami and Their Homeland 13
   Saami Groups 14
   Culture and Society 15
   Colonialism and Decolonialism in Saami Area 19
   Nature, Geography, and the Challenges of Climate Change in
      Saami Area 21

3 Skolt Saami 25
   Migrant History of the Skolt Saami During the Twentieth Century 26
   Characteristics of Skolt Saami Culture 30
   Skolt Saami Representations in Research 31

4 Perspectives of Indigenous Studies 37
  Knowledge Construction 38
  Saami Research 40
  Indigenous Dance and Music Studies 42

PART TWO SKOLT SAAMI DANCE CULTURE UNTIL THE SECOND WORLD WAR

5 Dance-Loving Communities 47
  Pleasure of Dance 48
  Earliest Descriptions of Dancing among the Eastern Saami 50
  Features of Early-Twentieth-Century Skolt Saami Dance Culture 53

6 Dancing Year 57
  First Dancing Season, from Christmas to the Shrove 57
  Second Dancing Season, after Lent 62
  Minor Dancing Season during Festivities in Summer and Autumn 64

7 Skolt Saami Music 67
  Own and Shared Music Cultures 67
  Dance Songs 69
  Music Instruments and Instrumental Music 75

8 *Ka'drel* 81
  From the French Court to Northern Village Dances 81
  Dancing the *Ka'drel* 87
  Ka'drel Music 89

9 Other Dances and Games 93
  Šestjårkka and *Vosmerkka* 93
  Couple Dances 96
  Dances in Different Formations 101
  Games 104

PART THREE RECESSION AND RECOVERY

10 Obmutescence 115
  Dancing in New Settlements (1940s–50s) 115

Challenge of Modern Culture (1950–60s) 117
Changes and Confusion 120

11 Revitalization of Skolt Saami Dance and Music 123
Early Steps 124
"Dance-Boom" of Če'vetjäu'rr 126
Njeä'llem Folklore Group 129
Impact of the Russian Saami 130
Film Recordings of the *Ka'drel* and Other Dances 134

12 Taking Dances to the Stage 137
Performances Home and Abroad 137
New Music for the *Ka'drel* 140
Costumes Used on Stage 143

13 Skolt Saami Dance Culture in the 2000s 147
Contemporary Contexts of the *Ka'drel* 147
Ka'drel book 148

PART FOUR MEANINGS AND TURNING POINTS

14 Innovative and Inclusive Culture 153
Emerging Agency 154
Skolt Saami Identities 155
Cultural Appropriation and Stereotypes 157
Cultural Survival 161
Pleässjeei meer "Dancing People" Exhibition 2024 163

15 Conclusion: Revitalized and Retaken Dance Culture in the 2020s 167

Appendices 171
   Appendix 1: Comparison of Folk Quadrilles 171
   Appendix 2: Structures of Couple Dances 176
   Appendix 3: *Ainamilaadu* Structure 180
References 181
Index 195

FIGURES AND MUSIC EXAMPLES

Figures

- **1.1** Petri Hoppu having a lecture about Karelian and Skolt Saami dances at the seminar "Karjalasta kolttien maille" (From Karelia to the Skolt Saami Land) in Oulu, Finland, October 2024 9
- **1.2** The Skolt Saami music group Suõmmkar 10
- **2.1** Saami languages at the beginning of the twentieth century 14
- **3.1** Skolt Saami *sijdd*s in the Murman coastal area in Northwest Russia 26
- **3.2** Suõ'nn'jel *sijdd* in Pechenga in 1913 27
- **3.3** Paččjokk *sijdd* in Pechenga 27
- **3.4** Risttǩe'dd *sijdd* 28
- **3.5** The evacuation of the Skolt Saami from Pechenga to the eastern parts of the municipality of Inari after the Second World War 29
- **3.6** Skolt Saami 34
- **5.1** Saami from Luujäu'rr *sijdd* 51
- **5.2** A Skolt Saami girl 54
- **5.3** Mari Gauriloff 55
- **6.1** Riding with a *saan*-sled in Suõ'nn'jel, 1936 59
- **6.2** Playing a rope-game in Suõ'nn'jel, 1932 60

6.3	Teacher Hilja Vartiainen and Liisa Feodoroff in the winter of 1928–9 63
7.1	Utts Evvan or Evvan Semenoff (b. 1908) plays "Armonico Italiano"—accordion, 1938 77
7.2	Dancers shake hands with the accordion player after a dance 78
8.1	Square formation for eight dancers (black pin = male, white pin = female) 82
8.2	The *l'été* ("summer") figure of the quadrille dance, a print engraved by Lebas (1818) 84
8.3	*Ka'drel* dancing in Suõ'nn'jel 87
8.4	*Ka'drel* dancing in Če'vetjäu'rr in 1979 90
9.1a and b	*Šestjårkka* dancing in Če'vetjäu'rr in 1979 94
9.2	*Ainamilaadu* (Sowing of Buckwheat) 105
9.3a and b	The start figure of *Ainamilaadu*. As the dance progresses, women go through men's gate 106
11.1	Če'vetjäu'rr *ka'drel* group performing in Utsjoki in 1982 128
11.2a and b	Two articles describing Irja Jefremoff's work on revitalizing Skolt Saami dance 131
11.3	Grigori Koputoff with his accordion in Njeä'llem 132
11.4	Grigori Koputoff accompanying dance in Njeä'llem 132
11.5	Vaa'ssel (Vasili) Titoff plays a harmonica in a bus in the 1970s 133
11.6	Grigori Koputoff playing the mandolin with Martta Orttonen 133
12.1	Seman Jeffremoff and Grigori Koputoff playing harmonicas in Kaustinen Folk Music Festival in 1978 139
12.2	A musical notation of Če'vetjäu'rr Skolt *ka'drel* or Luujäu'rr *ka'drel* was published in *Sevettijärven kolttakatrilli* 142

12.3	The wedding festivities in Če'vetjäu'rr in the 1960s 143
12.4	Dancers at the Saami Soiree in 1973 144
12.5	Markus and Elina Moshnikoff dancing the quadrille and Sari Saxholm playing the accordion at the restaurant Peuralammen Paari in Če'vetjäu'rr, Inari, June 2018 145
12.6	Njeä'llem Folklore Group dances *Korobushka* in Njeä'llem, Inari, 1983 146
13.1	The cover of *Sevettijärven kolttakatrilli. Če'vetjääu'r ka'dre'l*, an instruction book for the Skolt *ka'drel* by Sari Saxholm, Minna Moshnikoff, and Mari Gauriloff 150
14.1	*Ka'drel* dancing in Njeä'llem during the 75-year anniversary of resettlement of Skolt Saami, August 25, 2024 158
14.2	*Ka'drel* dancers in Inari, 2014 159
14.3a and b	An overall view and dance costumes from the Skolt Saami dance exhibition Pleässjeei meer "Dancing People," March 13, 2024 164

Music Examples

1. *Vo sadu li v ogorode* 71
2. *Vo sadu li v ogorode* 71
3. *Mâid kuulak niõđ* 74
4. A Russian song *Yabloko* 74
5. An excerpt of *Miklai da Täđjjan* 75
6. *Jä'ǩǩem Feodoroff's Ka'drel* 79
7. *Mäšš viilljaž Meeđrai â'lǧǧ* 91
8. *Reeii Evvan â'lǧǧ* 92
9. *Šestjårkka* 98
10. *Vintjårkka*-melody (*Rom krenitsa*) performed by Grigori Koputoff with the harmonica 101

11 *Oira* performed by Grigori Koputoff with the harmonica 102
12 *Korobushka* performed by Grigori Koputoff with the harmonica 103
13 *Ripaska* performed by Grigori Koputoff with the harmonica 104
14 *Ainamilaadu* 109
15 *Okldu'na* performed by Skolt Saami dancers in 1979 110

FOREWORD

As a Skolt Saami, music and dance have always been part of how I experience the world. I grew up surrounded by singing, the sound of the accordion, and the rhythms of dance resonating at community gatherings. Among these dances, the *ka'drel* holds a special place in my heart. It is not only a quadrille—not only steps and figures—but also laughter, closeness, and the joy of moving together. It is the heartbeat of our people.

When I read the pages of this book, I hear those familiar sounds again. I see the circle of dancers, the sparkle in people's eyes when the music begins. For us, the *ka'drel* is a memory carried in the body and a promise that our culture continues. Even when much was taken from us—our lands, our language, our confidence—dance gave us strength and reminded us that we still belong together.

This book tells the story of how Skolt Saami dance has been preserved, revitalized, and continues to live. It is also a recognition of our voices and our creativity. As director of the Skolt Saami Museum *Ä'vv*, I am grateful that future generations can turn to this book and find both history and encouragement. But I also write as someone whose own feet have stepped the figures of the *ka'drel* and whose own voice has joined in the singing.

I hope that readers of this book will feel the vitality of Skolt Saami dance. For us, dance is, above all, alive, flowing in this very moment. When we dance the *ka'drel*, we carry forward the resilience of our ancestors and give our children joy and pride. That is why we are the "Dancing People."

Hanna-Maaria Kiprianoff
Director, Skolt Saami Museum *Ä'vv*

ACKNOWLEDGMENTS

This book project has been made possible through the generous support of the **Jenny and Antti Wihuri Foundation**, whose contribution we gratefully acknowledge.

We extend our heartfelt thanks to the **Skolt Saami institutions** that have supported and collaborated with us throughout this work. In particular, we wish to thank the **Skolt Saami Siida Council (Saa'mi siidsååbbar)**, **Skolt Saami Cultural Foundation**, and **Skolt Saami Museum** Ä'vv for their invaluable assistance, insights, and commitment to preserving and revitalizing Skolt Saami culture.

We are also deeply grateful to the **Giellagas Institute at the University of Oulu** and the **Oulu University of Applied Sciences** for their support and for providing a platform for interdisciplinary collaboration and research. These institutions also serve as the academic homes of the authors: **Marko Jouste** is affiliated with the Giellagas Institute, and **Petri Hoppu** with the Oulu University of Applied Sciences. We also gratefully acknowledge the support of the **Finnish Folk Music Institute**, whose archival resources and long-standing commitment to the documentation and promotion of traditional music and dance have been of great value to this research.

We wish to express our sincere appreciation to the many individuals who have contributed to this project through their expertise, encouragement, and collaboration. In particular, we thank **Irja Jefremoff**, **Heikki Laitinen**, and **Hanna-Maaria Kiprianoff** for their generous sharing of knowledge, archival materials, and fieldwork experience. Their contributions—ranging from expertise in Skolt Saami language and culture to long-standing engagement with traditional music and dance—have enriched this work in countless ways.

Special thanks go to **Kia Olin**, **Markus Juutinen**, and **Miika Lehtinen**, who have transcribed and proofread the Skolt Saami language in this publication.

Finally, we thank all the individuals and members of the Skolt Saami community who shared their knowledge, stories, and traditions with us through interviews and cooperation, especially **Anna Lumikivi, Elias Moshnikoff, Seija Sivertsen, Katri Jefremoff, Reino Fofonoff, Simo Jefremoff, Heini Wesslin, Terhi Harju, Anna-Katariina Feodoroff, Veikko Feodoroff, Sari Saxholm, Minna Moshnikoff,**

Erkki Lumisalmi, Eeva Nykänen, Tanja Telkkälä, Kauko Lietoff, Tauno Lietoff, Satu Moshnikoff, Riitta Feodoroff, Sirkka Hakkola, Aud Mathissen, Anja Hivand, Herluf Nymoen, Ahti Similä, and Vladimir Feodoroff. This book would not have been possible without your trust and generosity.

1 INTRODUCTION

This book explores the extraordinary role of dance within the Skolt Saami, a small indigenous group in the far north of Europe, offering fresh insights into broader themes such as the enduring impacts of colonization, the power of dance in defining cultural identity, and the evolving nature of dance research itself. The Skolt Saami, referred to as the "Dancing People" in this book, embody a unique cultural ethos where dance is not merely a social activity but also a defining element of their worldview. Unlike other Saami groups in Finland and Scandinavia, the Skolt Saami have woven dance deeply into their cultural fabric, reflecting resilience and adaptability in the face of historical challenges.

Central to this study is the traditional quadrille, *ka'drel*, which stands as both a cornerstone of Skolt Saami identity and a vibrant, living tradition. This book highlights how dance has remained a dynamic force in Skolt Saami life—rooted in the past, yet continually evolving. Beyond its historical significance, dance now serves as a bridge to the present, embracing various forms of cultural transmission that reshape how traditions are understood and practiced today.

By situating Skolt Saami dance in a historical and contemporary context, this book challenges the notion of tradition as merely preserving a distant past. Instead, it portrays dance as an adaptive medium that continues to thrive, connecting the Skolt Saami's rich history with their present and future. This approach underscores why the story of the "Dancing People" matters—not just as an ethnographic account but also as a lens through which to view the dynamic interplay of culture, identity, and resilience in an ever-changing world. The book analyzes various aspects of dance in the Skolt Saami culture: dance as a movement, accompanying music, costumes, and dance situation, its rules and cultural significance in the historical context. These elements are related, and they are crucial in understanding how dance situations are constructed. Dance is not a separate phenomenon, but musical accompaniment, dress, space, and the historical and geographical contexts create necessary conditions for an activity to be called dancing.

When studying the dance and music cultures of the Saami people, the question of how to define dance and music as concepts inevitably comes up. Historically, Western scholars have examined the Saami culture through Western concepts and claimed that the Saami have not had their own "original" dance culture, since all dancing has been interpreted as merely borrowing of the neighboring cultures. Moreover, the perception of dance being absent among the Saami likely reflects the narrow view of outside observers, because the Saami apparently did not have couple-based dance forms (man-woman) common in other parts of Western and Northern Europe before the end of the nineteenth century. A similar idea can also be found in Henrik Gabriel Porthan in the eighteenth century, when he wrote in his doctoral thesis that the Eastern Finns did not dance at all and that the Western Finns had learned to dance from the Swedes.[1] However, documents about dance in Finland date back centuries before Porthan's time, highlighting significant differences in how dance is perceived.

The perspective of this book is limited in time from the latter half of the nineteenth century. However, the book considers the fact that the dance culture of the Skolt Saami at the turn of the nineteenth and twentieth centuries did not emerge spontaneously, nor was it solely influenced by external sources. Although earlier dancing is not covered in this study—and it would be challenging in any case due to the paucity of documentation—its existence is self-evident, and it must have influenced later developments. The roots of the Skolt Saami dancing people go deeper than just in modern culture.

The main research questions of this study are discussed in the following sections.

What Are the Dance Activities That the Contemporary Skolt Saami Regard as Their Own?

The first question covers the aspects of dance as practice and movement forms at different points in history. It also addresses the acceptance of shared cultural activities and the openness to receive new ones, which have characterized Skolt Saami communities throughout recorded history. The communities have never lived in complete isolation from the outside world; their original homelands lay at a culturally diverse crossroads where peoples of varied ethnic and linguistic backgrounds—along with merchants, fishermen, and state officials—converged,

---

[1] Henrik Gabriel Porthan, "De Poësi Fennica" (PhD diss., Regia Academia Aboensis [Royal Academy of Turku], 1766), 77.

most often arriving from the east and southeast. This influence is evident in local dance culture.

However, the dances—particularly quadrille, *ka'drel*—have not just been "copied" from foreigners but have also been indigenized, "Skolt Saamized": they have been adapted to the local culture and the seasonal cycle of the communities. Thus, the dances are not seen as a collection of external influences, but following the principles of dance anthropology, ethnomusicology, and cultural anthropology, they are studied as an integral part of the ever-changing web of cultural activities.

What Discourses Concern Dance in the Skolt Saami Community?

The second question focuses on various forms of communication concerning dance. This includes two parts. We must keep in mind that the primary "language" or "media" of dance is the movement itself, both expressing individuality and interaction. As it is a nonverbal, embodied form of communication, studying it is challenging. This is also linked to the other aspect of dance as the accompanying music is similarly a nonverbal activity. Both are experienced, learnt, and operated mainly by "doing," not discussing it.

When these are discussed in verbal form, they represent various other aspects, like the social organization of dance. It offers us contemporary experiences, memories, hopes, and wishes, as well as more analytical thinking of the role and meaning of the dance. The question, how dance is talked about, offers us more sources on understanding the dance and its role in the Skolt Saami community throughout the historical period of our investigation. This is highly important as it is a part of how Skolt Saami's own narrative of dance is formulated. Moreover, on the other end of this communicational line are the Skolt Saami writings of dance, especially the recent guidebook *Sevettijärven kolttakatrilli*.[2] Besides a general description of *ka'drel*, it functions as a defining normative aspect of dance, like names for the various dance figures, describing figures and transcribed examples of dance music.

Interestingly, when it comes to other Saami groups in Finland or Scandinavia, one rarely includes dance in discourses surrounding them. An often-repeated narrative in the Nordic countries has been that the Saami do not have their own dance culture at all. However, the situation is different for the Skolt Saami because they themselves emphasize the importance of dance in their communities in their narratives, and the people who visited them and lived in the same regions have

---

[2]Sari Saxholm, Minna Moshnikoff, and Mari Gauriloff, *Sevettijärven kolttakatrilli. Če'vetjääu'r ka'dre'l* (Inari: Sámi Duodji, 2022).

also done the same. The image of the Skolt Saami as a dancing people has been created for more than a hundred years, and at the same time their mutual talk about dance has always been positive and encouraging to dance. For other Nordic Saami groups, the history and contemporary practices of dance are yet to be re-interpreted by present-day perspectives.

What Is the Role and Significance of Dance in Keeping and Preserving the Skolt Saami Embodied Culture, Communities, and Society?

The third question combines embodied and discursive dimensions shifting focus to meanings of dance. The meanings of dance emerge in the activity itself and in the discussion about dance. The levels of discourse and embodiment are not independent of each other but are shaped by mutual interaction. Through them, dance becomes a solid and constructive part of culture and society, as well as people's identity. For the Skolt Saami, a central part of the process of giving meaning is the strong symbolic position of the *ka'drel* in the culture. Interestingly, however, in the twenty-first century, other dances have clearly faded into the background, when the *ka'drel* has emerged as a central and explicitly recognized symbol of identity.

The processes of inclusion and exclusion, through which the people entitled to dance are determined, are also a key part of the meaning of dance. At these intersections of discourses and activities, solutions have varied in many ways over time and are driven by historical, social, cultural, and political factors. The dance has been the subject of continuous negotiations, and in this process individuals and communities have sought to define their identities in situations where the existence of the entire Skolt Saami culture has been threatened.

The Skolt Saami have sought a balance between openness and protection of their dance culture. Historically, they have been willing to adopt external dance influences and share their own dances with others; on the other hand, they have recognized the contemporary threats of cultural appropriation that total openness exposes them to. Negotiations on these issues have also been long-term, and they continue even today.

The book emphasizes a variety of source materials. However, the research of the history of Skolt Saami dance is challenging, as the source material is inconsistent in regarding different dances as well as local dance activities, cultural contexts, and time periods. The complexity of the general history of the Skolt Saami and the whole region of the Murman coast in the border area of Russia, Norway, and Finland offers an uneven number of sources of different localities. A special feature is that there are a limited number of contemporary sources. These are mainly outsiders' descriptions of the events they have seen and experienced. Although outsides may lack an understanding of the Skolt Saami culture—and the interpretations may sometimes be biased—they serve as witnesses to an event. Contemporary descriptions exist practically of only two dances, *ka'drel* and *Ainamilaadu*. In addition to this, our research has revealed up to fifteen different dances that have been in use during the twentieth century by the Skolt Saami. An important source of material consists of interviews of the Skolt Saami conducted between the 1950s and the 1970s—contemporary for that time while also serving as testimonies of the past by individuals who lived during the late nineteenth and early twentieth centuries. In them, the Skolt Saami describe the actual dancing culture and reminisce about dancing before the Second World War as well as performing songs, which were used to accompany dancing. There are also historical photographs from at least 1913 onward. A selection of these reveals the clothing used while dancing, as well as dance occasions and dance postures. However, the first film recordings from which the dance figures and movement can be observed are only from the 1970s.

Based on these sources, we have attempted to build a description of the Skolt Saami dance culture during the twentieth and early twenty-first centuries. We have combined contemporary sources and historical dance, but in a majority of different dances, we must resort to later sources and state that historical dance has most likely also followed these models. This is due, first, to the fact that the Skolt Saami did not themselves document materials related to dance in the early twentieth century, and the recorded information—for example, recordings and photographs—are all made by outside researchers. Although the dance was already considered a special and interesting cultural feature in the 1930s, it was not recorded comprehensively.

Naturally, this does not mean that the Skolt Saami do not have a perspective on its own culture and history. In some cases, history opens a window through which the indigenous voice can be heard. For example, recordings discovered from the Bolshevik occupation of the Pechenga area in 1920 highlighted the Skolt Saami's account of the historical events.[3] Correspondingly, there are scattered sources pertaining to the Skolt Saami dance culture. An interesting material is found from a local journal called *Sää'moddâz*, in which the members of the Skolt Saami community write about culture and activities around dancing during the 1970s and 1980s.

By combining different source materials from different periods, we have tried to create a description of the Skolt Saami dance culture during the twentieth and

---

[3] Marko Jouste, "Skolt Saami Leu'dd: Tradition as a medium of individual and collective remembrance." In *The Sámi World*, ed. Sanna Valkonen, Áile Aikio, Saara Alakorva, and Sigga-Marja Magga (London: Routledge, 2022), 59–67.

early twenty-first centuries. The very fact that the Skolt Saami dance is the central focus presents a new avenue for research, as it is a phenomenon that is yet to be comprehensively studied. In addition to cultural studies and historical methods, our research is also based on Saami research and indigenous research, both of which emphasize a method of working with the community. This incorporates various methods of acquiring information. We have gathered information from the Skolt Saami people through interviews, which is significant given the limited number of earlier interviews focusing on dance. Naturally, personal and experiential information from the first half of the twentieth century are no longer available. However, the memory of current generations goes back to the 1950s. This era is not extensively explored in archival interviews, even though they are dated close to this time. In addition, historical interviews from archives provide significant information about dance before the Second World War and form an important part of this research. The interviewees are part of the Skolt Saami community, and bringing their voices for the use of modern generations is meaningful.

These interviews from the 1950s to the 1970s correspond to a period known for its crucial impact on Saami traditional knowledge and Saami languages, due to the disruption of knowledge transmission from older to younger generations. This was due to various reasons, of which the most significant is the introduction of a boarding school system in the Saami area, thus sending the children away from their parents during the school years.[4] General politics for the minorities were governed by a principle of a process of cultural acculturation, in which the dominant Finnish culture was hoped to replace the Saami culture and language. Furthermore, the 1960s witnessed a vast cultural change in Finland from a rural way of life to urbanization and educating the new generation for modern professions. However, the same period is also known for extensive linguistic recording activities, archival programs, and vast archive collections.[5] From today's perspective, it seems contradictory that the tradition holders were interviewed thoroughly while their main audience, the Saami children, were not present in learning the culture and strengthening the language. One can argue that the idea or the need of using archive materials supplementing the "natural" transfer of cultural heritage becomes an issue only in this period.

However, it was the same "boarding-school generation" that began to develop the modern Saami society and promoted the Saami national awakening, bringing

---

[4]Veli-Pekka Lehtola, *Saamelaiset suomalaiset – kohtaamisia 1896–1953* (Helsinki: SKS, 2012), 411, 453, 457.
[5]Marko Jouste, "Saamelaismusiikin tallennus Suomessa," in *Kohtaaminen – Gávnnadeapmi*, ed. Marko Jouste (Inari: Sámi Museum – Saamelaismuseosäätiö & Yhteispohjoismainen joikuarkistoprojekti, 2007), 27–35; see Pekka Sammallahti, *Vuõ'lǧǧe jåå'tted ooudâs*. Edited by Marko Jouste, Miika Lehtinen, and Markus Juutinen. Publications of the Giellagas Institute vol. 16 (Oulu: University of Oulu, 2021).

forward the active aim to develop, strengthen, and revitalize Saami cultures.[6] Modern culture also utilized the founding of new Saami art organizations, publishing companies, media, and festivals. New recording technologies (reel-to-reel tapes, C-cassettes) enabled recording activities not only for "academic" professionals but also for "ordinary" people. This opportunity was often utilized in Saami communities. Furthermore, the impact of the Yle Sápmi (founded in 1973) is notable as the radio work led to the creation of a sound archive in Inari. The revitalizing Skolt Saami dance was part of this process, and people used modern tools such as radio announcements to know the time and location of the dance group's next gatherings. Despite this fact, however, the archive material has often been used to compensate for at least some of the consequences by repatriating them to the present generations. Many interviews are significant for this research, as we can often hear the only examples of certain dance songs or descriptions of dance occasions; additionally, our aim is to support the repatriation process for the Skolt Saami community.

In general, repatriation is a broad interdisciplinary concept that includes various topics, activities, and events. It not only includes Saami access to traditional knowledge in, for example, archives and museums, but is also more broadly connected to the governance of cultural heritage and involves cooperation between researchers and indigenous communities and institutions.[7]

In this research, we have worked together with the present-day members of the Skolt Saami community and also past Skolt Saami generations through archives. The research data is produced for both research and the community. In general, many aspects of the revitalization of Saami culture and the development of modern culture and society can be considered success stories when viewed in a broader context. This does not mean that there are no challenges, especially related to cultural and political rights and land use. However, the teaching of Saami languages continues to produce new language-proficient generations in Finland, and more people work with Saami culture than ever before. Saami music has grown to become a major part of both culture and economy, with around 500 albums of Saami music already published over the past fifty years. In the media, there are newspapers, radio, TV, and active coverage across the internet and social media.

It is notable that the Skolt Saami dance itself is a success story. A small community, subject to subjugation and discrimination, have preserved an unbroken oral tradition for 150 years. A shift from dancing only in the community to a modern dance culture began with the establishment of two dance groups in the early 1970s: The *Njeä'llem (Nellim) folklore group* and the *Če'vetjäu'rr ka'drel group*

---

[6]Veli-Pekka Lehtola, *Saamelaisten parlamentti. Suomen saamelaisvaltuuskunta 1973–1995 ja Saamelaiskäräjät 1996–2003* (Inari: Saamelaiskäräjät, 2005).
[7]See Eeva-Kristiina Nylander, *From Repatriation to Rematriation: Dismantling the Attitudes and Potentials Behind the Repatriation of Sámi Heritage* (Oulu: Giellagas Institute, Universitys of Oulu, 2023), 39–41.

worked actively both within and beyond the community in not only reviving and strengthening the dance culture but also performing to the outsiders to raise awareness about the unique Skolt Saami culture. In the twenty-first century, *ka'drel* has gained a new status in culture, and through dance, a new "positive" story of the Skolt Saami is told. As the pioneer of the modern Saami art, Nils-Aslak Valkeapää, wrote in 1971, the goal is to be "authentic but not museum-like."[8]

It is notable that the view of the past is largely built through people's verbal interpretations, thus offering a model of constructivist theory. The understanding of Skolt Saami culture, art, and history must be seen in the context of the informants. One could also reflect on Skolt Saami teacher and craftsman Heini Wesslin's idea that most of the knowledge and research of the Skolt Saami culture is from the outsiders' perspective and does not always reflect the insiders' experience and traditional knowledge.[9]

The authors of this book identify the issue, as they are not Skolt Saami but rather dance and music scholars from the Finnish academic world. Focusing on Skolt Saami experiences and narratives has been a conscious strategy, helping to avoid a strong confrontation between the dominant and indigenous cultures. The tension related to power between the researcher and the group under study can never be completely removed, but it can be reduced and changed by an ongoing dialogue between the researchers and the community as well as through research transparency, which has been an important part of the current study. The focus on ethical questions and legal issues is vital while working with indigenous material, which highly includes culture-sensitive information and contains a significant amount of culturally and personally delicate data. The research has been conducted in accordance with the guidelines provided by the Ethical Guidelines for Research Involving the Sámi People in Finland (2024).[10] A significant portion of this work is linked to questions on the rights to the material gathered from indigenous peoples. On a general level, this is linked to the question of indigenous people's rights to their own cultural heritage. These themes have been emphasized in the work of UNESCO and the World Intellectual Property Organization, and they are part of both national and international agreements concerning the rights of the Saami people.

The authors have been interviewing Skolt Saami for several years on their own, and in March 2023, they also made a joint field trip to Inari. The interviews have been conversational in nature, with the authors aiming for open interaction with

---

[8] Nils-Aslak Valkeapää, *Terveisiä Lapista* (Helsinki: Otava, 1971).
[9] Heini Wesslin, "Ajatuksia berliiniläisen MEK-museon tutkimusprojektista" (paper presented at the Sámi National Day Seminar in Oulu, February 6, 2024).
[10] Lydia Heikkilä, Rauna Kuokkanen, Veli-Pekka Lehtola, Päivi Magga, Sigga-Marja Magga, Janne Näkkäläjärvi, Sanna Valkonen, and Pirjo Kristiina Virtanen, *Ethical Guidelines for Research Involving the Sámi People in Finland* (Oulu: Oulun yliopisto, 2024). Available online: https://urn.fi/URN:NBN:fi:oulu-202405294076 (accessed June 15, 2024).

the interviewees. During the interviews, for example, recordings of dances from previous decades—most of which are completely unfamiliar to the current Skolt Saami—have been shared and discussed. In this way, it has been possible to convey information about existing dance materials through the interviews.

Furthermore, in the spring of 2023, the authors were asked to plan an exhibition of Skolt Saami dance in the Skolt Saami Museum Ä'vv located in the village of Neiden in Norway. The exhibition, which opened in March 2024, represented an initial step in repatriating the traditional knowledge that has been obtained for the Skolt Saami community in Finland and Norway. Moreover, as a musician, Jouste is the founding member of the Skolt Saami music group Suõmmkar, which has performed and recorded material based on archive recordings including dance songs. In 2019, Jouste was hired by the Sámi Education Institute in Inari to give a course on Skolt Saami dance music. During the course, accompanying *ka'drel* by some of the traditional dance songs were tested, marking a steps in the development and modernization of dance accompaniment. There is an openness and willingness to redefine dance and explore new ways of dancing. Modernizing is not seen as a threat but as an opportunity to engage new generations of Skolt Saami. The small size of the community makes each activity very meaningful, and attracting young people to participate is important. Hoppu's contribution to Skolt

FIGURE 1.1. Petri Hoppu having a lecture about Karelian and Skolt Saami dances at the seminar "Karjalasta kolttien maille" (From Karelia to the Skolt Saami Land) in Oulu, Finland, October 2024.

Source: Photograph by Marko Jouste.

FIGURE 1.2. The Skolt Saami music group Suõmmkar. The author Marko Jouste is the second from the left.

Source: Photograph by Terhi Tuovinen.

Saami dance is also notable and consists of teaching and consulting activities. He has studied archival information about dance in depth and shared this information with the Skolt Saami. He has worked as a consultant in projects related to the Skolt Saami dance, for example, in the publication of the *ka'drel* book. He has also tried to bring out little-known and almost lost dances, of which, however, there is archival information and video recordings. In this way, he has inspired the Skolt Saami themselves to take control of their own dance material and use it in a way that suits the community. This book also gathers the authors' scientific and archive work consisting of various articles and teaching.

PART ONE

CONTEXTUALIZING SKOLT SAAMI STUDIES

In this part, the language groups, historical living environment, society, and culture of the Saami people, the indigenous peoples of northern Europe, are introduced. Special attention is paid to the Skolt Saami, who are one of Finland's three Saami groups but whose culture differs in many ways from the other two groups. In addition, the perspectives and approaches of indigenous studies, especially regarding dance and music, as well as the position of Saami studies as part of a wider field of research will be reviewed.

2 SAAMI AND THEIR HOMELAND

The Saami are an indigenous people living in Scandinavia, northern Fennoscandia, and the Kola Peninsula. The land of the Saami is located on the territories of Norway, Sweden, Finland, and Russia.[1] During the Middle Ages, the Saami inhabited wide areas as compared to the present situation, covering considerably larger areas of modern Scandinavia and parts of northwestern Russia. In historical sources, the Saami are often referred to as Phinnoi, Scrithifinoi, or Lapps. The current number of the Saami is estimated to be about 60,000–100,000 people. However, due to many centuries of forced assimilation in the above-mentioned four countries, it is difficult to estimate the exact number of the Saami. In the Nordic countries, there are national Saami parliaments, which have a representative role in the administration of the Saami areas. In these countries there is also a system of schooling and higher education for the Saami.[2]

The Saami are recognized as an indigenous people in Norway, Sweden, Finland, and Russia. The indigenous status of the Saami is secured in the constitution in Finland (1995/1999) and Norway (1988). In 1977, the Swedish Parliament recognized the Saami as an indigenous people; in addition, the Swedish Form of Government generally provides for the right of ethnic, linguistic, and religious minorities to preserve and

---

[1] The concept *Sápmi* is often used to define the area where the Saami live. However, as the word *Sápmi* comes from the North Sámi language and the theme of this book focuses on Skolt Saami, we do not use North Sámi concepts but more general terms such as "Saami area" or "Saami region." For similar reasons, we prefer the spelling *Saami* over *Sámi*, following the recommendation of The Giellagas Institute for Saami Studies at the University of Oulu.

[2] Veli-Pekka Lehtola, *Saamelaiset – historia, yhteiskunta, taide* (Inari: Kustannus-Puntsi, 2015), 10; Pekka Sammallahti, "Saamelaisten juuret," in *Ennen muinoin: Miten menneisyyttämme tutkitaan*, Tietolipas 180, ed. Riho Grünthal (Helsinki: SKS, 2004), 168; Christian Carpelan, "Saamelaisten esihistoriaa ja saamelaisarkeologiaa," in *Lappi 4 – Saamelaisten ja suomalaisten maa*, ed. Martti Linkola (Hämeenlinna: Karisto, 1985), 36; Marko Jouste, "The Historical Skolt Saami Music and the Two Types of Melodic Structures in Leu'dd-Tradition," *Folklore–Electronic Journal of Folklore* 68 (2017): 69–84, 69.

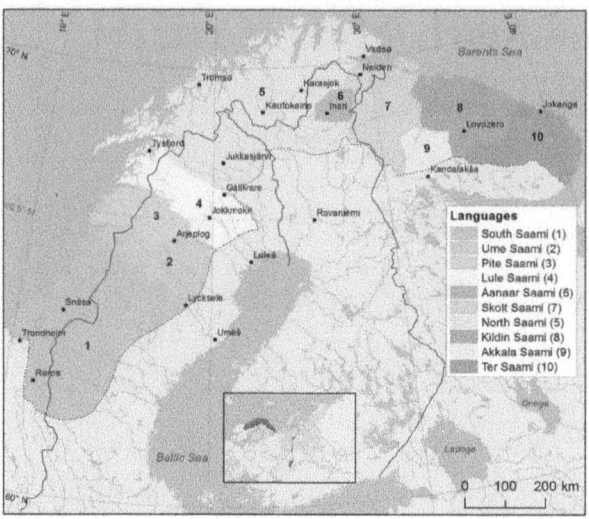

FIGURE 2.1. Saami languages at the beginning of the twentieth century.

Source: Rantanen, T., H. Tolvanen, M. Roose, J. Ylikoski, and O. Vesakoski (2022), "Best Practices for Spatial Language Data Harmonization, Sharing and Map Creation – A Case Study of Uralic," *PLoS ONE* 17(6): e0269648. Available online: https://doi.org/10.1371/journal.pone.0269648; Rantanen, T., O. Vesakoski, J. Ylikoski, and H. Tolvanen (2021), "Geographical Database of the Uralic Languages (v1.0) [Data set]," *Zenodo*. Available online: https://doi.org/10.5281/zenodo.4784188, https://sites.utu.fi/urhia/language-maps/, https://commons.wikimedia.org/w/index.php?curid=144643516 (CC BY 4.0).

develop their cultural and social life. In the Nordic countries, during the period after the Second World War, the Saami have established a modern Saami society with all main components of cultural and political governance, for example, Saami parliaments, Saami education, Saami culture organizations. At the level of the Russian Federation, there are several laws and regulations concerning the Kola Saami, such as the 1993 constitutional provision guaranteeing the rights of indigenous peoples in accordance with international agreements ratified by Russia, as well as the 1999 provision guaranteeing the rights of minority indigenous peoples within the federation.[3]

Saami Groups

Historically, the Saami can be divided into several groups according to language, source of livelihood, and the degree to which local environmental characteristics

---

[3]Irja Seurujärvi-Kari, "Alkuperäiskansatutkimus, alkuperäiskansaliike ja saamelaiset," in *Saamentutkimus tänään*, ed. Irja Seurujärvi-Kari, Petri Halinen, and Risto Pulkkinen (Helsinki: SKS, 2011), 21.

have influenced their cultures. Linguistically, Saami is currently divided into nine main languages, each with its own dialects. Over centuries, these languages have diverged so much that, for example, a North Saami speaker would struggle to understand Skolt Saami or Aanaar Saami without difficulty. Regionally, the largest language group is the North Saami, and it is also the strongest literary language, although Southern, Lulejan, Aanaar (Inari), Skolt, and Kildin Saami have their own literary languages as well. In Finland, there are three main Saami languages: Aanaar Saami, Skolt Saami, and North Saami.[4]

In a historical and cultural sense, there is a pronounced difference between the Western and Eastern Saami. The Western Saami have had connections with Scandinavian and Finnish cultures, as well as with the Lutheran Church. The Eastern group, to which the Skolt Saami belong, is mostly influenced by Russian and Karelian cultures, as well as by the Orthodox Church.

The Eastern Saami cultures in Russia can be divided into three main groups by language and cultural characteristics. However, due to the radical cultural and social changes in this area, especially during the Soviet era, definitions used here refer mainly to the cultural situation in the first half of the twentieth century. The traditional Ter Saami areas are in the easternmost part of the Kola Peninsula. Kildin and Akkala Saami have inhabited the central part and Skolt Saami the westernmost part in the border area of Russia, Finland, and Norway. The Akkala Saami language became extinct in the early 2000s. In Finland, there are also the Aanaar Saami people, belonging to the Eastern Saami group but having historically been under Swedish and Finnish, as well as Lutheran, dominance.[5]

Culture and Society

The Saami culture, rich and diverse, is intricately tied to the northern regions of Scandinavia and Russia, spanning across Norway, Sweden, Finland, and Russia's Kola Peninsula. Despite the shared geographical area, Saami culture has developed unique characteristics influenced by the varied environments and historical contexts within these countries. Language is a crucial part of Saami identity, but it has faced significant suppression, particularly during periods of forced assimilation in all Nordic countries and Russia. All Saami languages are

---

[4]Lehtola, *Saamelaiset*, 13.
[5]See Tero Mustonen and Kaisu Mustonen, *Eastern Saami Atlas* (Tampere: Snowchange, 2011), 29–52; Marko Jouste, "Katsaus Venäjän saamelaisten musiikkiperinteiden keräykseen ja tutkimukseen," in *Song and Emergent Poetics*, ed. Pekka Huttu-Hiltunen, Frog, Karina Lukin, and Eila Stepanova, Runolauluakatemian julkaisuja, no. 18, Juminkeon julkaisuja, no. 119 (Kuhmo: Juminkeko, 2014), 361–2; Elisabeth Scheller, "The Sámi Language Situation in Russia," in *Ethnic and Linguistic Context of Identity: Finno-Ugric Minorities*, ed. Riho Grünthal, Magdolna Kovács. Uralica Helsingiensia 5. (Helsinki: Société Finno-Ougrienne 2011), 79–95.

minority languages in countries where they are spoken. UNESCO has classified all of them as endangered languages. In addition to language, significant identity markers have been handicraft—including clothing—along with music, and, with Skolt Saami and Saami in Russia, dance as well.

Efforts to revive and protect Saami languages have been increasing during the past decades, with language education and media playing important roles. In Finland, these revitalization efforts began mainly with North Saami language workers already in the 1970s but soon expanded to include other Saami languages as well. The revitalization of the Aanaar (Inari) Saami language and culture has been an internationally recognized process; it is documented in *Revitalising Indigenous Languages: How to Recreate a Lost Generation* by Marja-Liisa Olthuis, Suvi Kivelä, and Tove Skuttnab-Kangas.[6] Over the past decade, these efforts were also addressed to Skolt Saami.

It is noteworthy that archive material can also have a strong supportive role for present-day Saami generations in revitalizing and strengthening their local culture. Furthermore, the themes and actions of both language and culture revitalization were the focus of the project "Skolt Saami Memory Bank - A Pilot for Data Management and Revitalization of Endangered Skolt Saami Music, Language, and Culture" funded by the Academy of Finland and led by Marko Jouste (2016–18). The idea of the project was to create a path of repatriation between the Saami Culture Archive and Skolt Saami community.[7] The impact of Saami cultural studies and ethnomusicological research on culture revitalization can also be observed in the case of Aanaar Saami livđe. Jouste's doctoral thesis *Tullâčalmaaš kirdâččij* ("The One Who Flew with the Fire-Eyes") was published in 2011,[8] and since then the already active Aanaar Saami teachers and culture workers have included the Aanaar Saami livđe tradition as a part of their work in language nests and schools, as well as in materials used at school.

Besides culture and language, the traditional forms of livelihood have defined the essence of the Saami. Reindeer herding is perhaps the most iconic Saami livelihood, especially in Norway, Sweden, and Finland. In Russia, reindeer herding remains significant but has been heavily impacted by former Soviet policies and ongoing economic challenges. In addition to reindeer herding, the Saami have traditionally engaged in fishing, hunting, and small-scale farming. These activities

---

[6]Marja-Liisa Olthuis, Suvi Kivelä, and Tove Skutnabb-Kangas, *Revitalising Indigenous Languages: How to Recreate a Lost Generation* (Bristol, Buffalo, and Toronto: Multilingual Matters, 2013).
[7]See Marko Jouste, Markus Juutinen, Miika Lehtinen, Anna Lumikivi, and Hanna-Maaria Kiprianoff, "Sää'mǩiõl da kulttuur jeälltummuš Skolt Sää'm mosttbaŋkk - ha'ŋǩǩõõzzâst," *Dutkansearvvi dieđalaš áigečála* 2, no. 1 (2018): 11–16. Available online: https://www.dutkansearvi.fi/volume-2-issue-1-fi/ (accessed August 6, 2024).
[8]Marko Jouste, "Tullâčalmaaš kirdâččij – 'tulisilmillä lenteli'. 1900-luvun alun musiikkikulttuuri paikallisen perinteen ja ympäröivien kulttuurien vuorovaikutuksessa" (PhD diss., School of Social Sciences and Humanities, University of Tampere, 2011).

are adapted to the harsh Arctic and sub-Arctic environments of Saami region, with a deep respect for nature being a central tenet of Saami life. The modernization of reindeer herding began in the 1960s with the introduction of snowmobiles; since then, motorization has revolutionized the field.[9]

Saami craft tradition is an important cultural expression, and it has a particular connection to dance. It encompasses items made from natural materials like wood, bone, and reindeer hides. These crafts are both functional and artistic, often decorated with symbolic designs that reflect Saami heritage. Saami traditional clothing is perhaps the most visible part of the Saami culture in modern times; its position, therefore, is significant and recognized. Saami clothing is perceived as a tradition that connects individuals to the past generations and strengthens their identities. Saami groups have different names for their clothing: for example, in Finland, it is known as *gákti* in North Saami, *mááccuh* in Aanaar Saami, and *pihttâz* or *määccak̓* in Skolt Saami.[10] In addition to protecting and decorating the body, clothing also signifies communication, a way of expressing things that are important to the Saami. Saami craft researcher Sigga-Marja Magga states that Saami clothing can also be described as a kind of social performance, an act that includes the display of craftsmanship and aesthetics as well as a reading, an image conceived by the recipient of its message, where, in addition to the situation, the person's age, gender, and family background form a set of meanings.[11]

Saami clothing is characterized by a dominant color adorned with bands of contrasting colors, plaits, pewter embroidery, tin art, and often a high collar. Clothing traditionally includes a belt, shoes, and shoe bands, as well as a shawl of silk or wool. Accessories such as high collars, jewelry, gloves, pants, and hats are often used. The appearance of traditional clothing varies between different Saami groups. The basic shape and cut of the dress differ depending on the gender presentation and in some areas also depending on the wearer's age and marital status.[12]

---

[9]Vladislava K. Vladimirova, "'We are Reindeer People, We Come from Reindeer.' Reindeer Herding in Representations of the Sami in Russia.'" *Acta Borealia* 28, no. 1 (2011): 89–113. Available online: https://doi.org/10.1080/08003831.2011.575661 (accessed 15 August, 2024); Gabriel Kuhn, *Liberating Sápmi: Indigenous Resistance in Europe's Far North* (Oakland, CA: PM Press, 2020); Hanna Guttorm, "Becoming Earth: Rethinking and (Re-)Connecting with the Earth, Sámi Lands and Relations." In *Bridging Cultural Concepts of Nature: Indigenous People and Protected Spaces of Nature*, ed. Rani-Henrik Andersson, Boyd Cothran and Saara Kekki (Helsinki: Helsinki University Press, 2021). Available online: https://doi.org/10.33134/AHEAD-1-8 (accessed 15 August, 2024).
[10]Áile Aikio, "Gákti – sukujen puku," *Fáktalávvu* (2018). Available online: https://faktalavvu.net/2018/02/27/gakti-sukujen-puku/ (accessed August 15, 2024) ; *Say It in Saami*, 'Quick Guide to Saami Culture'. *YLE (The Finnish Broadcasting Company)* (2018). Available online: http://sayitinsaami.yle.fi/quick-guide-to-sami-culture/ (accessed August 15, 2024).
[11]Sigga-Marja Magga, "Nurinpäin käännetty gákti saamelaisen vastarinnan muotona," *Politiikka* 60 (2018): 260–4.
[12]Roman Kozakand, "Overview of Saami Costume," *Blog: Folk Costume & Embroidery* (2013). Available online: http://folkcostume.blogspot.com/2013/05/overview-of-saami-costume.html (accessed July 28, 2024).

Traditional clothing is an important cohesive identity symbol and "a way of being a Saami," and it has a particularly great significance in festive contexts. At baptisms, funerals, weddings, confirmations, and other solemn occasions, many Saami wear traditional clothing. Saami people regard their attire as an integral part of a cultural identity, and, therefore, it is emphasized that they should be worn only by those who understand and appreciate them.[13]

There are three Saami music traditions in Finland: Northern Saami, Aanaar Saami, and Skolt Saami; today, we find all these groups coming together, forming a contemporary Saami music culture in Finland and sharing the same stages at concerts and festivals. As Finland is in the border area of Northern and Eastern Saami cultures, it offers a possibility to examine the diversity and complexity of both the historical and present-day transnational Saami community. Traditional Saami music has been investigated since the late nineteenth century, and modern music acquired scientific interest already during the 1970s. More recent studies of modern Saami music[14] have focused mainly on the Saami culture in Norway, which is understandable since the Saami community in Norway is the largest and has a leading role, for example, in the number of artists and recordings of Saami music. However, the North Saami music is often considered as dominant form of the modern Saami music, which can lead to biased renditions.

Music also plays a complex role in cultural and political self-determination as well as in the politics of indigeneity in the process of building a transnational Saami community.[15] Within this process, Saami traditional music—especially the North Saami chant called "luohti (yoik)"—became a central national symbol of Saami culture already during the 1970s.[16] In the context of modern Saami music, various traditional forms of music can serve as elements inherited from the living traditions of different Saami localities, which are combined with modern music to create a novel, unprecedented fusion.

Contemporary Saami music culture can be seen as a local, national, transnational, and international phenomenon. Approximately five hundred albums of Saami music were released since 1960s in four countries (Finland, Norway, Sweden, and Russia). For a relatively small indigenous population, this is a significant amount,

---

[13]*Sámi Duodji*, "Puvut." Available online: https://www.samiduodji.com/puvut (accessed August 15, 2024); Lehtola, *Saamelaiset*, 15–17.

[14]See Thomas R. Hilder, *Sámi Musical Performance and the Politics of Indigeneity in Northern Europe* (London: Rowman & Littlefield, 2015); Annukka Hirvasvuopio-Laiti, "Gárddi luhtte lávddi ala - Poroaidalta esiintymislavalle. Saamelaiset elementit tenonsaamelaisessa musiikissa kolmen sukupolven aikana" (MA diss., Department of Music Anthropology, University of Tampere, 2008); Richard Wiren Jones-Bamman, "As Long As We Continue to Joik, We'll Remember Who We Are: Negotiating Identity and the Performance of Culture: The Saami Joik" (PhD diss., Department of Music, University of Washington, 1993). Available online: https://digital.lib.washington.edu/researchworks/items/22ed0e8e-f525-41f5-b071-16c0c9f3e4d1 (accessed August 6, 2024).

[15]Hilder, *Sámi Musical Performance*, 65.

[16]Lehtola, *Saamelaiset*, 169.

highlighting the role of music in cultural, political, and socio-economic life. Over the past decades, the Saami cultural sector has grown to be an important part of Saami society, and it is *modern Saami music*—born as a part of the national awakening of the Saami people in 1960s and 1970s—that is the most well-known product of Saami culture globally, with many globally acclaimed Saami artists.[17]

In Norway, Sweden, and Finland, Saami culture is increasingly recognized and celebrated, but this has not always been the case. These countries have historically tried to assimilate the Saami, leading to significant cultural loss. Today, as mentioned, there are Saami parliaments in Norway, Sweden, and Finland, which aim to preserve Saami culture and advocate for their rights. In addition, Skolt Saami have a special administrative organization called *Saa'mi siidsååbbar*, "Skolt Saami siida council" in Finland. It has a centuries-long continuity from the Russian era to monitor and promote the realization of the rights of the Skolt Saami and exist as the official representative of the Skolt Saami people.[18]

Despite these advancements, Saami culture still encounters challenges, including ongoing discrimination, pressures from land and resource exploitation, and the impacts of climate change on traditional livelihoods. In Russia, the situation is more precarious, with less institutional support for Saami cultural preservation and more significant economic pressures on their traditional ways of life.

Colonialism and Decolonialism in Saami Area

All Saami people have a complex history with colonialism, characterized by centuries of assimilation efforts, land dispossession, and cultural suppression by various colonial powers. Colonialism in Saami territories began with the expansion of Sweden, Norway, and Russia into the northern regions where the Saami traditionally lived. These colonial powers sought to assert control over land and resources, often at the expense of indigenous peoples, the Saami.[19]

---

[17]See Jones-Bamman, "As Long as We Continue to Joik, We'll Remember Who We Are," 268, 284–9; Marko Jouste, "Áillohaš ja uuden joiun synty," in *Minä soin – Mun čuojan. Kirjoituksia Nils-Aslak Valkeapään elämäntyöstä*, ed. Taarna Valtonena and Leena Valkeapää (Rovaniemi: Lapland University Press, 2017), 233; Jorma Lehtola, *Laulujen Lappi* (Inari: Kustannus-Puntsi, 2007), 279.

[18]Sonja Tanhua, "Kolttasaamelaisen kyläkokousjärjestelmän vaikuttamisen strategiat ja taktiikat 1920–1979," PhD diss., Faculty of Humanities, University of Oulu, 2023. Available online: https://urn.fi/URN:ISBN:9789526235745 (accessed August 15, 2025).

[19]Veli-Pekka Lehtola, "Sámi Histories, Colonialism, and Finland," *ARCTIC ANTHROPOLOGY* 52 (2015): 22–36 (25–6); Carl-Gösta Ojala, "East and West in Sápmi: – Borders and Identities in Sámi Historical Archaeology," *META – Historiskarkeologisk Tidskrift* (March 2021): 143–60 (148–52). Available online: https://doi.org/10.59008/meta.vi.10924 (accessed August 19, 2024).

One of the key aspects of colonialism experienced by the Saami was the imposition of cultural assimilation policies. Especially since the late nineteenth century, governments pursued a policy of forced assimilation, which aimed to eradicate indigenous languages and cultures in favor of a dominant culture. Saami children were often forcibly removed from their families and sent to boarding schools where they were prohibited from speaking their native languages or practicing their traditional customs.[20]

Land dispossession was another significant aspect of colonialism for the Saami. As colonial powers expanded their territories and sought to exploit natural resources such as timber, minerals, and, later, hydroelectric power, Saami lands were often encroached upon or outright seized. This disrupted traditional Saami ways of life, such as reindeer herding and fishing, and led to economic marginalization. Furthermore, colonialism brought about environmental degradation in Saami territories, as industrialization and resource extraction projects had adverse impacts on the natural environment that the Saami depended upon for their livelihoods.[21]

In recent decades, there has been a growing recognition of the historical injustices faced by the Saami due to colonialism. Efforts to address these injustices include initiatives aimed at land restitution, language revitalization, and promoting Saami cultural rights. The 2007 UN Declaration on the Rights of Indigenous Peoples marked a significant milestone for indigenous peoples, including the Saami, symbolizing the beginning of the end of marginalization and the opportunity for self-governance. Saami people critique Western research traditions and ethnocentrism, advocating for methodologies that reflect their own perspectives and experiences. Inspired by works like Linda Tuhiwai Smith's "Decolonizing Methodologies," Saami researchers and activists emphasize the importance of indigenous perspectives in research.[22] In indigenous studies, decolonization refers to a process that reveals and dismantles the forms of colonial power, as well as the

---

[20]Henry Minde, "Assimilation of the Sami - Implementation and Consequences." *Acta Borealia* 20, no. 2 (2003): 121–46; Eva Alerby, "In School You Learn to Get On in Life: Sámi Children in Sweden," in *Voices from the Margins*, ed. Eva Alerby and Jill Brown (Leiden: Brill, 2008), 31–2; Ulla Aikio-Puoskari, "The Ethnic Revival, Language and Education of the Sámi, an Indigenous People, in Three Nordic Countries (Finland, Norway and Sweden)," in *Social Justice through Multilingual Education*, ed. Tove Skutnabb-Kangas, Robert Phillipson, Ajit Mohanty, and Minati Panda (Bristol, Blue Ridge Summit: Multilingual Matters, 2009), 242–3.

[21]Magdalena Naum and Jonas Nordin, "Introduction: Situating Scandinavian Colonialism," in *Scandinavian Colonialism and the Rise of Modernity: Small Time Agents in a Global Arena*, ed. Magdalena Naum and Jonas Nordin, Contributions to Global Historical Archaeology, vol. 37 (New York: Springer, 2013), 8; Lehtola, "Sámi Histories, Colonialism, and Finland," 25–9; Åsa Össbo, "Hydropower Company Sites: A Study of Swedish Settler Colonialism," *Settler Colonial Studies* 13, no. 1 (2023): 115–32.

[22]Irja Seurujärvi-Kari, "'We Are No Longer Prepared to Be Silent': The Making of Sámi Indigenous Identity in an International Context," *Suomen Antropologi: Journal of the Finnish Anthropological Society* 35, no. 4 (2010): 5–25.

consequences of such practices. Likewise, the goal of the decolonization process is to create new structures and practices based on one's own values.[23] The Saami parliaments in Nordic countries play important roles in advocating for Saami rights and representation in decision-making processes. However, challenges remain, and ongoing efforts are needed to address the legacies of colonialism and support the self-determination and cultural survival of the Saami people.[24]

Nature, Geography, and the Challenges of Climate Change in Saami Area

The nature and geography of Saami area are diverse, depending on the region. As a geographical area, Saami area covers the northern parts of Finland, Sweden, Norway, and Russia. The area is characterized by fells, forests, lakes, and wilderness. In Finnish Lapland's fells, for example, the vegetation mainly belongs to the subalpine zone, where moss and lichen are common. In the plains, the vegetation is patchy and low. In the Saami region, there are periods of complete darkness in winter—when the sun does not rise at all—and "nightless nights" in summer—when the sun does not set. This phenomenon occurs due to the tilt of the Earth's axis of rotation.[25]

The climate of Saami area varies across different regions, but, in general, it is arctic. In Norwegian Lapland, the climate is maritime subarctic. Compared to other regions, temperatures in the Tromsø area are milder thanks to sea currents. In Swedish Lapland, while the climate is also subarctic, it is colder inland than on the coast. In Finnish Lapland, the climate is continental subarctic. In Kola, Russia, the climate is arctic. What these areas have in common is a long winter, short summer, and diverse but vulnerable nature.[26]

---

[23]Sanna Valkonen, *Poliittinen saamelaisuus* (Tampere: Vastapaino, 2009), 201–3.
[24]Rauna Kuokkanen, "The Problem of Culturalizing Indigenous Self-determination: Sámi cultural autonomy in Finland," *Polar Journal* 14, no. 1 (2024): 148–66.
[25]Lapin ELY-keskus, "Luonnon monimuotoisuus turvaa elämän edellytykset maapallolla," *ymparisto.fi* (2023). Available online: https://www.ymparisto.fi/fi/luonto-vesistot-ja-meri/luonnon-monimuotoisuus/luonnon-monimuotoisuus-lappi (accessed July 31, 2024); Daisy Dobrijevic, "Midnight Sun: What It Is and How to See It," *Space.com* (2024). Available online: https://www.space.com/midnight-sun-facts-where-and-when-to-see (accessed July 31, 2024).
[26]*Climates to Travel*, "Weather and Climate in Tromso (Norway)," *World Climage Guide*. Available online: https://www.climatestotravel.com/climate/norway/tromso (accessed July 31, 2024); "Swedish Lapland Climate," *Luleå Guided Tours & Activities*. Available online: https://www.laplandtours.se/Lapland_climate.html (accessed July 31, 2024); "Climate in Lapland (Finland)," *WorldData.info*. Available online: https://www.worlddata.info/europe/finland/climate-lapland.php (accessed July 31, 2024); World Wildlife Fund, "Kola Peninsula Tundra," *WildWorld* (2001). Available online: https://web.archive.org/web/20100308074247/http://www.nationalgeographic.com/wildworld/profiles/terrestrial/pa/pa1106.html (accessed July 31, 2024).

The nature of the Saami region is determined by large seasonal variations, a harsh climate, and a small number of species. However, many arctic species can be found in the area, and the abundance of many species groups is at its greatest specifically in the northern regions. The Saami people live on the border between forest and open land, and the location of the forest border largely determines where the reindeer graze. Reindeer-herding culture in its current form emerged in Western Norway during the thirteenth century and gradually spread across the region over the next few centuries. The reindeer's family roots are deep in the northern foothills, and it has adapted to withstand the harsh conditions of the north.[27]

The natural environment of the Saami region has also been subject to colonialist measures. For example, in the twentieth century, there were colonialist attitudes toward Lapland's nature in the Finnish public debate. The end of the Second World War and the reconstruction period of Lapland were significant watersheds in the history of nature use in Lapland. At that time, the value of Lapland's natural resources, such as forests, hydropower, farmland, and ore resources, was relatively small. However, the state's postwar industrialization of Lapland fulfills the hallmarks of a predatory economy and ecological colonialism; it is also the cause of Lapland's current problems. In the texts of the 1940s and 1950s, the natural conditions of Lapland were clearly interpreted in the national and national territorial context. The gaze was directed from south to north, and then the north loomed as a desolate, immeasurable, uncleared, and unproductive area that needed to be integrated into national unity and developed. In this view, the natural conditions of Lapland were not an obstacle, but only a retardation.[28]

Climate change has a significant impact on Saami area, which affects Saami peoples' culture, livelihoods, and health. The average temperature in Saami area has risen by 2.3°C since the postindustrial period. This warming trend is altering the region's snow conditions: for example, changes in snow and ice conditions have made it increasingly difficult for reindeer to dig underneath thick snow and ice crusts for lichen, threatening the Saami's traditional reindeer-herding culture.[29] Unpredictable environmental conditions have also led to fatal accidents in Saami communities. Many herders have been forced to change their livelihood models, introducing modern technologies and providing additional food for reindeer herds to survive. They have experienced increasingly severe and rapidly shifting,

---

[27]Tuomas Heikkilä and Antero Järvinen, "Saamelaisalueen luonto ja sen muutokset," in *Saamentutkimus tänään*, ed. Irja Seurujärvi-Kari, Petri Halinen, and Risto Pulkkinen (Helsinki: SKS, 2011), 59–63.

[28]Jarno Valkonen, *Lapin luontopolitiikka. Analyysi vuosien 1946–2000 julkisesta keskustelusta* (Tampere: University of Tampere, 2003). Available online: https://urn.fi/urn:isbn:951-44-5775-7 (accessed July 31, 2024).

[29]Klemetti Näkkäläjärvi, "Climate Change = Culture Change: What Happened to the Snow?," *The Circle: WWF magazine*, no. 1 (2019): 6–7. Available online: https://arcticwwf.org/site/assets/files/2127/thecircle0119_web_2.pdf (accessed July 31, 2024).

unstable weather with associated changes in vegetation and alterations in the freeze-thaw cycle, all of which affect reindeer herding.

As the climate changes and the snow-free season grows longer, it is triggering changes to Saami culture, language, and livelihoods. Climate change, combined with other pressures, has led to increased stress, anxiety, worry, and depression. Physical and psychological stress has emerged as a growing concern for reindeer herders and their families. Climate change in Saami area has increased the risk of not only hazards and injuries but also food insecurity and disease associated with, for instance, altered diets.[30]

In a warming climate, the Saami will likely survive as a linguistic minority, but their unique culture and knowledge system may fade away. While the Saami people are adapting to these changes, the impacts of climate change pose significant challenges to their traditional way of life, forcing them to adapt and adjust their activities and cultural practices.[31]

Nature is part of the Saami cultural heritage, knowledge, and traditions.[32] For Saami youth, nature is an important part of everyday life. Since childhood, they have spent time in nature, for example, collecting bark with their mothers, making a fire, or sledding down a hill. In their youth, they have, for example, gone hunting with their fathers, snowmobiling, or berry picking with friends. They are, therefore, worried about the impacts of climate change, especially on reindeer husbandry and living conditions. According to them, the exceptionally heavy snowfall caused by climate change, along with the subsequent spring floods, threaten all of this. In addition to climate change, they are also concerned about land use plans that challenge the carrying capacity of northern nature and Saami culture.

---

[30]Ibid.; Inkeri Markkula, Minna Turunen, Taru Rikkonen, Sirpa Rasmus, Veina Koski, and Jeffrey M. Welker, "Climate Change, Cultural Continuity and Ecological Grief: Insights from the Sámi Homeland," *Ambio* 53 (2024): 1203–17. Available online: https://doi.org/10.1007/s13280-024-02012-9 (accessed August 3, 2024).
[31]Näkkäläjärvi, "Climate Change = Culture Change."
[32]Helena Ristaniemi, 'Saamelaisnuoret ja historian läsnäolo', *Lähihistoria* 2, no. 1 (2023): 96–107. Available online: https://lahihistoria.journal.fi/article/view/131054 (accessed August 3, 2024).

3 SKOLT SAAMI

In the Skolt Saami original homeland between Lake Inari and Murmansk Bay, the society was organized through the system of *sijdd*s (Saami villages). A *sijdd* consisted of the inhabitants of a village and the area owned by them. Within *sijdd*s, the inhabitants followed their traditional way of life, based on seasonal migration, moving between communal winter residencies and individual family territories for fishing and hunting. There were some local and specific cultural characteristics in various *sijdd*s. For example, the people of Suõ'nn'jel *sijdd* lived in an inland forest area, made their living by reindeer herding and lake-fishing, and had close contacts with the people of Inari. The neighboring Peäccam *sijdd* was located on the mountainous shore of the Arctic Ocean, and sea-fishing was therefore a natural source of income that supported reindeer herding. There was also a strong Russian element in their local culture, manifested by the influence of the Russian Orthodox monastery nearby. There were seven *sijdd*s in the Skolt Saami land in the early twentieth century. The farthest *sijdd* to the west was Njauddâm. It was the first to be separated from others when its area became a part of Norway in 1826, while Suõ'nn'jel, Paččjokk, Peäccam, Njuõ'ttjäu'rr, Mue'tǩǩ, and Sââ'rves were governed by Russia.[1]

---

[1] Mustonen and Mustonen, *Eastern Saami Atlas*, 24–5; Anni Linkola and Martti Linkola, "Kolttasaamelaiset: Vähemmistön vähemmistö," in *Siiddastallan: Siidoista kyliin. Luontosidonnainen saamelaiskulttuuri ja sen muuttuminen*, ed. Jukka Pennanen and Klemetti Näkkäläjärvi, Inarin saamelaismuseon julkaisuja 3 (Jyväskylä: Pohjoinen, 2000), 158–67; Martti Linkola and Pekka Sammallahti, "Koltanmaa, osa Saamenmaata," in *Koltat, karjalaiset ja setukaiset. Pienet kansat maailmojen rajoilla*, ed. Tuija Saarinen and Seppo Suhonen (Kuopio: Snellman-instituutti, 1995), 39–51; Jouste, "Katsaus Venäjän saamelaisten musiikkiperinteiden," 361–2.

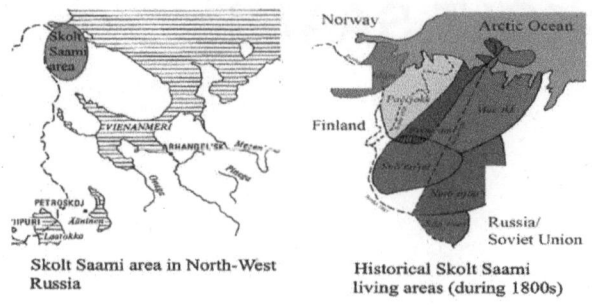

FIGURE 3.1. Skolt Saami *sijdd*s in the Murman coastal area in Northwest Russia.

Migrant History of the Skolt Saami During the Twentieth Century

The history of the Skolt Saami was marked by significant changes and challenges in the twentieth century. Based on the Treaty of Tartu, the Skolt Saami territories were divided by the border between the newly independent Finland and Soviet Russia in 1920. Skolt Saami village areas of Paččjokk, Peäccam, and Suõ′nn′jel were incorporated into Finland and the area named Pechenga (in Finnish: *Petsamo*). During the same period, the inhabitants of Njuõ′ttjäu′rr, Mue′tǩǩ, and Sââ′rves became Soviet citizens under Soviet rule. Soviet Skolt Saami were forced to relocate from their home areas during the 1930s. The collectivization process dismantled the traditional Skolt Saami society when all of them were relocated into eleven *kolkhozy* together with other local inhabitants.[2] As a result of these historical events, Skolt Saami contacts across the Russian border began to decline and gradually ceased to exist entirely.

After 1920, only the Skolt Saami of the Suõ′nn′jel *sijdd* in Pechenga followed their migration pattern, and the *sijdd* was seen as representative of ancient Skolt culture. Consequently, there was a strong intention to protect it from Finnish settlement, with discussions even arising about establishing an autonomous Skolt territory or reservation in Suõ′nn′jel.[3] Two other Skolt *sijdd*s on the Finnish side of the border, Paaččjokk and Peäccam, were not protected, as it was believed that

---

[2]Lukas Allemann, *The Saami of the Kola Peninsula: About the Life of an Ethnic Minority in the Soviet Union*, Senter for samiske studier, Skriftserie nr. 19 (Tromsø: University of Tromsø, 2013), 67–8. Available online: http://dx.doi.org/10.7557/sss.2013.19 (accessed July 31, 2024); Mustonen and Mustonen, *Eastern Saami Atlas*, 88.

[3]Lehtola, *Saamelaiset suomalaiset*, 268–77, 331–9.

FIGURE 3.2. Suõ'nn'jel *sijdd* in Pechenga in 1913.
Source: T. I. Itkonen. Museovirasto, Suomalais-ugrilainen kuvakokoelma (SUK117:51).

FIGURE 3.3. Paččjokk *sijdd* in Pechenga.
Source: Museovirasto, Suomalais-ugrilainen kuvakokoelma (SUK1162:81).

their traditional livelihood had already collapsed and that the inhabitants were adapting themselves to the values and customs of a new society.[4]

---

[4]Veli-Pekka Lehtola, *The Saami People – Traditions in Transition*, trans. L. Weber Müller-Wille (Inari: Kustannus-Puntsi, 2002), 66.

FIGURE 3.4. Risttke'dd *sijdd*.
Source: T. I. Itkonen 1914. Museovirasto, Suomalais-ugrilainen kuvakokoelma (SUK188:15).

Finally, the Second World War devastated the Finnish Skolt Saami lives as well. According to the peace treaties signed in Moscow (1944) and Paris (1947), the last Skolt homelands were ceded to the Soviet Union. Moreover, the war led to a ten-year period of nearly constant migration for the Skolt Saami, beginning with the first evacuation to the west in 1939 when the Finnish Winter War broke out. As Finnish citizens, the Skolt Saami of Pechenga decided to move to Finland permanently after the war. The re-settling of the traditional living areas, which were now a part of the Soviet Union, would have been impossible. People were relocated to the new home areas of Njeä'llem and Če'vetjä'urr in Inari district in 1949.[5]

In their new settlement, the Skolt Saami could no longer continue their annual migration since their new residences were permanent. This resulted in a remarkable shift in the livelihood of the former Suõ'nn'jel Skolt Saami compared to that in Pechenga. Similarly, many Skolt traditions, including dancing, began to deteriorate since the Skolt Saami found themselves in a culturally different—and often hostile—environment, where distinctive cultural features could irritate other

---

[5]Linkola and Linkola, "Kolttasaamelaiset," 158–67; Mustonen and Mustonen, *Eastern Saami Atlas*, 220–41; Veli-Pekka Lehtola, *Saamelainen evakko* (Inari: Kustannus-Puntsi, 2004), 33, 44–62, 128–43.

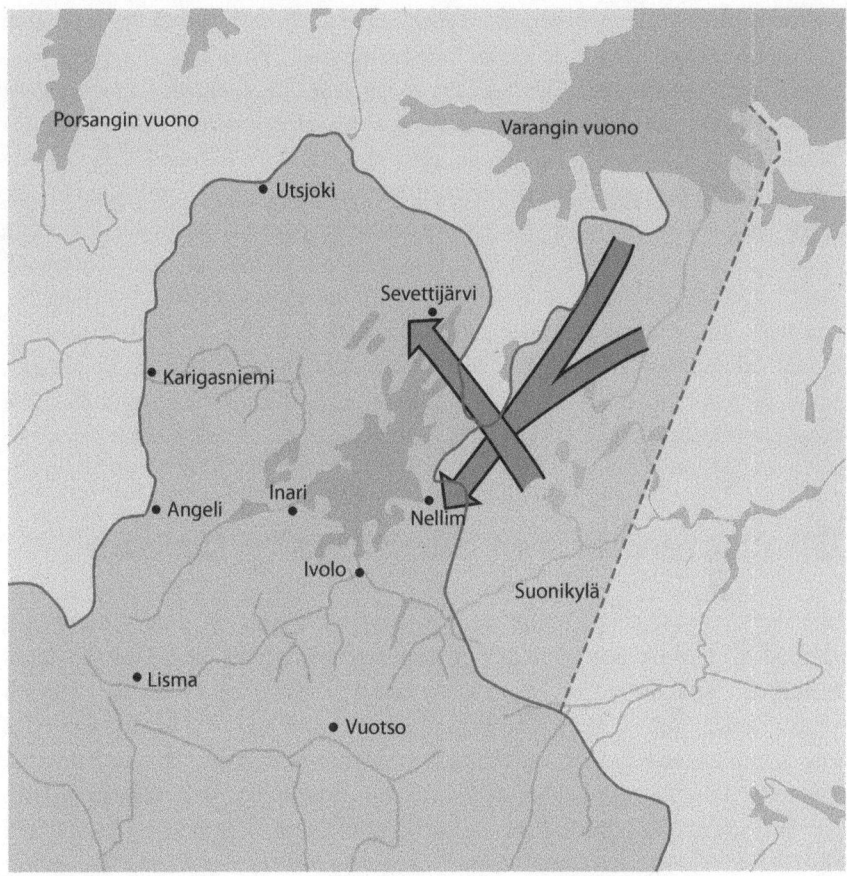

FIGURE 3.5. The evacuation of the Skolt Saami from Pechenga to the eastern parts of the municipality of Inari after the Second World War. Inhabitants from Suõ'nn'jel (Suonikylä) were settled to Če'vetjäu'rr (Sevettijärvi) area and those from Paččjokk and Peäccam to Njeä'llem (Nellim)-Keväjärvi area. The dotted line is the Finnish-Soviet border, 1920–40.

Source: Saami Museum Siida map, https://www.samimuseum.fi/saamjiellem/english/kolttaalue.html.

people around. One interviewee from Inari stated that in the village of Njeä'llem, for example, the Skolt Saami perceived themselves as having the lowest social status among the multiple ethnic groups of the village.[6] The situation was better in the village of Če'vetjäu'rr where the Skolt Saami were a majority. However, their children were not allowed to speak Skolt; rather, they were forced to use Finnish at school until the 1970s.

---

[6]Irja Jefremoff, interview by Petri Hoppu in Keväjärvi, Inari, Finland, August 15, 2014.

Today, there are about five hundred Skolt Saami in Finland. The traditional culture of the Skolt Saami has suffered from forced migration during and after the Second World War. However, they have been able to keep the traditional music culture alive. It is noteworthy that archive material can have a strong supportive role for present-day Saami generations in revitalizing and strengthening their local culture. This has already been shown in the revitalization process of Aanaar Saami language and culture.[7] The "Skolt Saami Memory Bank" project also explored practical methods for making archival recordings and other materials accessible and relevant to contemporary Skolt Saami life. This included developing ways to integrate archived music, language resources, and cultural documentation into community use, as well as fostering collaborations between researchers, archivists, and community members. By doing so, the project aimed to ensure that repatriated materials would not remain static historical records, but instead become active tools in everyday cultural and linguistic practices.[8]

Characteristics of Skolt Saami Culture

The Skolt Saami history, culture, and religion is unique in Finland. As Saami and Orthodox, they are also a minority within a minority. The Skolt Saami cultural history is characterized by frequent contact with Russians. From the sixteenth century until 1920, a great majority of Skolt Saami were under Russian rule. For centuries, the Russian government and the Orthodox Church primarily maintained friendly relations with Skolt Saami's own institutions. Russian features can be seen in Skolt Saami dance and music, clothing, and food traditions, and the Orthodox religion is even today an essential part of their society and culture.[9]

The early-twentieth-century Skolt Saami culture can be seen as essentially Skolt Saami; in the analysis, however, one must also consider the strong impact of the shared traditions of the neighboring Karelian, Russian, Norwegian, and Finnish cultures, as the traditional living areas of the Skolt Saami are located in a cultural melting pot of various northern peoples.[10] However, the culturally diverse environment, which had existed in this area for centuries, disintegrated during the twentieth century.[11]

---

[7]Olthuis, Kivelä, and Skutnabb-Kangas, *Revitalising Indigenous Languages*.
[8]See Jouste et al., "Sää'mǩiõl da kulttuur."
[9]Linkola and Sammallahti, "Koltanmaa, osa Saamenmaata"; Lars Ivar Hansen and Bjørnar Olsen, *Hunters in Transition: An Outline of Early Saami History*, The Northern World Series Nr. 63 (Leiden: Brill, 2014), 173.
[10]Jouste, "Katsaus Venäjän saamelaisten musiikkiperinteiden," 362–3; Heikki Laitinen, "Suonikylän laulut vuonna 1961: Tutkielma kolttasaamelaisten musiikkiperinteestä" (MA diss., Department of Musicology, University of Helsinki, 1977), 12–14; Juha Pentikäinen, "Lappalaisten perinnealuejako," in *Vanhaa ja uutta Lappia*, ed. Hannes Sihvo, Kalevalaseuran Vuosikirja 51 (Porvoo & Helsinki: Söderström, 1971), 142.
[11]Jouste, "The Historical Skolt Saami Music," 69–71.

The Skolt Saami are an exceptional people group among the Saami in the Nordic countries, because they have had a strong group and couple dance culture since the nineteenth century. The background of the dance culture is the contacts with the Russians and Karelians, from whom their dances mainly originate. Similar dances are also known among the Saami groups of Kola. Their music and clothing traditions are closely related to dance culture.

The impact of Russian and Karelian is shown in many areas of the Skolt Saami life. In the second half of the nineteenth century, the Saami women of Kola gradually began to wear the sarafan of the Karelians and Northern Russians. This practice continues today among the Skolt Saami. The attire also includes a pearl-decorated belt and a Russian soroka-type headdress for married women, the *šaamšik̆* (Russian шамшура), whose forehead imitates the decorations of the soroka but is made with pearl embroidery. Unmarried women wear *pee'rvesk* (Russian перевязка) and widows *po'vdnek̆* (Russian повойник). Pearl embroidery is a traditional way of decorating for the Skolt Saami. Small glass beads are sewn into decorative patterns, usually on red wire. Some of the embroidery designs are influenced by Orthodox religion, such as icons and church patterns. Different Skolt families have had their own embroidery patterns, which, over time, have merged with decorative designs common to all.[12]

The clothing of Skolt Saami men has evolved in recent years, appearing to align more with the costume styles of other Saami groups. Like other Saami attire, the Skolt Saami clothing was used as festive garments and, as they wore out, became everyday clothing. Today, it is mostly used as festive wear.[13]

Skolt Saami Representations in Research

With the annexation of Pechenga to Finland in 1920, the Finns encountered a new ethnic group—the Skolt Saami—who became a part of the recently independent state. In Finland's minority policy at the time, attitudes varied. Still, racist discourses based on colonialist thinking played a significant role in the encounters between the Finnish majority and the Skolt minority. Finnish Pechenga literature in the 1920s and 1930s is full of contemptuous descriptions of the Skolt Saami, who were typically presented as undeveloped as well as physically and mentally weak, and they needed to be instructed like little children.[14] They were frequently considered

---

[12]Ibid.
[13]*Sámi Duodji*, "Kolttasaamelainen puku." Available online: https://www.samiduodji.com/16 (accessed July 20, 2024); *Oktavuohta*, "Saamen puku kertoo monta asiaa." Available online: https://www.oktavuohta.com/gakti (accessed July 20, 2024).
[14]Lehtola, "Sámi Histories, Colonialism, and Finland"; Elina Arminen, "'Seikkailu Jäämerellä', Kaarlo Hännisen Jäämeren sankari ja suomalainen kolonialismi," *Historiallinen aikakauskirja* 118, no. 4 (2020): 481–93. Available online: https://erepo.uef.fi/handle/123456789/24083 (accessed July 20, 2024).

criminals, especially reindeer thieves, although, in reality, the Finns often hunted Saami reindeer without permission—a fact that was typically overlooked.[15]

In Finland, the annexation of Pechenga was, above all, viewed from the perspectives of economy and security policy, and it was seen as the duty of the native population to adapt to the demands of the new rulers. Even before the Treaty of Tartu, the social democratic politician Väinö Voionmaa (1869–1947) viewed the protection of Finland's interests on the shores of the Arctic Ocean as paramount:

> The Arctic Ocean is no longer a Lappish Sea, and the question of the Arctic Ocean is no longer only about the fish soup and lichen soil of a few Lappish people. There is no sense or right in withholding for the benefit of a hundred regressed and backward living beings, no matter how interesting and worthy of preservation their language and culture may be, large economic benefits that can be used by hundreds of thousands of people and entire states. The Lappish issues must be and undoubtedly can be resolved in a satisfactory way without sacrificing important interests for our entire country.[16]

Many scholars have studied Skolt Saami society and culture since the early twentieth century. The Skolt Saami were perceived as an ethnic group in need of cultural protection to survive or as representatives of an ancient culture whose inevitable fate was to fade away. The latter view was presented, for example, by T. I. Itkonen (1891–1968). He was a linguist, ethnographer, and researcher of religion who collected material objects from *Sää'mjânnam* ("Saami land")—especially Pechenga and Kola Peninsula—at the beginning of the twentieth century. A great majority of his collections are of Skolt Saami origin.[17]

Like many scholars of his time, Itkonen approached Saami culture through the lens of cultural evolution, which influenced his collecting practices. He focused particularly on the Skolt Saami, documenting their material culture during his field trips. Rather than emphasizing contemporary changes, his work concentrated on recording traditions and practices that were at risk of disappearing. Through his research, publications, and collections, Itkonen played a central role in shaping the understanding of Skolt Saami heritage.[18]

---

[15] Veli-Pekka Lehtola, "Aito saamelainen ei syö haarukalla ja veitsellä. Stereotypiat ja saamelainen kulttuurintutkimus," in *Pohjoiset identiteetit ja mentaliteetit. Osa 1: Outamaalta tunturiin*, ed. Marja Tuominen, Seija Tuulentie, Veli-Pekka Lehtola, and Mervi Autti, Lapin yliopiston taiteiden tiedekunnan julkaisuja C:16 (Rovaniemi: Lapin yliopisto, 1999), 157.

[16] Väinö Voionmaa, *Suomi Jäämerellä* (Helsinki: Edistysseurojen Kustannusosakeyhtiö, 1918), 135.

[17] Eeva-Kristiina Harlin and Veli-Pekka Lehtola, "Skolt Sámi Heritage, Toivo Immanuel Itkonen (1891–1968), and the Sámi Collections at the National Museum of Finland," *Nordic Museology* 27, no. 3 (2019): 45–60.

[18] Ibid., 57.

It must be added that while Itkonen inevitably reflected the framework of cultural evolution characteristic of lappology at the time, his fieldwork demonstrates a more complex engagement.[19] His publications preserve extensive vocabulary and cultural knowledge across nearly all areas of traditional Skolt Saami life, ensuring that intangible aspects of culture were not lost. Moreover, his travel journals and photographs are considered unique first-hand records of places later destroyed or abandoned, such as the winter village of Suo'nn'jel.[20]

A somewhat different view on the Skolt Saami is presented by another Finnish researcher, geologist and geographer Väinö Tanner (1881–1948), who created a picture of an authentic ancient community that had been disrupted by modern society.[21] Tanner largely overlooked the fact that the Skolt Saami's reality had significantly changed over the past century; instead, he emphasized the harmonious ideal he believed he had discovered among the Skolt Saami. Tanner's study greatly influenced later research and Skolt Saami's attitudes toward their history and culture, as he was one of the first scholars to recognize Skolt Saami's rights to their own society and culture.[22]

Tanner's famous report contains numerous descriptions of the Skolt Saami "character" and advice on how they could best maintain their "happiness." He collected information from his Skolt Saami guides and included Saami voices in his book, albeit in a controlled manner. He aimed for a relativistic gaze, acknowledging the intrinsic value of the Skolt Saami culture. However, his gaze was purist and normative, containing numerous colonial tropes. He used reindeer and reindeer herding as a tool to endow the Skolt Saami with cultural potency and agency, praising them for their successful adaptation to their environment. However, his conception of the Skolt Saami culture as a reindeer-herding culture became a cultural straitjacket and a source of vulnerability. His report also conveyed a politics of identity, with passages where the Skolt Saami—elevated in status–show the Finns their lowly place along the Arctic coast. Despite his sympathetic and relativistic colonial representations, he failed to produce a consistently considerate report on the Skolt Saami, instead depicting them as being on the lowest developmental rung—the weakest of the peoples struggling to survive and adapt.[23]

---

[19]Veli-Pekka Lehtola, "Vanishing Lapps, Progress in Action. Finnish Lappology and Representations of the Sámi in Publicity in the Early 20th Century," *Arctic and North* 2, no. 27 (2017), 83–102 (88–93).
[20]See Marko Jouste, "'Maailman pienin kansa musiikissa rikkain'. A. O. Väisänen saamelaisten musiikkiperinteiden kerääjänä ja tutkijana." In *Kalevalaseuran vuosikirja* 90 (Helsinki: Kalevalaseura, 2011).
[21]Väinö Tanner, "Antropogeografiska studier inom Petsamo-området: 1 Skoltlapparna," *Fennia* 49, no. 4 (1929): 1–518.
[22]Hansen and Olsen, *Hunters in Transition*, 168–74; see also Jukka Nyyssönen, "Väinö Tanner, saamentutkimus ja uudelleen herännyt kansainvälinen kritiikki," in *Saamenmaa. Kulttuuritieteellisiä näkökulmia*, ed. Veli-Pekka Lehtola, Ulla Piela, and Hanna Snellman (Helsinki: SKS, 2012).
[23]Jukka Nyyssönen, "Nation-Building and Colonialism: The Early Skolt Saami Research of Väinö Tanner," in *Finnish Colonial Encounters: From Anti-Imperialism to Cultural Colonialism and Complicity*, ed. Raita Merivirta, Leila Koivunen, and Timo Särkkä (Cham: Palgrave Macmillan, 2021), 133–7.

FIGURE 3.6. Skolt Saami. Antti Hämäläinen.
Source: Museovirasto, Suomalais-ugrilainen kuvakokoelma (SUK529:469).

Several Finnish scholars shared the view that the Skolt Saami faced the threat of extinction.[24] This kind of attitude was often linked to racism. The history of independent Finland includes racial studies targeting all Saami groups, reflecting views that the Saami are racially inferior and less developed. Physical anthropology was an important area of medical research in the 1920s and 1930s. Researchers categorized the Finns as a "cultural race" and the Saami as an "inferior race." Many researchers and politicians saw the Saami as a people who had no future in a modernizing society. Relying on cultural evolutionist ideas, they considered the Saami as a less developed and doomed group. At the turn of the 1960s and 1970s, studies were still carried out in which the racial characteristics of the Skolt Saami among other Saami were mapped by measuring and photographing their bodies.[25]

As late as in the 1970s, British anthropologist Tim Ingold argued that the future of the Skolt Saami was endangered not so much by acculturation as by logistical challenges: he suggested that the Skolt community might be too small to survive as a distinct ethnic entity, although the Skolt people could find new ways to adapt their living conditions.[26] However, since the 1970s, the Skolt Saami themselves

---

[24]For example, Samuli Paulaharju, *Kolttain mailta* (Helsinki: Kustannusosakeyhtiö Kirja, 1921), 198.
[25]Suvi Keskinen, "Kolonialismin ja rasismin historiaa Suomesta käsin." In *Rasismi, valta ja vastarinta: Rodullistaminen, valkoisuus ja koloniaalisuus Suomessa*, ed. Suvi Keskinen, Minna Seikkula and Faith Mkwesha (Helsinki: Gaudeamus, 2021), 80–81.
[26]Tim Ingold, *The Skolt Lapps Today* (Cambridge: Cambridge University Press, 1976), 252–53.

began demanding changes to their status, and the attitudes of Finnish scholars toward them shifted. The earlier patronizing mentality gradually transformed into a desire to enter into dialogue with them, and their agency began to be strongly emphasized.

4 PERSPECTIVES OF INDIGENOUS STUDIES

Saami research can be seen as part of the whole of indigenous research, the goals of which are decolonization, emphasizing ethics, and bringing indigenous knowledge production to the center of the research. In addition to examining the diversity of the present, it creates opportunities to understand historical continuities and power relations. The states dominating indigenous peoples' territories inevitably destabilize their worldview, for example, through research and education. To counter this development, it is necessary to integrate the indigenous perspective into research, recognizing local values and aspirations, and to secure real opportunities for participation and influence among the members of such communities.[1]

Indigenous studies provide a critical lens to understand the diverse experiences and perspectives of indigenous peoples. It underscores the importance of indigenous knowledge and methodologies in shaping sustainable livelihoods and contributing to the broader field of knowledge. Indigenous studies today is a multidisciplinary field that explores the history, culture, politics, issues, and contemporary experience of indigenous peoples. It draws on disciplines such as anthropology, sociology, history, literature, political science, arts research, and education. Indigenous studies also critically engage with local concepts and ideas that draw from different experiences and standpoints.[2]

---

[1] Michael Anthony Hart, "Indigenous Worldviews, Knowledge, and Research: The Development of an Indigenous Research Paradigm," *Journal of Indigenous Voices in Social Work* 1, no. 1 (2010): 1–16. Available online: http://hdl.handle.net/10125/15117 (accessed June 12, 2024).

[2] Stephen Bocking, "Indigenous Knowledge and Perspectives," in *Handbook of the Historiography of the Earth and Environmental Sciences*, ed. Elena Aronova., David Sepkoski, and Marco Tamborini. Historiographies of Science (Cham: Springer, 2023). Available online: https://doi.org/10.1007/978-3-030-92679-3_20-1 (accessed June 12, 2024); Pirjo Kristiina Virtanen and Irja Seurujärvi-Kari, "Introduction: Theorizing Indigenous Knowledge(s)," *Dutkansearvvi dieđalaš áigečála* 3, no. 2 (2019): 1–19. Available online: https://www.dutkansearvi.fi/volume-3-issue-2-en/pirjo-kristi

To a certain extent, the study of indigenous peoples has been biased in that it has mainly focused on the rural population, even though an increasingly large part of the world's indigenous population lives in cities.[3] The same also applies to the Saami, whose largest communities are today in cities. As a result of urbanization, the economic structure of the Saami people has changed radically, especially outside the Saami region, but also within it. Today, the Saami population largely reflects the professional and educational structure of the majority population.[4] For indigenous studies, urbanization creates challenges because it calls into question essentialist views of ethnic groups, their societies, and cultures. The development does not reduce the need for research; on the contrary, it increases it, because in the cities, the representatives of the indigenous peoples must struggle with the definition and recognition of their own identity.

Moreover, there has also been growing criticism of the term "indigenous peoples." Indigenous scholars argue it essentializes and politicizes indigenous identities. Indigeneity can be seen as incoherent in the sense that its features cannot be generalized globally. However, as a concept, it can be used as an analytical tool to resist the colonial system and move toward more equal relations and recognition of differences. Therefore, despite challenges, the indigenous peoples, including the Saami, have used indigeneity as a political resource to advocate for their rights and cultural preservation.[5]

Knowledge Construction

A critical examination of the forms of knowledge construction is an important part of indigenous studies, and it forms the starting point for new perspectives that enable equality to be realized in research. Recognizing biases in research requires a scientific-philosophical re-evaluation of the formation of knowledge.

Indigenous onto-epistemologies refer to the totality of indigenous ways of understanding their existence and knowledge. These epistemologies are informed by indigenous cultural and ethical frameworks specific to the nations with whom the research is being conducted. Indigenous epistemologies play a pivotal role

---

ina-virtanen-irja-seurujarvi-kari-introduction-theorizing-indigenous-knowledges-en/ (accessed June 12, 2024).
[3]Dana Brablec and Andrew Canessa, "Introduction: Indigenous Peoples in the Cities of the World," in *Urban Indigeneities: Being Indigenous in the Twenty-First Century*, ed. Dana Brablec and Andrew Canessa (Tuczon: University of Arizona Press, 2023), 3–4.
[4]Mikkel Berg-Nordlie and Anna Andersen, "Cities in Sápmi, Sámi in the Cities: Indigenous Urbanization in the Nordic Countries and Russia," in *An Urban Future for Sápmi? Indigenous Urbanization in the Nordic States and Russia*, ed. Mikkel Berg-Nordlie, Astri Dankertsen, and Marte Winsvold (New York and Oxford: Berghahn Books, 2022).
[5]Seurujärvi-Kari, "'We Are No Longer Prepared to Be Silent.'"

in development and are applied in many facets of sociocultural foundations and modern scientific discourses.[6]

Indigenous onto-epistemologies in research are recognized as a holistic and plural concept. They are shaped by experiential knowledges in traditional, storied places where distinct collectivities of humans and other-than-human nations/peoples intersect, interact, and coexist. These onto-epistemologies not only encompass how sources of knowledge are attributed but also serve as one of the ontological pillars that uphold honesty and truth-telling within a relationally oriented epistemology. They are grounded in indigenous ways of knowing, being, and doing, and are underpinned by culturally contextualized ontologies, epistemologies, and value systems developed over millennia.[7]

Indigenous research methodologies articulate how researchers and aboriginal communities engage in research together. These methodologies are fundamentally rooted in the traditions and knowledge systems of indigenous peoples themselves. Very specific indigenous methods emerge from language, culture, and worldview. Indigenous research methodologies offer a pathway for translating indigenous perspectives on academic integrity into the university classroom and institutional culture. These methodologies are systematic approaches to research that are embedded within an ethic of truth-telling and relational accountability. They represent a diverse and enduring knowledge system.[8]

Indigenous research methodologies uphold principles of relevance, respect for indigenous knowledges, responsible relationships, holism, and indigenous ethics. These principles guide the research process, ensuring that research partnerships with indigenous communities create sustained meaningful change. For instance,

---

[6] Juan Camilo Cajigas-Rotundo, "Ontoepistemologías indígenas," *Tabula Rasa* 26 (2017): 123–39; Michelle Pidgeon and Riley Tasha, "Understanding the Application and Use of Indigenous Research Methodologies in the Social Sciences by Indigenous and Non-Indigenous Scholars," *International Journal of Education Policy and Leadership* 17, no. 8 (2021): 1–17. Available online: https://doi.org/10.22230/ijepl.2021v17n8a1065 (accessed June 15, 2024); Edward Shizha, "Indigenous Epistemologies and Decolonized Sustainable Livelihoods in Africa," in *The Palgrave Handbook on Critical Theories of Education*, ed. Ali A. Abdi and Greg William Misiaszek (Cham: Palgrave Macmillan, 2022). Available online: https://doi.org/10.1007/978-3-030-86343-2_26 (accessed June 15, 2024).
[7] Paul L. Gareau and Molly Swain, "Indigenous Knowledges," *Oxford Research Encyclopedia of Religion* (2024, January 30). Available online: https://oxfordre.com/religion/view/10.1093/acrefore/9780199340378.001.0001/acrefore-9780199340378-e-1178 (accessed June 15, 2024); Gabrielle L. Lindstrom, "Accountability, Relationality and Indigenous Epistemology: Advancing an Indigenous Perspective on Academic Integrity," in *Academic Integrity in Canada. An Enduring and Essential Challenge*, ed. Sarah Elaine Eaton and Julia Christensen Hughes (Cham: Springer, 2022). Available online: https://doi.org/10.1007/978-3-030-83255-1_6 (accessed June 15, 2024).
[8] Lindstrom, "Accountability, Relationality and Indigenous Epistemology"; Pidgeon and Tasha, "Understanding the Application and Use of Indigenous Research Methodologies"; Mike Evans, Adrian Miller, Peter Hutchinson, and Carlene Dingwall, "Decolonizing Research Practice: Indigenous Methodologies, Aboriginal Methods and Knowledge/Knowing," in *Oxford Handbook of Qualitative Research*, ed. Patricia Leavy (Oxford: Oxford University Press, 2014). Available online: https://doi.org/10.1093/oxfordhb/9780199811755.013.019 (accessed June 15, 2024).

in indigenous participatory action research projects, indigenous communities determine their research needs and assert their rights to self-determination over research and programs that directly impact them.[9]

Indigenous knowledge systems constitute a conglomerate of various disciplines and intersecting epistemologies and value systems. The accumulated knowledges have emerged from trial-and-error experimentation as well as tested empirical practices and paradigms related to ecological, geographical, economic, social, and other traditions of existence. The ecological system in the form of biodiversity and local environment contributes to sustainable livelihoods among indigenous peoples. Indigenous knowledge systems are defined as the total of all knowledge and skills that people in a particular geographic area possess, enabling them to get the most out of their natural environment. These systems encompass a wide range of categories, including agricultural, meteorological, ecological, medicinal, pharmaceutical, textile manufacture, metallurgy, and food technology.[10]

In research, indigenous knowledge systems are recognized as valid resources for education and development, as well as a valid framework for research among and with indigenous peoples. They provide a culturally specific lens through which to view and understand the world. Their application helps to ensure that research is culturally sensitive, relevant, and beneficial to the indigenous communities involved. It also contributes to a deeper understanding of indigenous perspectives, fostering respect for indigenous knowledge and contributing to meaningful change for indigenous peoples and their communities.[11]

Saami Research

Over the past five decades, the modern field of Saami research—or Saami studies—has emerged as an interdisciplinary area of scholarship. Its main task is to conduct research that centers the Saami perspective and critically examines both Saami communities and the dominant societies in which Saami live.[12] It emphasizes "the community-driven nature of research as well as the significance

---

[9]Pidgeon and Tasha, "Understanding the Application and Use of Indigenous Research Methodologies."
[10]Shizha, "Indigenous Epistemologies and Decolonized Sustainable Livelihoods"; Kai Horsthemke, "Indigenous (African) Knowledge Systems, Science, and Technology," in *The Palgrave Handbook of African Philosophy*, ed. Adeshina Afolayan and Toyin Falola (New York: Palgrave Macmillan, 2017). Available online: https://doi.org/10.1057/978-1-137-59291-0_38 (accessed June 15, 2024).
[11]Constance Khupe, "Indigenous Knowledge Systems," in *Science Education in Theory and Practice. An Introductory Guide to Learning Theory*, ed. Ben Akpan and Teresa J. Kennedy (Cham: Springer, 2020). Available online: https://doi.org/10.1007/978-3-030-43620-9_30 (accessed June 15, 2024).
[12]Anni-Siiri Länsman, "Kenelle saamentutkija tutkii?," in *Tutkijan kirja*, ed. Kirsti Lempiäinen, Olli Löytty, and Merja Kinnunen (Tampere: Vastapaino, 2008), 87–8, 90.

of research from the community perspective. Taking cultural values, norms, and Indigenous peoples' collective right to self-determination into consideration receives significant emphasis." Saami research stresses that the Saami have the right to influence the production of information about themselves and their public image.[13]

Because of this, Saami research has direct consequences for the Saami people—consequences that must always be taken into account. According to Harald Gaski, Saami people should be actively involved in Saami research. In line with the broader movement of Indigenous methodologies, he argues for a shift from the Saami being objects of research to becoming subjects who participate in shaping the premises of scholarship.[14]

Professor Veli-Pekka Lehtola identifies the main feature of this approach as recognizing the Saami as active agents in their own history and culture.[15] Professor Rauna Kuokkanen emphasizes the important role of Indigenous scholarship not only in guiding academic work but also in supporting modern Saami society by educating professionals.[16]

In Saami culture, the ability to read nature and its inhabitants—both animal and human—has long been an important skill. This cultural knowledge is highly valued, and those who possess it are regarded as learned individuals. This respect for traditional knowledge is also reflected in Saami approaches to research, where such skills and perspectives are integrated into the process.[17]

Saami research is conducted in various research institutions and universities, primarily in the Nordic countries but also internationally. Both Saami and non-Saami scholars contribute to the field, and Gaski sees this as a positive development. He notes that the Saami have welcomed diverse perspectives and scholars from different backgrounds, without feeling the need to separate Saami research from Western academic traditions:

> It's been more about getting Sami perspectives into research --i.e., Sami empiricism --and not, to the same degree as in North America and Oceania, a question of taking our own epistemology as a point of departure, of theorizing from our own knowledge traditions. Such theorizing, Sami scholars have argued, may proceed not necessarily in place of the Western tradition, but

---

[13] Heikkilä et al., *Ethical Guidelines for Research*.
[14] Harald Gaski, "Indigenism and Cosmopolitanism: A PanSami View of the Indigenous Perspective in Sami Culture and Research," *AlterNative: An International Journal of Indigenous Peoples* 9, no. 2 (2013): 113–24. Available online: https://doi.org/10.1177/117718011300900201 (accessed June 15, 2024).
[15] Lehtola, *Saamelaiset*, 17.
[16] Rauna Kuokkanen, "Sami Higher Education and Research: Toward Building a Vision for Future," in *Indigenous Peoples: Self-determination - Knowledge - Indigeneity*, ed. Henry Minde (Utrecht: Eburon, 2008), 267–9.
[17] Gaski, "Indigenism and Cosmopolitanism," 115.

rather in addition to it: the aim has not been framed as an "either/or" question, but rather as a "both/and" proposition.[18]

Because Saami research is so multifaceted, there has been a recognized need for common ethical guidelines across its various areas. These guidelines for research involving the Saami have been developed in cooperation with Saami communities and researchers. They aim to help ensure that research is conducted in a sustainable and respectful manner.[19]

The purpose of the guidelines is to create culturally safe methods and conditions for research. In addition to Saami communities, researchers and experts from various fields have contributed to their development. Since the 1970s, the Saami people and the research community have discussed the creation of sustainable research practices and the central importance of research ethics. Increasingly, there is a shared recognition—both within Saami communities and among researchers—of the importance of producing ethical guidelines for Saami research in collaboration with the Saami themselves.[20]

Indigenous Dance and Music Studies

Dance and music are a vital part of indigenous cultures and societies, serving as a medium for expression, resistance, and the preservation and regeneration of indigenous knowledge and ontologies. The categories of indigenous music and dance are subjects to a constantly shifting public discourse based on the continuing ideological struggle between institutional control and indigenous self-determination. Therefore, the role of indigenous dance and music in research is not just about the dance and music themselves but also about understanding the cultural, social, and political contexts in which they are created and performed. Research provides insights into the ways in which indigenous dancers and musicians navigate and negotiate their identities within the broader field of arts and society. It also helps in challenging and reframing notions of indigeneity.[21]

---

[18]Gaski, "Indigenism and Cosmopolitanism," 116.
[19]Heikkilä et al., *Ethical Guidelines for Research*.
[20]Ibid.
[21]Clint Bracknell, "Identity, Language and Collaboration in Indigenous Music," in *The Difference Identity Makes: Indigenous Cultural Capital in Australian Cultural Fields*, ed. Lawrence Bamblett, Fred Myers, and Tim Rowse (Canberra, ACT: Aboriginal Studies Press, 2019). Available online: https://ro.ecu.edu.au/ecuworkspost2013/6643 (accessed June 15, 2024); María Regina Firmino Castillo, "Dancing the Pluriverse," *Dance Research Journal* 48, no. 1, Special Issue: Indigenous Dance Today (April 2016): 55–73.

Ethical engagement with indigenous dance and music involves recognizing and respecting the cultural diversity and self-determination of indigenous communities. It is about understanding and respecting the cultural, social, and political contexts in which the dance and music are created and performed. It is also about challenging and reframing notions of indigeneity. Researchers must be aware of the potential impacts of their research on the communities involved and strive to ensure that their work benefits these communities. Building trust with indigenous communities in research is a process that requires respect, understanding, and collaboration. Non-indigenous researchers can build trust with indigenous communities by approaching them as equals, developing a relationship of trust, showing respect, and taking steps to avoid cultural misunderstandings. It is also important for researchers to be open to learning from the indigenous communities they are working with, as well as to be committed to conducting their research in a way that benefits these communities. Addressing power imbalances involves recognizing and respecting indigenous diversity, challenging dominant discourses, collaborating on equal terms, and avoiding cultural misunderstandings. Research should not be a one-way process. Scholars should aim to give back to the communities they study, whether through sharing their findings, providing resources, or other means.[22]

In education, scholars have made significant progress in exposing the colonial violences that pervade dance and music curricula, pedagogical approaches, and teacher education. However, the research processes used to identify, understand, and evaluate anti-colonial or decolonizing work often embody colonial logics themselves. The politics of knowledge production between indigenous epistemes and the academy raises questions about the methodological responsibility of dance and music education research in indigenous settings, especially when conducted by non-indigenous researchers. Understanding research as a relation of possibility found in relation with others can open new avenues for decolonizing dance and music education. The history of decolonization in dance and music is a journey of reclaiming indigenous practices and re-centering them in the teaching and learning of dance and music. This involves leveraging resources, communities, and experiences within the local environments of indigenous dance practices to develop competences and skills of perceiving, teaching, and sharing knowledge. In essence, researchers can contribute to decolonizing dance and music education by challenging the dominant narratives, highlighting the colonial violence, taking methodological responsibility, and actively participating in the process of reclaiming and re-centering indigenous practices.[23]

---

[22]Bracknell, "Identity, Language and Collaboration in Indigenous Music"; Firmino Castillo, "Dancing the Pluriverse"; Jacqueline Shea Murphy, "Editor's Note," *Dance Research Journal* 48, no. 1, Special Issue: Indigenous Dance Today (April 2016): 1–8.

[23]Alexis Anja Kallio, "Decolonizing Music Education Research and the (Im)possibility of Methodological Responsibility," *Research Studies in Music Education* 42, no. 2 (2020): 177–91.

The study of Saami music has seen significant evolution over the years. The modern history of collecting and researching Saami music began in the early twentieth century when Finnish musicologist Armas Launis (1884–1959) and folklorists Väinö Salminen (1880–1947) and T. I. Itkonen collected music from various regions where the Saami people reside. Itkonen also carried out the first sound recordings of Skolt Saami language and music. A period of "mass collections" of the Saami languages and music began in the 1950s and lasted until the 1970s.[24] However, it was not until the mid-1970s that new analytical research began. In recent years, the study of Saami music has responded to globalizing music practices by shifting analytical and ethnographic attention from music within nation-states to music across borders. This shift has been a disciplinary trend since the 1990s. Saami popular music has been linked with indigenous political assertions for greater sovereignty, minority language sustainability, new historical narratives, and environmental challenges in the transnational sociocultural contexts of the Nordic world. Following the revival of traditional Saami music from the 1960s onward, Saami musicians were increasingly engaging with popular music genres and new digital technologies, combining the traditional Saami vocal genres with ambient sounds, metal, rock, and rap, and reaching global, virtual audiences. This evolution of the study of Saami music reflects the changing times and the increasing recognition of the importance of preserving and promoting indigenous cultures and their music traditions.[25]

Available online: https://doi.org/10.1177/1321103X19845690 (accessed June 30, 2024); Alfdaniels Mabingo, Gerald Ssemaganda, Edward Sembatya, and Ronald Kibirige, "Decolonizing Dance Teacher Education: Reflections of Four Teachers of Indigenous Dances," *African Postcolonial Environments. Journal of Dance Education* 20, no. 3 (2020), 148–56. Available online: https://doi.org/10.1080/15290 824.2020.1781866 (accessed June 30, 2024).

[24]Marko Jouste, "Saamelaismusiikin tallennus Suomessa," in *Kohtaaminen - Gávnnadeapmi*, ed. Marko Jouste (Inari: Sámi museum - Saamelaismuseosäätiö & Yhteispohjoismainen joikuarkistoprojekti, 2007), 28.

[25]Tina K. Ramnarine, "Aspirations, Global Futures, and Lessons from Sámi Popular Music for the Twenty-First Century," in *The Oxford Handbook of Popular Music in the Nordic Countries*, ed. Fabian Holt and Antti-Ville Kärjä (Oxford: Oxford University Press, 2017). Available online: https://doi.org/10.1093/oxfordhb/9780190603908.013.0015 (accessed June 30, 2024).

PART TWO

SKOLT SAAMI DANCE CULTURE UNTIL THE SECOND WORLD WAR

From the end of the nineteenth century, a flourishing dance culture developed among the Skolt Saami, which was combined with a new kind of instrumental music, especially through the introduction of the accordion. Old and new cultural influences merged into a unique culture that was intertwined with the Skolt Saami seasonal cycle. For several decades, new dance and music influences came in abundance, especially from Russia and Russian Karelia. After the border with Soviet Russia was closed in the early 1920s, the cultural exchange ended, but the Skolt Saami dance culture remained unique in many respects until the Second World War.

5 DANCE-LOVING COMMUNITIES

There is no information about the Skolt Saami dance culture before the end of the nineteenth century. One has commonly thought in the Nordic countries that Saami groups do not have any known dance culture,[1] although some mentions of Saami dance can be found in historical documents.[2] Apparently, for decades, the research conducted by non-Saami scholars did not recognize phenomena related to dance, and they were not considered worthy of study from the perspective of Western sciences. This is related to the presupposition that such aspects of culture, which were interpreted to be borrowed from neighboring people, were not relevant as objects of research. Dance was one of such cultural activities, which was not considered an original form of Saami culture. Similar interpretations were made of many other cultural features (e.g., language, music, clothing), and often collecting information about these was not considered significant.

---

[1] Interestingly, while stating that the Saami do not have a recognized dance culture, Kari Bergholm adds that Skolt Saami have some dances "borrowed from Murmansk region Russians," thus downplaying the value of their dances. Practically every documented Finnish folk dance in Finland can be described as "borrowed," yet Bergholm regards them as Finnish although he acknowledges their foreign background. He writes "that material of folk tradition has been constantly transported from one country to another, but each nation has modified and melted them to suit its own tradition according to its own special style vision." Apparently, he does not feel the Skolt Saami have had any similar vision of style. Kari Bergholm, "Suomalaisen kansantanssin tyylipiirteitä," in *Tanhuvakka. Suuri suomalainen kansantanssikirja*, ed. Pirkko-Liisa Rausmaa and Esko Rausmaa (Helsinki: Suomalaisen Kansantanssin Ystävät, 1997), 24–6.

[2] For example, Bulstrode Whitelocke, *Bulstr. Whitelockes Dag-Bok öfver dess ambassade til Sverige åren 1653 och 1654*, Öfversatt ifrån engelskan (Uppsala: Johan Edman, 1777).

Pleasure of Dance

The situation of dance among the Saami since the late nineteenth century has varied a lot. In the cultures of the Saami people under Russian rule, dance had a strong position, and the Russian influence was dominant in the dance culture. On the other hand, similar dance cultures did not emerge among the Saami in Sweden, Norway, and Finland, being especially influenced by the Laestadian movement within the Lutheran Church, especially in Northern Scandinavia and Finland, which was very anti-dance. After the Skolt Saami moved to their new places of residence in Inari, among Finns and Inari and Northern Saami, the positive attitude toward dance was very exceptional.

The basis of our research has also been to question the conventional research concept that the Saami have not danced or that the Saami have not had dances. The interpretation presented in the previous study is based on the idea that dance was not seen as an original but a borrowed form of culture and therefore was not considered part of authentic Saami culture. However, the Saami have danced like everyone else, despite the disapproval of the Christian church and local revival movements (e.g., Laestadism). Likewise, traditional forms of music such as the Northern Saami luohti (yoik) were frowned upon, but people continued performing luohtis. However, it is good to remember that dance in a "modern" context is not a centuries-old tradition, but a form of culture that only became a part of the Saami's life during the nineteenth century. Thus, it corresponds to many other forms of culture that have strong connections with dominant cultures.

The general attitude toward dance and music changed at the end of the nineteenth century. Dancing was common in Northern Finland and among the Kven people at least as late as the 1860s, following which a Laestadian religious revival movement began to spread in Lapland. Dancing and all kinds of revelry were viewed very negatively within the revival movement. At the same time, condemning Saami music traditions as a sin was strengthened. Finnish journalist G. A. Andersson describes the situation during 1880s as follows:

> Apart from spell songs, other old poems and songs were already very rare in Lapland 30 years ago. Maybe the strong religious current that moved in Lapland swept them so completely from people's memory. It was also due to religious reasons that even modern folk songs had not gained a foothold among younger people. When public opinion condemned all secular songs, such "sorrowful" songs were not played, at least in the hearing of older people.[3]

---

[3] Gustaf Adolf Andersson, *Tietoja Sodankylän ja Kittilän pitäjien aikaisemmista ja myöhemmistä waiheista* (Kemi: Kemin uusi kirjapaino, 1914).

Furthermore, travelogs of the astronomical research group, the so-called *Tähtiherrat*,[4] from 1882 to 1884 also discuss the effects of Sodankylä's religious revival on the culture of the keepers. In addition to the Saami tradition, the revival movement in Laestadius also had an impact on the region's Finnish folk poetry. This must have destroyed the last shreds of the old music tradition, which was no longer available at the beginning of the twentieth century when the actual music collection began. These attitudes continued and strengthened during the following decades. Väinö Salminen recalls his experiences in Kittilä in 1904 as follows:

> On the banks of the Muoniojoki, both on the Finnish and Swedish sides, folk poetry has disappeared. The sermons of Laestadius, the "great prophet" of the South-Lapland, killed off the lasting remains of folk poetry. [General attitude was expressed] so that it is not good to "spoil your mouth" by telling and singing "crap" as is the common way of speaking.[5]

The Laestadian movement had a significant impact on the Saami cultures in Nordic countries, and because of this, dancing and other "earthy pleasures" were considered as a sin. This attitude was also accepted widely in many Saami communities, in which the Christian religion played an important role. However, this did not stop people dancing in many social events but as the context was often Finnish, Swedish or Norwegian, dance was not considered as part of the Saami culture. This can be interpreted as a form of "the colonialisation of mind," articulated widely in the indigenous studies. However, the situation in the Skolt Saami culture differs considerably as the Nordic religious movements did not affect the Russian Orthodox church, in which dancing was not considered as a sin after the lifting the ban over dancing during the late nineteenth century, imposed earlier by the Orthodox Old Believers (старообрядство). This is the opposite policy compared to the Scandinavian Lutheran Church's negative attitudes toward dancing. Lutheran priests and especially the members of the highly popular Laestadian revivalist movement considered dancing as a sin. Thus, from the mid-nineteenth century to the mid-twentieth century, the Saami areas were divided into two completely opposite cultures regarding dance.

However, the Orthodox Church imposed some restrictions as dancing was strictly forbidden during Lent. Instead, one could play various games outside. *Jõnn lä'znpei'vv*—"St. Mary's Day"—was specially dedicated for these games. According to Jaakko Pohjola, Suõ'nn'jel's last schoolteacher, everyone tried to be involved on that day, whether in a ball game, a game of rope, or other games.[6] Similarly, if

---

[4] "Star gentlemen": astronomers.
[5] Väinö Salminen, "Lappalaisten 'joikaus'-lauluista," *Valvoja* 27, no. 1 (1907): 1–9.
[6] Jaakko Pohjola, "Käynnillä Koltta-Lapissa, miesväen 'paratiisissa,'" *Turun ylioppilaslehti*, March 15, 1939, 15–16.

someone passed away in the *sijdd*, all dancing ceased. Antti Hämäläinen (1897–1976), a Finnish ethnographer, described this as follows:

> After the death of an adult, e.g., in Suõ'nn'jel, no one works until the deceased is buried in the bosom of the earth. The death of even a small child causes all kinds of joy and fun seizes in the whole village. The dances, which the Skolt Saami are so fond of, and «siõrr» (games) are stopped immediately.[7]

In earlier times, dancing was almost exclusively performed by adults, as it was restricted from children. This information comes from several interviews. Katri Jeffremoff stated that youngsters under 15 did not dance and were not allowed to join dances. In 1986, Ee'led Semenoff and Då'mnn Sanila stated in an interview that one could join the *ka'drel* dances after turning 15.[8]

Earliest Descriptions of Dancing among the Eastern Saami

Skolt Saami have known common couple and group dances since the second half of the nineteenth century. Dancing was an essential form of entertainment for them when they lived in their winter villages in their original homeland. The Skolt Saami dance culture has many features like those of the Karelian and Northern Russian dance cultures, and, to some extent, even with Northern Finns. It is evident, however, that most of their traditional dances—maybe all—have come from Russian Karelia and Russia. Similar dances have also been known among the other Saami in the Kola Peninsula. The Russian influence has been remarkable among all of them due to the Orthodox religion, Russian military service, and the numerous contacts with Russian merchants. It is assumed that the birth of the dance culture is connected to the liftting of the earlier mentioned ban on dancing imposed by the Orthodox Old Believers (старообрядство), who had previously considered it a sin.

---

[7] Antti Hämäläinen, *Koltta-Lappia sanoin ja kuvin. Uutta Lapin lääniä I* (Helsinki: WSOY, 1938), 69–70.
[8] Hannele Tulonen, "Popmusiikki nousi pelimanni-ja tanhuperinteen rinnalle Sodankylän Jutajaisjuhlilla," *Helsingin Sanomat*, July 7, 1986, 11. This rule has changed radically over the last forty years. In the 1990s, the *ka'drel* became a part of Če'vetjäu'rr elementary school's program. On the fiftieth anniversary of Če'vetjäu'rr settlement in 1999, there were both adults and children's groups performing the *ka'drel* at the celebration party. In 2009, the headmaster of Če'vetjäu'rr school stated in an interview that the children would not leave Če'vetjäu'rr school without the basic knowledge of the language, handicrafts, and *ka'drel* dancing. According to Satu Moshnikoff, the former teacher of the Če'vetjäu'rr school, there were three dance groups dancing simultaneously in the Če'vetjäu'rr sixty-year anniversary celebration. The members of the groups represented diverse age groups.

FIGURE 5.1. Saami from Luujäu'rr *sijdd*.
Source: Photograph by J. A. Palmén in Luujäu'r, August 11, 1887.

Early descriptions in Finnish literature show how the influence of Russian culture was strong in the late nineteenth century all over Russian Lapland. In terms of music tradition, the most easily recognizable Russian features were the appearance of dance, dance music, and accordions among the Kola Saami people at the end of the nineteenth century. There are several descriptions of dances and the use of accordions in the travelogs of contemporaries. Accordions can also be seen in a few photos taken from the Kola Peninsula. For example, the photograph seen in Figure 5.1 was taken by J. A. Palmén on August 11, 1887, in the Kildin Saami village of Luujäu'rr, "Lovozero." In the picture is what appears to be a "Cherepovka" accordion. This type of accordion began to be manufactured in the 1860s and 1870s in the Russian town of Cherepovets.[9]

When the Western travelers describe dance occasions in the nineteenth and early twentieth centuries, there is almost always an accordion player mentioned as well. The use of accordion was introduced by the Russians. The earliest dance descriptions found in Finnish literature is from Finnish linguist Arvid Genetz (1848–1915). In 1876, he spent the year in Kola Peninsula gathering material for his Kola Saami dictionary (published in 1891). Genetz writes in his journal of a dance event in Ponoi village in the eastern part of Kola, where both Russians and Teri Saami lived at the time:

---

[9]Marko Jouste, "Lampaitako olette, kun ette osaa edes katrillia tanssia?," in *Venäläisen musiikkikulttuurin vaikutuksia historiallisessa Suonikylän musiikkiperinteessä. Seminar Proceedings of Runolaulu Akatemia* (Kuhmo: Runolaulu-Akatemia & Juminkeko, 2013); Альфред Мирек, "Череповка, черепашки обыкновенные," *Аккордеонист.Ру* (2017). Available online: http://www.akkordeonist.ru/history_view.php?id=24 (accessed August 3, 2024).

On the 8th of October [1876] I was invited to an evening entertainment; a few young men had set up a dance party in a neighboring house for one ruble and gathered girls there. There was plenty of music; the best singer among the girls started the song with a terribly loud and sharp voice and soon the other girls joined in. At the same time, different notes were played on two, occasionally on three accordions. It is easy to guess what kind of harmony was born from this. The house was full of scabs, the table was full of stomachs; there were a few drunken hoes enjoying themselves. There was very little space for the dancers in the middle of the floor, and not much was needed, because the dance was very monotonous and at the beginning there was only one, later two couples on the floor. The boy demanded the girl to dance, hitting her on the head; then they "figured" in turns facing each other and spinning together. After the dance, they departed, the boy took his place, but the girl asked another young man to dance, etc.[10]

However, accordions were used not only by Russians but also by Norwegians and Finns who worked in the Pechenga and Kola regions. For example, Finnish traveler and journalist August Wilhelm Ervasti (1845–1900) described accordion playing in a merchant's house at Port Vladimir (Jeretnika), a Russian harbor in *Urrvuõnn* (Finnish: Uuravuono), during his trip to Kola in 1883:

Inside we met a young lieutenant from Bakan, a ship captain, a priest, I think there was someone else too. Then an accordion was played, and the ship's captain played the Norwegian national anthem 'Ja vi elsker detta landet', which the lieutenant did not like, so he suggested and sang "Booshe tsarjaa hranii" [*Bože, Tsarja Hrani*, Russian national anthem].[11]

Skolt Saami likely adopted dancing in the 1870s or 1880s. Finnish geologist Väinö Tanner speculated that the dance tradition began in the winter village of Kõllaž'jokk in Paaččjokk, which was in use from 1875 to 1888.[12]

Samuli Paulaharju (1875–1944), a Finnish ethnographer, described how Skolt Saami Eastern festivities ended in *ka'drel* dancing in 1914:

And with his whole family, even the little ones, he says long prayers in front of God [the home icon and a candle], crosses himself and bows, and someone in the crowd can even sing a holy verse, while the others also try their best to keep

---

[10] Arvid Genetz, "Kuolan niemimaan asukkaiden oloja tutkimassa vuonna 1876," in *Kuolan niemimaalla käyneiden suomalaisten tiedemiesten matkakertomuksia*, ed. and trans. Leif Rantala, Acta Lapponica Fenniae 20 (Rovaniemi: Lapin Tutkimusseura, 2008), 31–2.
[11] August Wilhelm Ervasti, *Suomalaiset jäämeren rannalla. Matkamuistelmia* (Oulu: Wickström, 1884).
[12] Tanner, 'Antropogeografiska studier inom Petsamo-området', 111.

up with him. Even after a little while before the repetition, he turns to the God to bow and pray and pray, and then turns off the fire, leaving only a tiny spark to flicker. But already in the afternoon, young man of the house blows it out, takes an accordion and starts playing the "kaatrel."[13]

The multicultural environment with shared dance traditions among the neighboring Karelian, Russian, Norwegian, and Finnish collapsed as the First World War (1914–1918), Russian revolution (1917), Russian civil war (1917–1922), and the Finnish paramilitary expeditions (1918 and 1920) entered the Murman Coast and Skolt Saami living areas. However, the wartime brought new cultural influences as Skolt Saami men served in the Tzar's army and later in the White and Red armies. Those who returned home from the war had learned new dances and dance music, and they began to teach these in their local communities. During the 1920s, these new dances spread through Skolt Saami society, esspecially Suõ'nn'jel *sijdd*—or, at least, numerous historical sources describe the *sijdd*'s vivid dance culture until the beginning of the Second World War in 1939.

Features of Early-Twentieth-Century Skolt Saami Dance Culture

At the beginning of the twentieth century, the Skolt Saami dance repertoire included both older square dances and other group dances from the latter part of the nineteenth century, as well as new couple dances. The *ka'drel* became a vital part of the Skolt Saami culture, and its skills were highly valued. In Suõ'nn'jel, *ka'drel* dancing continued uninterrupted until the Second World War. This is the period from which there is the most archive material.

Although dancing existed in the past, there was likely a hiatus in the early 1920s, when the people of Suõ'nn'jel did not have a winter village. The *ka'drel* craze seemingly began with the construction of the new Suõ'nn'jel in 1927, and it lasted until the winter war of the 1930s. The dance seasons were particularly timed after the fasting seasons, and There are numerous accounts of dancing, especially from the 1930s.

It is notable that the concept of "dressing well" is an important part of the dance culture in Skolt Saami society, and this was the case in the early twentieth century as well. A description written by Jaakko Pohjola, Suõ'nn'jel's last schoolteacher, reveals how people dressed up specially for dances in year 1939:

---

[13]Paulaharju, *Kolttain mailta*, 138–9.

FIGURE 5.2. A Skolt Saami girl.
Source: Pohjola, "Käynnillä Koltta-Lapissa," 15–16.

Skolt Saami women pay special attention to their dressing. However, the fashion trends from Paris do not reach here, and they would not be received here either. They are very old-fashioned people who stick to their customs. When choosing fabrics, the deciding factor is the color of the fabric and, as a side note, the quality of the fabric. As variegated as possible, as well as bright red, blue and yellow fabric is popular. The party dress also includes an apron. The headpiece is very beautiful. Married women have a tall cap, šaamšik̆, made of felt and vera, which is also beautifully embroidered with pearls. Girls also wear this kind of headdress "pervest," which is much more modest. There must be a limit to the girls' desire to dazzle, instead, there are no obstacles for the hostess. Women attach all kinds of rattling trinkets and a long knife to their belts. Men dress in the same way as elsewhere in Lapland. Everyone wears home-woven, beautifully embroidered woolen socks and fur shoes made of reindeer hooves (in addition to the socks, softened grass, shoe grass is also used in the shoes.) Having become accustomed to this kind of outfit, the shy youth, who prefer to be in a group, arrive at the dance hall. (It is someone's residential building.)[14]

---

[14]Pohjola, "Käynnillä Koltta-Lapissa."

FIGURE 5.3. Mari Gauriloff.
Source: Kalevala Foundation, A. O. Väisänen, 1926.

6 DANCING YEAR

Although the dance was a culturally vital part of the Skolt Saami way of life during the first part of the twentieth century, it was not practiced throughout the year. In the following, a model of dancing seasons of the Skolt Saami culture will be presented. The two main seasons are located at the time when Skolt Saami were gathered in the winter villages. This is frequently mentioned in contemporary sources:

> Winter is a time for socializing. The diligent youth then take advantage of the opportunity either to dance (ka'drel) or, during the lent, play games like rope- or running games etc. Even the older population takes part in them.[1]

First Dancing Season, from Christmas to the Shrove

The first dancing season, which can be dated to the period from Christmas to the Shrove, was the time when Skolt Saami had just moved to the winter village from autumn residences. Only before the Russian Christmas did people move to the winter village.[2] Social life began to bloom as all the people of the *sijdd* were gathered in the same place after each family had lived in their own areas since the spring. Social life consisted of various activities, but the descriptions, which include dance, often refer to three specialties: riding the reindeer sledges, playing games outside, and dancing indoors. As often, there are various historical sources

---

[1] Pohjola, "Käynnillä Koltta-Lapissa," 15.
[2] Uno Holmberg, "Kolttain omistusoikeuksista ja -merkeistä," in *Kalevalaseuran vuosikirja* 7 (Helsinki: Kalevalaseura 1927), 8.

from the Suõ'nn'jel *sijdd*; some of the accounts found in these sources may also reflect conditions or events in other Skolt Saami *sijdd*s of the time.

According to T. I. Itkonen, the Skolt Saami used to race in their winter villages with sleds pulled by three or four reindeer. The tradition likely began at the turn of the nineteenth and twentieth centuries as the Komi *nartta* sleigh—also called *saan*—was only introduced at the end of the nineteenth century. For the first time, there was a *saan*-sleigh in Suõ'nn'jel in the early 1890s.[3] Samuli Paulaharju, who visited Suõ'nn'jel in 1914, writes:

> It has been almost thirty years since this remarkable way of transportation was seen for the first time in Suõ'nn'jel. A Skolt Saami boy, who had worked as a hired hand for Komi in the Muotka-sijdd, had learned to ride a reindeer sled with him. The boy immediately showed the people of Suõ'nn'jel his wonderful skill: he harnessed two of the village men's reindeer alongside his trained reindeer bull and then galloped handsomely around the village, guiding with a long stick. The whole village looked in awe at this remarkable event, which was like a great revelation in their wilderness. Now the Skolt Saami are almost as great a master in the art of sleigh riding as the Komi. In front of a long sled, he harnesses either a troika, three reindeer, or a tzitverka, four, five reindeer, even sometimes a tsetse, six bulls side by side, one tied to the other.[4]

Paulaharju writes about the beginning of the Lenten week that "the wildest thing is to live Lent, the beginning of Lent, when you prepare yourself with dances, intrigues and rides, as well as hearty meat soups to face the harsh fast." Paulaharju elaborates the description of Shrove as follows:

> But when Shrove comes, followed by a long and severe fasting period, joy, and carefree rejoicing rise to the top. Because during the holy fast, you can't dance or rummage, and that's why you must have enough of it beforehand. The days of the week are a continuous frenzy, the more severe the closer the beginning of Lent comes. We dance, we drink and drive, five, six, even eight reindeer are harnessed in front of the herd, and the herd is full of men, women, children, people of all ages, even the little cradleboard "k̆iõtkâm" children, and then we fly at full speed through the village from one end to the other, so that the snow is thrown like snow , the reindeer's antlers click and the bells clang. We shout and caress, sing and sing, whatever voice comes out of the throat. And the man whose reindeer sleigh goes ahead. At the edge of the village, we stop, turn the teams, take the rumps, and then with the same commotion, we gallop through

---

[3] Toivo Immanuel Itkonen, *Suomen lappalaiset vuoteen 1945 II* (Porvoo: WSOY, 1948), 445.
[4] Paulaharju, *Kolttain mailta*, 84–5.

FIGURE 6.1. Riding with a *saan*-sled in Suõ'nn'jel, 1936.

Source: Photograph by Karl Nickul. Museovirasto, Suomalais-ugrilainen kuvakokoelma (SUK366:73).

to the other side of the village. And again, the rumblings and a rumbling rush through the village. It's a celebration of the fell folk.[5]

The entire week of Shrove was significant. The last day of Shrove called *Mäiddpâ'sslašttâm* was also the last day before Lent; people had fun driving reindeer and playing *nue'rrsiõrr*—"rope-game"—outside during the day and dancing and celebrating *prää'zneǩ*, a religious feast, afterwards inside a house. There is an expression, *siõrrpõõrt nårrai*—"the dance house came together"—for organizing dance events, which continued until morning. Jääkk Sverloff (1894–1977), in an interview conducted by a Finnish linguist Mikko Korhonen (1926–1991) in 1959, recalled a celebration in *Mäiddpâ'sslašttâm*. The events can be dated to have happened at the latest in the mid-1930s, since he mentioned his brother Ǩiurrâl Sverloff (1891–1941), who passed away in 1941:

> Well, at Christmas there wasn't much reindeer-driving or anything like that. But *Mäiddpâ'sslašttâm* "Shrove (Tuesday)," as they say *laskiainen* in Finnish, that week was all about driving, people driving. Then whoever had a good driving reindeer brought the best driving bulls. For a week, saan-sledges were

[5]Ibid., 41.

FIGURE 6.2. Playing a rope-game in Suõ'nn'jel, 1932.
Source: Photograph by Karl Nickul. Museovirasto, Suomalais-ugrilainen kuvakokoelma (SUK262:15a).

driven with four or five reindeer bulls. Then Ǩiurrâl [Sverloff] had such a trained driving reindeer that he didn't need a leash, only a driving rope. Five reindeer bulls are driven with only a driving stick to indicate which way to turn.

He came to the village. They are playing rope-game. He just throws his driving stick. All the reindeer stand. Others ride, the reindeer stay standing, you didn't even have to tie them up.

Then evening came, and then there was a party, Mäiddpâ′sslašttâm. They take their reindeer to the forest and the "dance hall gathers" and they dance until morning. They drink and dance there until morning and stop dancing. At four o'clock in the morning they still drank and drank until six o'clock in the morning. Then they stop and start fasting. That was the end of it.[6]

There is also a *Mäiddneä′ttel leu′dd* —"A shrove *leu′dd*"—recorded in Suõ'nn'jel in 1926 by A. O. Väisänen (1890–1969). The lyrics describe the first part of the day when people drove reindeer. It was performed by Paa'vvel Sverloff (b. 1878), the eldest brother of Jääkk and Ǩiurrâl.

Lo-loo-lol	Lo-loo-lol
Pue′tt-e-li joukk siid-a uu′lca,	A group of people rushed to the village road,
jâlkk uu′lca. Mäiddneä′ttel.	a smooth village road. [It is] Shrove week.

---

[6] Jääkk Sverloff, interview by Mikko Korhonen. The Institute for the Languages of Finland, Kotus 00631_1a.

Lal-lal-lal-lal-jo	Lal-lal-lal-lal-jo
Nuõrre villj-a vižž-i-li	The young brother gathered
tiudd kutt-e-lokutt jeärgažed	66 reindeer bulls.
Ǩeässti nuõrr villj-a koolmi jeärgai	The young brother harnessed three bulls,
i neeljji jeärgai,	four bulls (front of a saan-sledge)
vuäbba nuõrre	for the young sister
išttlâ'stted kälkksaani ool.	to sit on the painted saan-sledge.
Veâl ǩeässti tää'l-e	Brother drives fiercely
peridovoi jeärgaid	and steers the lead bulls.
Pue'ttal joukk riist uu'lcai mie'ldd.	A group of people came crossing the road.
Ha-ha-ha-haa-jo	Ha-ha-ha-haa-jo
Joortee'l, ǩie'zztee'l,	They drive circles.
pue'ttal joogg rââst	they drive over the (icy) river
uu'lcai mie'ldd-e-a-ga-ga-gon.	and along the village road.
Mäiddneä'ttel,	The week of Shrove,
Mäiddpâ'sslašttâm pei'vv.	Shrove holiday.[7]

Skolt Saami dances—especially *ka'drel*—were often mentioned in Finnish newspapers and journals during the 1930s and 1940s. Some of these contain recallings of the dance during the Shrove. Though these are not comprehensive descriptions, they often offer additional and important information about the dance practices and dance occasions, as they are the only contemporary written sources. A Finnish periodical *Suomen Kuvalehti* published an article on the travels of Louise Boyd and Barbara Donohoe from California and how they spent Christmas of 1933 and New Year of 1934 in Pechenga. While returning to South Finland from the shore of the Arctic Ocean, they passed through Suõ'nn'jel during the "dance season" after the "little lent" of Christmas. The Americans witnessed how the whole day was spent dancing and how guests were warmly welcomed to dance:

> On the way back, we stopped in Suõ'nn'jel. The arrival of the guests was known in the village, and so there were 150 people waiting, all of whom had to be greeted by hand according to custom. The whole village was dancing, because the [little] lent had just ended, and according to the custom, the dancing season continued for two weeks at a time. At 11 o'clock in the morning the ka'drel began, and it only ended late at night. And each house took turns as a dance hall. Miss Boyd and Donohoe also got caught up in the whirlwind of the dance

---

[7] Paa'vvel Sverloff, "*Mäiddneä'ttel leu'dd* 'Laskiaislaulu,'" interview by A. O. Väisänen in Suõ'nn'jel, 1926, Finnish Literature Society (SKS), ph 4/192.

and assured that they have never had such success in the male world like among Suõ'nn'jel's cavaliers.⁸

Shrove was followed by the Lent, and during that time, dancing was prohibited for religious reasons. However, outdoor games were permitted, and as the darkest and coldest period of the winter ended in March, people entertained themselves with these activities.

Second Dancing Season, after Lent

The Second dancing season during the winter began after Lent had ended. It appears that dancing followed mainly the same phases as seen earlier after Christmas. People first played games outside before coming inside for *ka'drel*. Aslak Outakoski (1909–2006), who visited Suõ'nn'jel in 1934, describes the dance after Lent:

> On holidays like this, which are densely packed just after Easter, the rope game is immediately followed by dancing, a ka'drel, accordion player brings his instrument, from which tunes come out even until midnight. As a novelty, Skolt Saamis have adopted the Finnish ring game in these years, although it creates more difficulties in tight spaces than ka'drel, which is danced by only two couples at a time. Even weekday evenings are often part of the same revelry. Judging from the previous one, you would think that Skolt Saami do nothing but have fun during this time. However, this is not the case. They also take care of their tasks, although play is understandably pleasant too.⁹

Another description, by Jaakko Pohjola, Suõ'nn'jel's last Finnish schoolteacher, reveals social manners and how people behaved during the dance. The description is from the year 1939:

> When the [accordion] player sits down, the boys rush to find a girl or a [married] woman of their choice (in the past, it is said, the girls may have been bystanders while the married women danced). Four pairs at a time thread beautifully in the "whirl" of the ka'drel. When you enter a dance house, you'd think you'd come to the complete opposite place. It's quiet. The women sit looking very dignified, with a serious and noble expression on their faces. When asking someone to dance, boys are no better than girls when it comes to making beautiful "courtly gestures". Simply saying the name or a familiar touch is enough as a sign. I followed the activities of the married women in one house. She was asked for a

---

⁸*Suomen Kuvalehti*, "Lappiin joulu-ukkoa tapaamaan – Kaliforniasta asti," March 10, 1934, 330–1.
⁹Aslak Outakoski, "Kolttakylää paastosta kevätmuuttoon," *Kaleva*, May 27, 1934, 6.

FIGURE 6.3. Teacher Hilja Vartiainen and Liisa Feodoroff in the winter of 1928–9.
Source: Museovirasto, Suomalais-ugrilainen kuvakokoelma (SUK925:221).

ka′drel. In the middle of the dance, she ran to soothe her crying child. Between the dances, she would go up to breastfeed—quite a public service—her child, and to serve food and water to the rest of her family and nurse the tired ones. So a very versatile activity; work and fun side by side![10]

There were several dance occasions in everyday life. It was part of winter village life almost every night, except during Lent.

The period of most intensive dancing was brief as soon after Easter, the Skolt Saami departed for their spring and summer residencies. Nevertheless, whenever possible, it was carried out with immense enthusiasm, as can be seen Antti Hämäläinen's description from 1938:

> It was worth seeing when old, bearded men took their wrinkle cheek missuses with dance steps to the middle of the floor to dance there a few, sometimes rather complicated figures you know the ka′drel—in front of the opposite couple and brought their "lady" back to her seat. And this continued incessantly until the small hours, when everybody went to sleep, tired and sweaty, to be able to continue the same procedure the next evening with new energy.[11]

An elementary school was established in Suõ′nn'jel in 1928, and the first teacher was a Finnish woman, Hilja Vartiainen. During the winter of 1928–9, she followed the life of the village and wrote a memoir about her experiences. Vartiainen also confirmed the timing of two main dancing seasons:

---

[10]Pohjola, "Käynnillä Koltta-Lapissa."
[11]Hämäläinen, *Koltta-Lappia sanoin ja kuvin*.

The dances can be set up immediately, whenever there are a few couples. It's good if there happens to be a harmonica or accordion player in the crowd. If there isn't, people just "play with their mouths" and thump with their foot harder. For orthodox Skolt Saami, dances are allowed during the non-fasting period. Lent time, from Shrove Sunday to Easter, is a time of refusal even when it comes to dancing. Even more dancing is done before and after Lent.[12]

Minor Dancing Season during Festivities in Summer and Autumn

Until the Second World War, Skolt Saami lived with their own families for most of the year in their own family areas. It is natural that there were often not enough people in one's own family for the actual dance. During summer, the dance was connected to *prää'zneǩ*, the festivities organized in connection with church holidays. Many people from the entire *sijdd* gathered for these festivities. The most important of these celebrations were *Ee'lj pei'vv*—"Midsummer"—and *Peeddar pei'vv*— "Peter's Day"— both located in June.

There are very few sources documenting dance in these festivities. Occasionally, some information can be found from Skolt Saami oral history and *leu'dd* texts. Such is the following text fragment of Peeddar pei'vv—"Peter's Day"—a *leu'dd* performed by Če'vetjäu'rr's village elder Jääkk Sverloff in 1961. Sverloff describes the festivities of Peter's Day and mentiones accordion playing while dancing. It is most likely a performer's personal memory from the 1920s:

> Si'rǧǧi viilljaž lij Evvan â'lǧǧ gu siõrâ-d-eškuõ'đi garmaan-i siõri-ju-vui'm-a.
>
> Teä-ve't gulak mij u võlak-i siõrâ-de-škuõ'điim ka'drell vie'sslâi-gu siõ're.
>
> De mij vuänak muu siõrâ-de-škuõ'đi mâna lekkâljeära võ'l-i uu'rčeškuõ'đi Sauuʒâst-i tij leä'ped šõddâm? Jeä'ped ve't-i ni gu siõlgât ni ka'drell siõrr ni gu siõrrâd?[13]

'Brother Si'rǧǧi is Evvan's son.
He started to play accordion, and we began to dance.'
'We danced a fast ka'drel dance.'

---

[12]Hilja Vartiainen, *Koulupaikan neitinä kolttain parissa* (Jyväskylä: Gummerus, 1929), 154.
[13]Marko Jouste, Elias Mosnikoff, and Seija Sivertsen, *Maaddârääjji leeu'd - Historiallisia kolttasaamelaisia leu'ddeja. The Leu'dds of the Ancestors. Historical Skolt Saami leu'dds* (Inari and Kautinen: Saamelaismuseosäätiö & Kansanmusiikki-Instituutti & Kolttien kyläkokous, 2007).

'We begin to dance, like reindeer bulls in a barn, we ran around.'
'Were you born of a sheep? You can't even dance the ka′drel?'

In the text, people who don't know how to dance are called sheep. This same expression can be seen in another song performance by O′nddri Jääkk from the village of Boris Gleb. It was written down by the Norwegian Saami Isak Saba in the 1910s:[14]

Fefraš gúlak, Evvan algge	Ferfras, listen, son of Evvan.
son lej riggas barn,	He is a rich boy.
stokkanta son ij datto	Without a drinking glass,
júkkat čæi.	he doesn't want to drink tea.
"*Goargaš don læh, vaiko ijjestad,*	"You are proud, even though
læk gaddarak mofte viercast.	you have legs like a ram.
Mah di lepet, lepetgo di savʒast šaddam,	What are you?
vai lepetgo di šaddam	Have you been born from a sheep?
Sodjar′vuvde ⁿaldda	Have you grown up tied up
galmma lavʒǯe-maddagest	in the Så′ǧǧervuu′d area
Go ⁱepet šiela sierrat?"	as you can not dance?"
"*Mist læh guoft′núorra nieid′*	"We have two young girls
núbbe sidast boattam,	Who came from another village:
Šaška sammal nieid	Šaška Sammol's girl
i Maška Jakkim nieid	and Maška Jakkim's girl,
gúoft′ nubbe sidast boađâš oabah."	two "sisters" from the other village."

The earliest description of Skolt Saami weddings is made by Jens A. Friis, who travelled in the Kola Peninsula during the summer of 1867. He provides a detailed account of wedding ceremonies in the Paččjokk area, but there is no mention of dancing during the festivities that span several days.[15] However, in 1868, Finnish ethnographer J. F. Thauvón (Thauwon) (1828–1918) visited Kola Peninsula and documented Akkala Saami weddings that lasted three days; he concluded his report of the final day with a remark: "Now the dancing and singing begin."[16] It is notable that Arvid Genetz also gives a description of dancing in the Kola Peninsula

---

[14] Marko Jouste, Markus Juutinen, and Miika Lehtinen, "Isak Saba ja Paččjogas 1919:s čohkejuvvon nuortalaš leu′ddat. Isak Saba og de skoltesamiske leu′ddene som ble samlet inn i Paččjokk i 1919," in *Optegnelser. Isak Sabas folkeminnesamling. Čállosat. Isak Saba álbmotmuitočoakkáldat*, Norsk Folkeminnelags skrifter 173 (Oslo: Skandinavian Academic Press, 2019), 221–4.

[15] Jens Andreas Friis, *En Sommer i Finmarken, Russisk Lapland og Nordkarelen* (Christiania: Cammermeyer, 1871), 153–8.

[16] Johan Fredrik Thauwon, *Matka-muistelmia Wenäjän Lapista* (1870), 8. Available online: https://urn.fi/URN:NBN:fi-fd2010-00001764 (accessed August 4, 2024).

that same year.[17] It is evident that dance was becoming a part of the Skolt Saami culture in the 1860s.

The most detailed description of the Skolt Saami weddings before the Second World War are presented by T. I. Itkonen. According to him, dancing took place at three-day weddings at the end of the first day of festivities, which was spent at the groom's house. At that time, the young couple sat side by side on the bed, which was partitioned from the rest of the room by a curtain. Only their shoes were visible beneath it. The guests dined and occasionally danced the *ka'drel*. According to Itkonen, "This is how the party, and the dance continued all night."[18] In Paččjokk, the wedding guests gathered for dancing in the wedding house a few days after the wedding. "Earlier, instruments were not used, girls and women only accompanied dance singing in Russian."[19]

At Skolt Saami weddings, dance was not part of the rituals or ceremonies, but young people could gather at some point and dance among themselves. The Okldu'na singing game is particularly mentioned as popular entertainment on such occasions.

---

[17]Genetz, "Kuolan niemimaan asukkaiden oloja tutkimassa vuonna 1876," 32.
[18]Itkonen, *Suomen lappalaiset vuoteen 1945 II*, 421.
[19]Ibid., 417.

7 SKOLT SAAMI MUSIC

Since the Skolt Saami have always lived in a multicultural environment, their music tradition is inherently multilayered. Multiculturalism and influences from different music traditions are visible in the diversity of music genres described in the earlier research.[1] They are also found in the vast collection of archival material, gathered from the Skolt Saami during the twentieth century and preserved in archives in Finland, Russia, Sweden, Norway, and Estonia.[2] Furthermore, the researchers who visited the Skolt Saami area during the first decades of the twentieth century often remarked about the Karelian and Russian impact on the Skolt Saami culture.

Own and Shared Music Cultures

Many forms of Skolt Saami musical expression belong to a group of traditions shared with northwestern Russia. For example, songs from the early twentieth century have their stylistic origin in the neighboring Russian or Karelian song traditions. However, in the center of the Skolt Saami music tradition is the genre of vocally performed individual song called *leu'dd*, which is essentially Skolt Saami. *Leu'dd* is a genre of unaccompanied Skolt Saami songs, and as a genre, it

---

[1] See Laitinen, "Suonikylän laulut vuonna 1961," 27–65; Ilpo Saastamoinen, "Itäsaamelaisten musiikkiperinteestä," in *Beaivvi mánát. Saamelaisten juuret ja nykyaika*, ed. Irja Seurujärvi-Kari, Tietolipas 164 (Helsinki: SKS, 2000); Marko Jouste, "Venäläisen bylinan ja kolttasaamelaisen leu'ddin välisestä yhteydestä," *Musiikin suunta* 30, nos. 3–4 (2008): 11–31 (24–8); Marko Jouste, "Katsaus koltan- ja kuolansaamelaisiin musiikkiperinteisiin," in *Sommelon säikeitä. Runolaulu-Akatemian seminaarijulkaisu 2009–2010*, ed. Pekka Huttu Hiltunen, Janne Seppänen, Frog, Eila Stepanova, and Riikka Nevalainen, Juminkeon julkaisuja, no. 86 (Kuhmo: Juminkeko, 2011), 54.
[2] See Jouste, "Katsaus koltan- ja kuolansaamelaisiin musiikkiperinteisiin," 54; Saastamoinen, "Itäsaamelaisten musiikkiperinteestä," 96–7; Ilpo Saastamoinen, "Laulu – puu – rumpu: Saamelaismusiikin alkulähteillä" (Licentiate of Arts diss., Department of Musicology, University of Jyväskylä, 1998), 588–90.

has equivalents in other Eastern Saami individual song traditions, such as Kildin Saami *luvvjt* and Aanaar Saami *livđe*. It is notable that the *leu'dd* tradition differs significantly from the Northern Saami *luohti*, "yoik," which is the most known form of Saami music in scientific literature. With a *leu'dd*, the singer refers to actual people, their life stories, and other historical events, and these can be studied in the broader context of local oral tradition. It can be defined as "a history told by people's own voices" since *leu'dd*s have preserved oral history over generations. Skolt Saami singers also comment on the various aspects of life inside the local community, and for this reason, *leu'dd*s and the music tradition in general are a valuable source of information about the Skolt Saami life and experience. Within this material, it is possible to obtain a historical Skolt Saami perspective on their own history as well as individual and collective worldviews.[3]

There are various models for the Skolt Saami music genre classification formulated in former research.[4] Sometimes there are *leu'dd*s and songs (not connected with known members of the community) in fairy tales. A special genre found in the archival material is the use of voice in various signals, such as calls for animals and imitations of the sounds they make. This group includes secular songs (e.g., Karelian and Russian folk and dance songs) and Christian songs taken from the Orthodox Church. Laments are found in the Eastern Saami music traditions as well as those of Karelians and Russians, but not among the Saami living in Scandinavia. Skolt Saami lullabies often have *baju-baju*-syllables, reflecting the link to Karelian and Russian lullaby traditions. There was instrumental dance music performed on accordions and harmonicas, as well as the vivid tradition of Karelian and Russian dances.[5] The forms of musical expression used for accompanying dance include both "dance songs" and instrumental dance music, performed mainly on accordions and harmonicas as in the Russian and Karelian dances. During the 1930s, gramophones were also used.

It is notable that singers may vary songs and as well as combine elements of the above-mentioned "ideal" genres; it is this process that creates new meanings in

---

[3] Marko Jouste, "Suomen saamelaisten musiikkiperinteet," in *Suomen musiikin historia: Kansanmusiikki*, ed. Anneli Asplund, Petri Hoppu, Heikki Laitinen, Timo Leisiö, Hannu Saha, and Simo Westerholm (Helsinki: WSOY, 2006); Marko Jouste, Elias Mosnikoff, and Seija Sivertsen, *Maaddârääjji leeu'd - Historiallisia kolttasaamelaisia leu'ddeja. The Leu'dds of the Ancestors. Historical Skolt Saami leu'dds* (Inari and Kaustinen: Saamelaismuseosäätiö & Kansanmusiikki-Instituutti & Kolttien kyläkokous, 2007), 13–14.

[4] Jouste, "Suomen saamelaisten musiikkiperinteet," 295–301; Saastamoinen, "Laulu – puu – rumpu," 102–4; Laitinen, "Suonikylän laulut vuonna 1961"; Heikki Laitinen, "Saamelaisten musiikki," in *Kansanmusiikki*, ed. Anneli Asplund and Matti Hako, Suomalaisen Kirjallisuuden Seuran toimituksia 366 (Helsinki: SKS, 1981), 194–7; Paulaharju, *Kolttain mailta*, 194.

[5] On Russian and Karelian impact, see, e.g., Jouste, "Lampaitako olette, kun ette osaa edes katrillia tanssia?," 23–5; Irja Häkämies, "Kolttasaamelainen musiikkiperinne," *Kansanmusiikki*, no. 2 (1978): 16–21 (18–19); Karl Nickul, *The Skolt Lapp Community, Suenjelsijd, during the Year 1938*, Nordiska Museet: Acta Lapponica V (Stockholm: Hugo Gebers Förlag, 1948), 57; Laitinen, "Saamelaisten musiikki," 195.

performances, and it is a central way of communication. However, the singers have knowledge of the functions of genres; they are aware of the genre system, which is further accompanied by a cultural code that directs the use of tradition.

Dance Songs

Whenever possible, the dance was accompanied by musical instruments, however, if there was no instruments or a musician present, the dance was accompanied by singing. There are very few sources describing the use of instruments during the decades at the end of the nineteenth and early twentieth centuries, and it is relatively difficult to assess the use of musical instruments as a dance accompaniment during that period. The most abundant information related to musical instruments is from Suõ'nn'jel from the 1930s. However, it can be assumed that, alongside musical accompaniment, singing together with dancing has been a widely used practice of dance accompaniment. Accompanying dance by singing was common especially in the 1950s and 1960s: it was likely that there were no instruments used in Če'vetjäu'rr or in Njeä'llem during that period. Although the recording of Skolt Saami music began in 1913, the first examples of dance music were not recorded until 1955. At that time, Näskk Moshnikoff and Därjj Jefremoff visited the Finnish Broadcasting Corporation's studio in Helsinki and performed many songs and *leu'dd*s. The recording of dance songs by people who had lived in Pechenga continued during the following decades. From these archive recordings, it is possible to get a comprehensive understanding of the most used dance songs mostly in Suõ'nn'jel and Če'vetjääu'r, but there are also some examples of dance songs originating from other areas as well.

According to archive recordings, dance songs can be divided into three groups. In the first group, most of the songs are of Russian origin, which are also sung with Russian lyrics. The second group consists of songs that use Russian melodies but are sung in Skolt Saami language and describe Skolt Saami life. The third group includes *leu'dd*s, which the performer has modified to fit the dance accompaniment. In the following, we shall give a musical example of each group.

Songs of Russian Origin: *Vo sadu li v ogorode*, "In the Garden"

Vo sadu li v ogorode, "In the Garden," is an old Russian folk song originating from the eighteenth century.[6] Like many other Russian folk songs, it was known by Skolt Saami in the early twentieth century and used as an accompaniment for dancing.

---

[6]*Vo sadu li v ogorode* is a Russian folk round-and-dance song, first published in 1790 in the collection Lvov-Pracha. Собрание народных русских песен с их голосами. На музыку положил Иван Прач [СПб.], 1790.

There are several solo and group performances of the song in the archival material, all of which have Russian words.[7] It should be noted that sometimes the lyrics are a mixture of Russian and Skolt Saami: the language skills of many Skolt Saami declined over the decades, as the language gradually fell out of common use when Pechenga was annexed to Finland in 1920. Here is a version performed by Ååjjaž Fofanoff in 1961:

Vo sa-du li v ogorode,	In the garden
Baryshnj-a gulla, laa	The maiden was walking.
von na pravoj-a ruko-j,	A cavalier approached
kavaler oblal-i,	from the right
Vy pozhaluytes, mol-o,	Would you agree
snami proguljat'sja,	to walk with me?
nadoj-e-ly na dav-e-no,	I'm tired
po tropim hodit'-i,	of walking the forest paths.
uzh' li milen'ka ty moj,	My love,
zatshem litso melish'?	Why is your face pale?
Ya ljublju tebja s dushoj,	I love you from my heart
ty menja ne verish'.	but you don't believe me.
"Veru ja, veru ja dorog-o-ja,	I believe,
veru so zhulej,	I do, my love.
sotvoreli zhalob'ja,	Kiss me,
potseluj-a sto dvadtsat' pjat'.	one hundred and twenty-five.

According to Ååjjaž Fofanoff, on such occasions, boys and girls danced together, and everyone sang the accompanying song (Music Example 1).

The melody differs from the most well-known Russian version (Music Example 2).

Similar textual content, where a maiden walks in the garden with her groom, can also be found in the Karelian music tradition. This is, for example, the song *Käveliin mia kuldaažen ke saduižes d'o* performed by Lid'a Plusnina (1936–2006), which perhaps also opens the meaning of the text performed by Ååjjaž Fofanoff a little more. The translation of the text is as follows:

Kävelin minä kultani kanssa puutarhassa	I walked with my darling in the garden
Satutin minä jalkani varvikossa	I hurt my leg in the brushwood
Kipeytyi minun jalkaseni kovasti,	My leg hurt a lot,

---

[7] Solo performances: Där'jj Jefremoff, interview by Erkki Ala-Könni. The Folklife Archives in University of Tampere, AK/0865; Ååjjaž Fofanoff, interview by Erkki Ala-Könni. The Folklife Archives in University of Tampere, AK/0530; Group performance: Ååjjaž Fofanoff, Marina Gavriloff, and Där'jj Jefremoff, interview by Erkki Ala-Könni. The Folklife Archives in University of Tampere, AK/0531.

MUSIC EXAMPLE 1. *Vo sadu li v ogorode.* Ååjjaž Fofanoff, interview by Erkki Ala-Könni, 1961. Transcription by Marko Jouste.

Source: The Folklife Archives in University of Tampere, AK/0530.

MUSIC EXAMPLE 2. *Vo sadu li v ogorode.* Transcription by Marko Jouste.

Lempi minua kultaseni lujasti.
Lähti hän, minulle ei sanonut - minä suutuin.

Vaan kun tuli takaisin,
minä jo lauhduin.
Toi hän minulle sormuksen ylen kauniin.

My darling loved me hard.
He left, he didn't tell me—I got angry.

But when he came back,
I already calmed down.
He brought me a beautiful ring.

Itse hän murahti:	He himself growled:
"Tulet omakseni."	"You will become mine."
vaan enää varvikkoihin	but we didn't go
emme menneet.	to the brushwoods anymore.[8]

Skolt Saami Songs with Russian Melodies: *Yabloko*

One of the most popular melodies in accompanying *ka'drel* has been the Russian dance called *Yabloko*, "Apple." It is also known as the Russian sailors' dance and became widely popular during the First World War.[9] In the Skolt Saami tradition, the melody has been used in both dance songs and *leu'dd*s. One of the best examples of the use of this melody is the following *ka'drel* song performed by Jääkk Sverloff in 1961. The style of the lyrics resembles the Russian and Karelian dance song genre called *chastushka*, consisting of short four-line segments, each of certain topic.[10] In this song, there are recallings describing various happenings in Suõ'nn'jel-village: How youngsters are running around the house and hide under tables and beds; how Brother Säkkri is wearing a Russian military cap; how a frightened fox run into a hole of a rocky cliff.[11]

Mâi'd-e kuulak-a niõ'đe	Listen, why are girls
juu u'rčči-ju-gu-de-ja de?	running around?
Mâi'd-e, mâi'd-e, mâi'd-a di	Why, why, why
pää'rne võl go o'rčča di?	are boys running around?
Di ve't-i go leäk lei-ja	And you are.
Go ko'st go mu'st lij ŋ-ääkkaž di	Where do I have a woman?
Ko'st go la mu'st lij laaukâž de	Where do I have a little bag?
Ko'st go la mu'st lij laaukâž.	Where do I have a little bag?
Säkkri gu viilljâž	Brother Säkkri
di sääldat-a kooppaž vuäivaž-e di.	a military cap in his head
Son-a de pâi-i vä'ʒʒ-e-li	He just started walking
Di son-a de pâi-i vä'ʒʒ-e-li.	He just started walking

---

[8]*Pit'k Randaane Pajod, Lyydiläisiä lauluja* (Helsinki: Maailman musiikin keskus, 2008), 26.
[9]Izaly Zemtsovsky, "Russian Federation. II. Traditional Music. 1. Russian," in *The New Grove Dictionary of Music and Musicians*, ed. Stanley Sadie (New York: Macmillan, 2001), 9; Petri Hoppu, "Jablochko: dans, musik och revolution," *Folkdansforskning i Norden* 43 (2020): 34–7; Jouste, "Lampaitako olette, kun ette osaa edes katrillia tanssia?," 55–63.
[10]Jari Eerola, *Vepsäläiset lühüdpajot: perusrakenteet, esityskäytännöt ja tyylillinen muutos* (Tampere: Tampere University Press, 2012), 52.
[11]Jääkk Sverloff, interview by Erkki Ala-Könni. The Folklife Archives in University of Tampere, AK/0568.

Mâi'd päärna go lee u'rčče	What are you boys running around with?
de mâi'd-e go lee niõ'đe u'rčče de de	What are you girls running around with?
Luu-li lul-lii lullaa.	Luu-li lul-lii lullaa.
Di dul-de lul-lii lul-lii-lul	Di dul-de lul-lii lul-lii-lul
Di duu-li lul-lii lool-la …	Di duu-li lul-lii lool-la …
Pâldd-a go de reâmmjaž i[12]	A frightened fox
pähtta-i čaaŋi	went inside of a rocky cliff
pâldd-a go de reâmnjaž di	A frightened fox
pähtta go de čaaŋi,	went inside of a rocky cliff
da luul-li-da luul-li lullaa.	da luul-li-da luul-li lullaa.
Äänn-a-gaž go stuâla vue'lnn-a,	Äänngaž under a table,
di Huâttar-i luâddaž vue'lnn-a,	Huâttar under a bench,
duu-ve't-i duu de lullaa.	duu-ve't-i duu de lullaa.

According to Sverloff, this song has been used as an accompaniment to various dances such as *ka'drel*, *Šestjarkka*, and *Vosmerkka*.[13] It has a clear four-beat rhythm, which the performer emphasizes by stomping his foot. The repeating part of the melody consists of the following phrases (Music Example 3).

The Russian song *Yabloko* has a-b-c-c-structure, with the first part (a-b) moving in the upper register, followed by a descending phrase (c) repeated twice (Music Example 4). One can easily notice the similarity between these two examples.

Leu'dds Modified for Dance Accompaniment: *Miklai da Täđjjan*

Depending on the performance, the *leu'dd* can be used instead of dance songs as a dance accompaniment. In some *leu'dd*s, the overall idea is that many of the song-like melodies might have a melodic model taken from the song traditions of the neighboring peoples.[14] This can be seen in the next example of the *leu'dd Miklai da Täđjjan*. It was performed by Va'ss Semenoja in Kirakkajoki, during a field recording organized by the Finnish Broadcasting Company in 1961.

The *leu'dd Miklai da Täđjjan*, "Miklai and Täđjjan," describes a love story of a bride and her rival suitors from the 1920s. The melody consists of three phrases and follows clearly the structure of the Yabloko-melody. This is repeated throughout the

---

[12] *Pältta rie'mpaž* signifies a fox that had eaten poison, survived, and therefore knows to avoid poison.
[13] Jääkk Sverloff, interview by Erkki Ala-Könni. The Folklife Archives in University of Tampere, AK/0568. The origin of the melody was pointed to me by Russian musicologist Mikhail Lobanov. He transcribed the melody from memory after having heard the recording.
[14] For more examples, see Jouste, "Lampaitako olette, kun ette osaa edes katrillia tanssia?."

MUSIC EXAMPLE 3. *Mâid kuulak niõďˆ*. Jääkk Sverloff, interview by Erkki Ala-Könni, 1961. Transcription by Marko Jouste.
Source: The Folklife Archives in University of Tampere, AK/0568.

MUSIC EXAMPLE 4. A Russian song *Yabloko*. Transcription from memory by M. Lobanov in possession of the author. Transcription by Marko Jouste.

performance, though, so that all phrases clearly resemble each other. There is some variation also in this type, especially in the rhythm, caused by the use of different words in different text lines (Music Example 5).

An interesting question is whether there are any clues of how and when these song melodies were incorporated into the *leu'dd* tradition of the Skolt Saami. Naturally, there is the general notion of multiculturalism and influences from different musical traditions in the cultural melting pot in the western part of the Kola Peninsula. There is also well-documented historical data of how Skolt Saami men, who were recruited into the Russian army during the First World War, learned songs during their service, and when they returned, the new songs and melodies became a new fashionable part of the Skolt Saami music.[15] According to Elias Mosnikoff and Täđjjan Killanen, two First World War veterans, Jääkk Sverloff and Å'll (Olli) Gauriloff brought dances and games with them to Suõ'nn'jel when they returned home in the early 1920s.[16] The experiences of being a soldier in

---

[15] Armas Launis, *Kaipaukseni maa. Lapinkävijän matkamuistoja* (Jyväskylä: Gummerus, 1922), 30.
[16] Elias Mosnikoff, interviewed by Marko Jouste in 2001. Saami Culture Archive, The Giellagas Institute for Saami Studies, University of Oulu, A1.2001, 1; Jääkk Sverloff, interview by Mikko Korhonen. The

MUSIC EXAMPLE 5. An excerpt of *Miklai da Tädjjan*. Va'ss Semenoja, interview by Erkki Ala-Könni 1961. Transcription by Marko Jouste.
Source: The Folklife Archives in University of Tampere, AK/0563.

Russia is described also by Jääkk Sverloff, who later became the head of the Skolt Saami community in the postwar decades.[17]

Music Instruments and Instrumental Music

The use of musical instruments began in the latter half of the nineteenth century among the Skolt Saami. In short, this became a common practice by the Russians, Karelians, and the Saami of the Kola Peninsula. Naturally, the neighboring Norwegians and Finns used instruments as they moved to Pechenga in the mid-nineteenth century. However, there is no exact information on the arrival of accordions to Pechenga, but most likely the first ones came from Russia. According to Irja Häkämies, the Russian-born musicians Stepan Kirikov and Nikolai Amansini toured and played in the villages of the Pechenga region. Well-known Skolt Saami players of accordion or harmonica originating from Peäccam *sijdd* during the twentieth century have been e.g., Huâttar Kiprianoff, Vaa'ssel (Vasili) Titoff, U'cc-Åttaž (Antti) Jefremoff, Jouni Haltta, and Je'ffem Koputoff. During 1970s, many of these players were active in the Njeä'llem (Nellim) Folklore group. In Suõ'nn'jel, there were also several musicians in the Feodoroff, Fofanoff, and Semenoff families. Karl Nickul, a Finnish researcher, made an inventory of physical objects in village of Suõ'nn'jel in 1938. The list includes two harmonicas, four accordions (concertina), and three gramophones.[18] The first accordion on the

---

Institute for the Languages of Finland, Kotus 09842_a; Tädjjan Killanen, interview by Mikko Korhonen. The Institute for the Languages of Finland, Kotus 09842_1a.
[17]See Ingold, *Skolt Lapps Today*, 235–53; Martti Linkola, "Jaakko Sverloff," in *Lappi 4 – Saamelaisten ja suomalaisten maa*, ed. Martti Linkola (Hämeenlinna: Karisto, 1985), 99.
[18]Nickul, *The Skolt Lapp Community*, 68; about Skolt Saami instrumental music, see Laitinen, "Suonikylän laulut vuonna 1961," 61–5.

list is marked for Ǩiurrâl Moshnikoff. Two musical instruments were found in the houses of Evvan-Si'rggi and Evvan-Reeig, members of the Fofanoff family. The fourth was in the house of Evvan-Åådaž Semenoff (Figure 7.1).

The harmonica was also known early on, but it was especially popular during the Second World War. Hilja Vartiainen describes in her memories from the winter of 1928–9 how people crowded into small houses to dance and how one could hear both an accordion and a harmonica at the same time.

> Huotari's little hut was packed full of people. There were women, men and children sitting on the benches in each other's laps. On the floor, in an area of no more than a couple of square meters, ka'drel was danced. There was room only for two pairs, but when you really wanted to put it in a tight spot, you could fit four pairs. The seated men stomped to the beat or chattered with their mouths. Illep Jä'ǩǩem played the harmonica, Nikolai Gauriloff played the accordion. The soles of fur shoes squelched on the wet, dirty floor.[19]

During the 1920s and 1930s, the variety of musical instruments grew, and dance music was also played from gramophones. Täddjan (Tatjana) Killanen described to Finnish linguist Mikko Korhonen in 1971 about dancing in Suõ'nn'jel and how a gramophone was also used as an accompaniment for dancing.

> In the winter village, we first played rope games outside. Then, when the evening got dark, we started dancing inside. There was a gramophone, the parents gathered to watch the younger one's dance.[20]

Antti Hämäläinen describes the accordion player's role in 1938:

> When one looks at the countless ka'drel figures, which go on continuously one after another, he notices the accordion player, who sits and sweats in the corner and is ready to play the same notes again and again. Rarely he is replaced by someone less experienced for a few rounds of ka'drel. When this happens, the master accordionist joins himself into the twirls of dance. But after every dance, the players' hard work is rewarded, as all the male dancers arrange a line to shake the players hand for gratitude.[21]

It is notable that Finnish couple dances gained recognition in the 1930s through gramophone records and radio programs. However, Nickul's list does not mention

---

[19]Vartiainen, *Koulupaikan neitinä kolttain parissa*, 158.
[20]Tatjana Killanen, interview by Mikko Korhonen. The Institute for the Languages of Finland, Kotus 09842/a.
[21]Hämäläinen, *Kolttain mailta*.

FIGURE 7.1. Utts Evvan or Evvan Semenoff (b. 1908) plays "Armonico Italiano"—accordion, 1938.

Source: Nickul, *The Skolt Lapp Community*, Plate LVIII, kuva 209.

FIGURE 7.2. Dancers shake hands with the accordion player after a dance. Source: Photograph by Antti Hämäläinen.

any radios Suõ'nn'jel. The accordions that were in use in Suõ'nn'jel were apparently not taken along on the evacuation trip, and no new ones were acquired after the move to Če'vetjäu'rr. At least in the recordings made in the 1950s and 1960s, instrumental music was not recorded. Jä'ǩǩem Feodoroff (b. 1910), previously mentioned as a harmonica player in Hilja Vartiainen's dance memoir, resumed playing the two-line accordion in the 1970s.[22] Elias Mosnikoff recorded the following *ka'drel* from him, which is possibly reminiscent of the dance tunes heard at Suõ'nn'jel dances before the wars. A rather similar playing style, with even the same musical phrases, can be heard in all recorded events featuring him during the 1970s (Music Example 6).

---

[22]Laitinen, "Suonikylän laulut vuonna 1961," 65.

MUSIC EXAMPLE 6. *Jä'kǩem Feodoroff's ka'drel*. The melody of a two-line accordion. Recording by Elias Moshnikoff. Transcription by Marko Jouste.

Source: Elias Moshnikoff's collection.

8   KA'DREL

The Skolt Saami *ka'drel* belongs to a large group of social group dances, the contradances (French: *contredanse*). Thus, their dance history is connected to European cultural and social history, where dancing played a remarkable role from the sixteenth until the nineteenth century. These dances are performed in sets, usually composed of couples, and dancing consists of an ever-changing interaction between subgroups of those in the set.[1]

The roots of the *ka'drel* are in the eighteenth-century contradances, especially the *cotillion*. The *cotillion* became one of the most popular dances in European courts, and by the end of the century, several other dance forms developed from it. One of these, known as a quadrille, was established at the court of Napoleon I. The French quadrille soon spread among the European upper classes, also in Saint Petersburg. During the nineteenth and early twentieth centuries, different forms of the quadrille became popular in different parts of the world, from the Caribbean to Siberia.

From the French Court to Northern Village Dances

In the eighteenth century, several dance forms emerged that were danced in a square. These dances became very popular in Europe and America, especially in the nineteenth century. They had their roots in the *cotillion* dance or *la contredanse française*, and several of them became known as folk dances around the world, especially in the late nineteenth century.

---

[1] Petri Hoppu, "Introduction," in *The Nordic Minuet. Royal Fashion and Peasant Tradition*, ed. Petri Hoppu, Egil Bakka, and Anne Fiskvik (Cambridge: Open Book, 2024), 14.

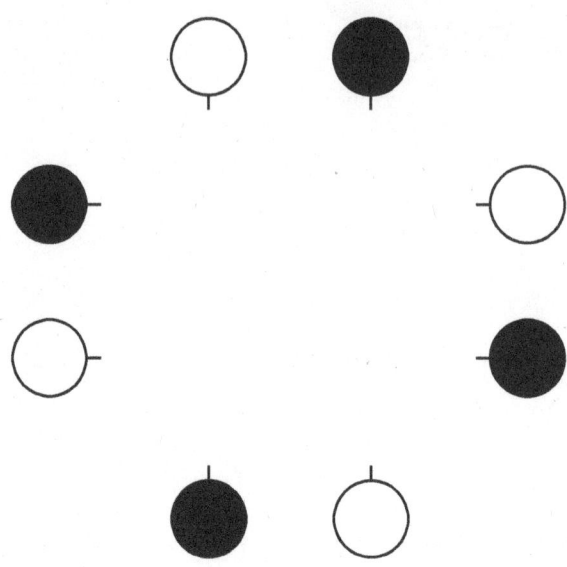

FIGURE 8.1. Square formation for eight dancers (black pin = male, white pin = female). Source: © Petri Hoppu.

The first written description of the *cotillon* (Le Cotillon, danse à Quatre) is from the French dance master Raoul Auger Feuillet's dance guide for the year 1706 (1705). Feuillet's *cotillion* was for two couples, as with many other early square dances. It had six figures, and each figure consisted of a changing part (*couplet*) and a permanent part (*refrain*). Alternating parts included similar figures as in later contradances and quadrilles: back and forth, turning around with one's couple, mills, and circles.[2]

This form became the basic form of the general *cotillion* dance in the eighteenth century, although the number of dancers grew to eight (Figure 8.1).

By the 1740s, the nine-figure *cotillion* became a standard form, and it was often called *la contredanse française*. The form was popular until the nineteenth century, although European dance masters also created several other square dances in the eighteenth and nineteenth centuries.

What became the standard form of the quadrille was a result of the development of the contradances at the end of the eighteenth and early nineteenth centuries. A significant new contradance form leading from *cotillion* toward the quadrille was the potpourri (*pot-pourri, pot-pourrée*). Potpourri was developed from the

---

[2] Raoul Auger Feuillet, *IIIIe Recueil de danses de bal pour l'année 1706* (Paris: 1705). The term "figure" corresponds to the French term *tour*. It was used in contradances to signify dance patterns corresponding to a musical reprise.

cotillion, but it did not have permanent parts. Potpourri was more of a chain of several contradances than a single dance. At the end of the eighteenth century, several potpourris were published in Paris, and their figures were often called *cotillions*: each figure was thus a dance, a *cotillion*, with its own parts that were not repeated.[3]

At the beginning of the nineteenth century, its features were incorporated into the most popular contradance of the century, the quadrille. Moreover, it further influenced Russian folk quadrilles during the latter half of the nineteenth century. Thus, despite its relatively modest popularity in European ballrooms, it left a lasting mark on European, and especially Russian, dance culture.

Following the French Revolution, potpourris were further developed, and by the early 1800s, during the era of Directory and the Napoleonic Empire after that, one began to call its new form a quadrille. This "imperial" French quadrille later became the standard form of a quadrille, and it became extremely popular throughout Europe. Napoleon's army had a significant role in spreading the quadrille in Europe. This also had its political dimension since the French government used dance balls as political propaganda: public balls in occupied regions were a sign that local society accepted their new rule.[4]

During the first years of the century, the quadrille's compositions varied significantly, although certain figures like *l'été* and *le pantalon* became more common than others. It was only toward the end of Napoleon's empire in the early 1810s that the quadrille began to take on a standard form, typically starting with these three figures in this order:

1. *Le Pantalon*
2. *L'été*
3. *La Poule*

In addition to these, a quadrille consisted of two or three figures that were not fixed. However, from the 1820s, the following last figures also became standardized:

4. *La Pastourelle* or *La Tréniz* (these could also follow each other)
5. *Finale* (or *La Polonaise*)[5]

As in potpourris, there were no permanent parts in the quadrille either, but each figure was an independent whole with its own music.

---

[3] Jean-Michel Guilcher, *La Contredanse et les renouvellements de la danse française* (Paris: Walter de Gruyter, 1969), 135.
[4] Cornelius Vanistendael, "Shaping Europe's First Dance Craze – The Role of Napoleon's Grande Armée in the Dissemination of the Quadrille (1795–1815)," *Dance Research* 36, no. 1 (2018): 91–111.
[5] Guilcher, *La Contredanse et les renouvellements*, 156.

FIGURE 8.2. The *l'été* ("summer") figure of the quadrille dance, a print engraved by Lebas (1818).

Source: Public domain. https://simple.wikipedia.org/wiki/Quadrille#/media/File:Quadrille-Ete-Lebas-ca1820.jpg.

Throughout the nineteenth century, several new quadrilles arose, and in these, apart from figures, the number of dancers could also vary. Instead of a square, for example, people started dancing in two lines facing each other: in Vienna, this became the most common way of dancing later in the century. However, the earliest record of this formation is from France in 1847. The most famous quadrille variation is perhaps *Les Lanciers*, which probably originated in Britain. There the dance was mentioned for the first time in 1817.[6]

From the courts and capitals of Europe, the quadrille began its triumphant journey around the world. During the nineteenth and early twentieth centuries, its different forms became common in the Western European colonies, and it reached a particularly strong position in many Caribbean Islands—for example, Greater and Lesser Antilles and Guyana—and within the sphere of the Indian Ocean. The dance was carried to the colonies by wealthy members of the plantocracy. The colonial powers had different rules to govern enslaved people in the colonies, leading to variations in the quadrille. The dance gained global popularity in the latter half of the nineteenth century, becoming a staple in colonial societies established by Europeans.[7]

---

[6]Ellis A. Rogers, *The Quadrille. A Practical Guide to Its Origin, Development and Performance* (Orpington: C & E Rogers, 2003), 87.

[7]John F. Szwed and Morton Marks, "The Afro-American Transformation of European Set Dances and Dance Suites," *Dance Research Journal* 20, no. 1 (1988): 29–36 (29–31); Brigitte Desrosiers, "Ile de la Réunion: musiques et identité," *Canadian Folk Music Journal* 20 (1992): 47–54 (51); Dominique O. Cyrille, "The Politics of Quadrille Performance in Nineteenth-Century Martinique," *Dance Research Journal* 38, no. 1 (2006): 43–60 (46–8); Yvonne Daniel, "An Ethnographic Comparison of Caribbean Quadrilles," *Black Music Research Journal* 30, no. 2 (2010): 215–40 (224–5); Ananya Jahanara Kabir, "Creolization as Balancing Act in the Transoceanic Quadrille: Choreogenesis, Incorporation, Memory,

The quadrille's European origins, its link with slavery, and its association with years of colonial rule have given the quadrille an uncertain status in some cultures, but it still holds a significant place in postcolonial island societies like Seychelles and St Lucia, symbolizing its vibrant life beyond Europe. The dance was not just replicated but also transformed in these societies, influenced by the cultural elements of African-heritage populations. While the quadrille has faded in contemporary Europe, it continues to thrive in the circum-Atlantic and Indian Ocean regions, Western and Southern African coasts, and South American gaucho cultures.[8]

Like many other European capitals, the French quadrille became popular in Saint Petersburg at the beginning of the nineteenth century. In 1811, it was introduced in the Russian court, although only a few knew how to dance it. It was initially considered a difficult dance and, therefore, met resistance among the dancing nobility. However, it soon gained immense popularity, and it could be danced for hours, repeating the figures many times. The Russian nobility danced the French quadrille in the capital and at the balls of large cities in different parts of the empire. The early-nineteenth-century Kharkiv ball, for example, was known as the "best in society."[9]

Later in nineteenth-century Russia, the French quadrille became the basic model for the dance among all classes of society. Especially after the emancipation reform, which abolished serfdom in Russia in 1861,[10] the rural dance culture began to flourish, and the quadrille became its cornerstone in many regions.[11] Over time, the quadrille evolved into a distinct form of Russian and other ethnic groups' folk dance, spreading widely throughout all regions of Russia in the nineteenth and early twentieth centuries. The dance was adapted to Russian dance songs and ditties, transforming from a complex classical dance to a lively folk quadrille. This transformation was influenced by popularizing Russian songs, dances, and themes at balls from the mid-nineteenth to the early twentieth centuries.[12]

Market," *Atlantic Studies: Global Currents* 17, no. 1 (2020): 135–57. Available online: https://doi.org/10.1080/14788810.2019.1700369 (accessed June 5, 2024).

[8]Cyrille, "The Politics of Quadrille Performance in Nineteenth-Century Martinique," 52–6; Daniel, "An Ethnographic Comparison of Caribbean Quadrilles," 233–5; Michael Hamlyn Dunseith, "Manifestations of 'Langarm': From Colonial Roots to Contemporary Practices," MA diss. thesis in Musicology (Stellenbosch University, 2017); Kabir, "Creolization as Balancing Act in the Transoceanic Quadrille."

[9]О.А. Захарова, *Русский бал XVIII — начала XX века. Танцы, костюмы, символика* (М.: ЛитРес, 2010), 9; Е. В. Первушина, "Французская кадриль 'на русские темы'," *Культура и искусство*, no. 11 (2021). Available online: https://nbpublish.com/library_read_article.php?id=34739 (accessed June 10, 2024).

[10]Michael Lynch, "The Emancipation of the Russian Serfs, 1861," *History Review*, no. 47 (December 2003). Available online: https://www.historytoday.com/archive/emancipation-russian-serfs-1861 (accessed June 10, 2024).

[11]See Виола Мальми, *Народные танцы Карелии* (Петрозаводск: Карелия, 1978).

[12]Первушина, 'Французская кадриль «на русские темы»'.

The French quadrille underwent several changes in Russia, including the shortening of the introduction, the replacement of complex French Pas with a simple step, the quickening of the tempo, and the addition of extra figures. In addition to the imperial French quadrille, other quadrille and contradance variations affected the development of folk quadrilles. One of the most popular variations of the quadrille, the *Lanciers* became popular in different local forms in the Russian empire.[13] In Russian Karelia, for example, it was known by different names like "lanssi" or "lantsik."[14] Figures from the *Lanciers*, especially circles that did not belong to the original French quadrille, could be incorporated into folk quadrilles. Additonally, the potpourri, often called the *cotillion* at the beginning of the nineteenth century, left a significant mark on Russian folk quadrilles.[15]

However, despite the influences from other contradances, the standard form of the quadrille largely remained the same in Russia, although local variations existed, and details of the figures differed between these variations. Among all the contradances, the quadrille, including its Russian name кадриль, is the best-known contradance in the late Russian Empire. In many places, it gained huge popularity, as can be seen in the following description from an Ingrian village in newly independent Estonia, near the Soviet Union border, in the 1920s:

> But suddenly, the accordion starts to pull at a slightly different pace; shouts of 'quadrille' are heard, one couple after another appear on the field, and soon the quadrille is going. - - Soon, the hands are clapped, the figure is over, the musician changes the tune, and the dance is in full swing again. A person like us would have to take many dance lessons before learning all the figures with their many different steps, changes and stops. They do everything instantly as if they knew it from birth. The quadrille is probably the favorite dance of Ingrians because it is almost every other dance.[16]

In the late 1800s and early 1900s, the quadrille was an essential part of folk culture in the Russian Empire, but despite the same name, its local variants differed from each other. The variants that most resembled the French quadrille typically had five or six figures—sometimes a few more—and they were most often danced in two opposite rows of couples, not in the square as in the original one. The French names of the figures were not used among the lower classes, but the figures were called by their respective numbers. Musicians played different melodies for the

---

[13]Ibid.
[14]Meri Ollikainen, *Karjalaisia leikkejä ja kansantanhuja* (Porvoo: WSOY, 1947), 63–66; Мальми, *Народные танцы Карелии*, 116–18.
[15]Pirkko-Liisa Rausmaa, "Purpuri suomalaisessa tanssiperinteessä," in *Suomalainen purpuri*, ed. Kari Bergholm (Helsinki: Suomalaisen Kansantanssin Ystävät, 2016), 12–13; Petri Hoppu, "Från kotiljong till Röntyskä. Franska kontradanser i Finland, Karelen och Ingermanland," *Folkdansforskning i Norden* 44 (2021): 34–9 (38–9); Первушина, "Французская кадриль 'на русские темы'."
[16]Heikki Hosia, "Ryssän rajalla juhannusta viettämässä," *Helsingin Sanomat Viikkoliite*, July 14, 1929, 3.

FIGURE 8.3. *Ka'drel* dancing in Suõ'nn'jel. Antti Hämäläinen, 1930s.
Source: Museovirasto, Suomalais-ugrilainen kuvakokoelma (SUK529:456).

figures of the folk quadrilles, and these were often popular Russian melodies. As with the French quadrille, there was a short break between each figure. In folk quadrilles, this could be indicated by dancers' hand clapping.[17]

Dancing the *Ka'drel*

The Skolt Saami *ka'drel (iigrâs-siõrr)* is the best-known of the Skolt Saami dances. The *ka'drel* probably entered the Russian Arctic regions during the last decades of the nineteenth century, similarly to many other regions in Russia at that time. The Northwest Russian Arctic shore was a meeting point for merchants not only from Karelia but also from other parts of Russia and Scandinavia, particularly Norway. The region was not a remote periphery, but at that time, it had a distinct international character. The Russian tradesmen brought the *ka'drel* and the accordion, the most popular instrument for dance accompaniment.

The *ka'drel* resembles Northwest Russian—especially Karelian—quadrilles, and it has maintained several features that originate from the early-nineteenth-century French quadrille. The Skolt name of the dance, *ka'drel*, comes from the Russian word for the quadrille (кадриль). Curiously, the dancing formation is a square—the original formation of the quadrille—and not two opposite lines,

---

[17]See Первушина, "Французская кадриль 'на русские темы'."

which is more common in Russian quadrilles. The *ka'drel* has six figures, and it has been traditionally danced by four couples. In most cases, the head couples facing each other start each figure, and the side couples repeat the same after them.

The description in Table 8.1 follows the description of the *ka'drel* in a video recording from the late 1970s. Unless stated otherwise, the description concerns head couples dancing, which is then repeated by side couples.

As with many folk quadrilles in Northwestern Russia and Karelia, the first four figures of the *ka'drel* have a lot in common with the respective figures in the French quadrille: *le pantalon*, *L'été*, *la poule*, and *la tréniz*. The *ka'drel* follows the original structure more strictly than many other folk quadrilles with little variation before the fifth figure. The last two figures of the *ka'drel* differ from the previous figures but in

Table 8.1. The Structure of the *Ka'drel*[1]

Figure	Description
1	Couples cross over and back, swing with a ballroom hold, and finally ladies cross over, move around the opposite gentleman with left hand in hand and return to their places where their move around their partner without holding hands.
2	The figure begins with gentlemen crossing over, swinging with the opposite lady, returning, and swinging with their partner, after which ladies cross over, swing, return, and swing.
3	The opposite gentlemen turn counterclockwise with left hands in hand, take their ladies with them and continue in the same direction, retreat with their ladies to the opposite places and cross over to their own places. The same is repeated so that ladies begin the figure.
4	Couple from one side takes a few side steps toward the center, swings around, raises joined hands, and the opposite gentleman goes under arch around the couple back to his partner. Couples swing in places.
5	The figure begins with all couples swinging in places, after which dancers make a circle with gentlemen facing out. The circle moves counterclockwise and clockwise so that everybody stays on the opposite side. The couples cross over to their places and swing, first head couples and side couples following immediately. The same is repeated.
6	Head couples start the figure, and sides follow immediately so that for the most time of the figure, everybody is dancing: Couples cross over with a ballroom hold, swing, return and swing. The gentlemen cross over and swing with the opposite lady, cross over with a ballroom hold with her, swing, return, and swing. The gentlemen cross over and swing with their own ladies, after which ladies cross over and back. The dance ends with the couples swinging in places.

1 Rausmaa, "Kolttien tanssiperinteet," 111–19.

different manners. The fifth figure consists mostly of circles while the last figure has similar parts as the first figures, but sides do not wait until head couples have finished all the parts of the figure. They do the same movements as the head couples but with a few steps after them. In musical terms, this could be described as a *stretto* figure.[18]

In terms of style, how the Skolt Saami dance their *ka'drel* is clearly distinct not only from the French quadrille but also from other folk quadrilles. The dance is restrained and dignified, and the dancers move in a steady flow without extra gestures, shouts, or whistles. However, in the fifth figure, dancers have the opportunity to showcase their "skills" through different steps, stampings, or turns while dancing in a circle.[19] As with other folk quadrilles in general, the number of steps in the turns is not precisely defined and the dance is characteristically free. The meditative character of the dance is highlighted by several eyewitnesses of the *ka'drel*.[20]

Ka'drel was extremely popular during the 1920s and 1930s. During that period, quadrilles were not actively danced in other parts of Finland, except for some regions in Orthodox Karelia; therefore, the dance was considered characteristically Skolt Saami. Although Skolt Saami danced other dances as well, there are very few descriptions of those from the early twentieth century. The *ka'drel* is mentioned frequently in Finnish ethnographic literature, which indicates that it was extremely popular among the Skolt Saami but probably also that outsiders considered it authentic and distinctive.

After the Second World war, the *ka'drel* was danced to some extent until the 1970s when it was revived as a dance performance. However, it was not until the 1970s that the dance was documented in detail.

Ka'drel Music

Jääkk Sverloff explains in the following interview in 1972 some of the ways of accompanying *ka'drel*.

Häkämies: Well, these ka'drels were danced there, and there are also words and songs to this ka'drel rhythm.

Sverloff: Well, of course it was done for like six of them [figures]. For the first, the second and the third, four, five, and six, and for each of them the song was made in this way and that way. And then they were sung in Russian and then so and so and so

---

[18] A more detailed comparative analysis of the *ka'drel*, Russian folk quadrilles, and the French quadrille is presented in Appendix 1.
[19] Rausmaa, "Kolttien tanssiperinteet," 117.
[20] E.g., Robert Crottet, *Lapplands andra ansikte*, trans. Gun Hägglund from French to Swedish (Stockholm: LTs förlag, 1966), 93–5; Heikki Laitinen, "Kokemuksia saamelaismusiikista viime vuosikymmeniltä," in *Kohtaaminen – Gávnnadeapmi*, ed. Marko Jouste (Inari: Sámi Museum – Saamelaismuseosäätiö & Yhteispohjoismainen joikuarkistoprojekti, 2007), 91–3.

FIGURE 8.4. *Ka'drel* dancing in Če'vetjäu'rr in 1979. An excerpt from the video "Dance in Če'vetjäu'rr" in 1979.
Source: The Finnish Folk Music Institute. Kik 44.

Häkämies: In Russian?
Sverloff: They sang in Russian.
Häkämies: So was it six verses or six stanzas?
Sverloff: Figures …
Häkämies: In dance, the figures were unique …
Sverloff: … and then those Skolt leu'dds were put into them, which was fun, they were put into instrumental music and then so and so into ka'drels
Häkämies: So all these songs were in Russian?
Sverloff: Yes, the songs were in Russian, but we haven't danced them for a long time.[21]

The sources reveal that different melodies played with accordion or various songs were used to accompany different parts of the *ka'drel*. Most of these songs use 6/4-meter instead of 4/4-meter, which has been a more popular meter for *ka'drel* during the last decades. The next two examples, both performed in 1961 by Jääkk Sverloff, highlight the style of these songs. Often the lyrics resemble the style of leu'dds describing certain real people and experienced events. In the first example, *Mäšš viiljaž Meeđrai âlǧǧ*, the most obvious feature referring to the *ka'drel* is the stomping rhythm and the *luuli-luulla*-refrains at the end of the verses. The lyrics describe life and people in the winter village of Suõ'nn'jel. The first character to be

---

[21]Jääkk Sverloff, interview by Irja Häkämies, 1972. The Folklife Archives in University of Tampere, Y/04479.

mentioned is Mä'šš. At the time of the incident, Mä'šš was a boy under 10 years old. In another recorded version of the same song, Mä'šš is remembered as he used to threw somersaults. Next, Evvan Mekk's son is remembered as the best man in the village, as he played the accordion, which is needed to accompany the dance. The lyrics continue with similar type of remarks of several persons[22] (Music Example 7).

The second example is the song *Reeig Evvan â'lǧǧ*, 'Reeig Evvan's son'. It has also a story similar to the *leu'dds* combined with the *ka'drel* song. As in the *leu'dds*, the main character of the story is presented first. A short description is related to Reeig's courtship in Suõ'nn'jel. The funny dimension of the recalling seems to be the fact that there were two women acting as matchmakers instead of a single man, as it was accustomed at that time.

MUSIC EXAMPLE 7. *Mäšš viilljaž Meedrai â'lǧǧ*. Jääkk Sverloff, interview by Erkki Ala-Könni 1961. Transcription by Marko Jouste.
Source: The Folklife Archives in University of Tampere, AK/0567.

---

[22]Jouste et al., *Maaddârääjji leeu'd - Historiallisia kolttasaamelaisia leu'ddeja*, 60.

MUSIC EXAMPLE 8. *Reeig Evvan â'lǧǧ.* Jääkk Sverloff, interview by Erkki Ala-Könni 1961. Transcription by Marko Jouste.
Source: The Folklife Archives in University of Tampere, AK/0551.

Riijgg-a-jaž go g-Evvan-i g-â'lǧǧ-a. Reeig Evvan's son.
Son-e ve't-e võl-e vue'lj-e-jo-di-ja He set off his path
Suõ'nn-i-'jel-le čuõkku go-la kuõrrâd. and traced the road to
 Suõ'nnjel-village.
Suõnn-a-põõ'nni ŋ-ääkk-a pä'cce vuõrrâd. Matchmaker-women remain
 delusional.
Äänn-a-kaž go de Huâttar-i nijdd-â. Ää'nnkaž Huâttar's daughter and
Ååjj-e-kaž-e Parfusaj-i nijdd-â: Åå'jjkaž Parfusaj's daughter:
"Ooddâl-e-vuõđâd-e ǩiõrggâd-i-vuõđad-i." "Your wit and diligence."
Lul-laa-lal-lee, laa-lel-loo, laa-la, jo. Lul-laa-lal-lee, laa-lel-loo, laal-la, jo.

In this short performance, the same melody is repeated eight times, with minor variations. The metric structure of the tune consists of six beats, which is a typical feature of Skolt Saami dance songs used to accompany ka'drel (Music Example 8).

9 OTHER DANCES AND GAMES

During the first decades of the twentieth century, the Skolt Saami dance repertoire covered a large selection of dance forms. In addition to the *ka'drel*, they danced other set dances in circles, squares, or rows, as well as couple dances, improvised solo dances, and singing games. There are also other games often mentioned in historical descriptions of Skolt Saami dances or other social outdoor activities. The Skolt Saami dance culture was never monolithic or static; however, with the advent of Western-style couple dances in Skolt communities in the latter half of the nineteenth, Skolt Saami adopted new dances as long as they lived in their original homeland. Moreover, the dance repertoire varied between different Skolt groups, and some of them were more eager than others to adopt new dance trends.

Šestjårkka and *Vosmerkka*

In addition to the *ka'drel*, Skolt Saami also danced other set dances with various compositions and in different formations since the late nineteenth century. Whenever their names are known, they most often originate from Russia, although there is information about dances whose names are in Skolt Saami language. As with the *ka'drel* and couple dances, most of these dances have counterparts in Karelian and Russian dance cultures.

Šestjårkka is a set dance whose name means "a dance for six" (Russian: Шестёрка), when danced with three couples. With four couples, the name is *Vosmerkka*, "a dance for eight" (Russian: Восьмерка). T. I. Itkonen mentions in his Skolt Saami dictionary dances *koummsiõrr*—"three dance"—and *nelljsiõrr*—"four dance"—and these could well be Skolt Saami names for

FIGURE 9.1A AND B. *Šestjårkka* dancing in Če'vetjäu'rr in 1979. An excerpt from the video recording in Če'vetjäu'rr in 1979.

Source: Finnish Folk Music Institute, kik 44.

Šestjårkka and Vosmerkka.¹ The Skolt Saami names may refer to the beginning of the dance with three or four dancers, whereas the Russian names can indicate the situation after the first round when there are six and eight persons or three and four couples dancing. The main part of the dance may have been the second round when the dancers moved in couples, since there is also mention in archival material that the dancers who joined later were "extra." This explanation makes the Russian names more conceivable.

Šestjårkka that was documented in the late 1970s begins in a square but differs otherwise from the *ka'drel*. Four dancers stand in a square. They start moving in figure eight, as in the reel. Every time they return, they ask someone to join the dance hand in hand. During the dance, four lines will be moving around incessantly.[2]

Notably, there is a discrepancy between the name of this dance and its execution, since at no point are six persons or three couples dancing it. However, a dance with a similar name, *Shestjorkka*, has been documented in Sumski Posad in Russian Karelia. It has a similar structure to Šestjårkka, but it begins with three, follows with six, and ends with nine ladies.[3] It is possible that Skolt Šestjårkka originally referred to a dance starting with three persons, similar to Sumski Posad, whereas Vosmerkka is the name of a similar dance but starting with four persons. Thus, Šestjårkka from the 1970s should be *Vosmerkka*, as the original choreography of Šestjårkka was no longer in use at that time. Obviously, the original references of the dance names disappeared when the knowledge of Russian language faded during the latter half of the twentieth century.[4]

Šestjårkka Music

As an example of the Šestjårkka style, here is Dä'rjj Jefremoff's performance from 1955, in which he humorously recounts the joys of his youth, that is, the 1920s. This text also reflects on the experience of belonging to the Finnish state.

Vuäbb-i-žan-i, Vuäbb-i-žan-a,	Sisters, sisters
da dii-di, did-di, dii-di, dii-da-da,	da dii-di, did-di, dii-di, dii-da-da,
dii-di, did-di, dii-di, dii-da-da.	dii-di, did-di, dii-di, dii-da-da.
Njui'ǩkest-njui'ǩk-e-sâ'sttep de,	Let's jump, let's jump,

---

[1]T. I. Itkonen defines *koummsiõrr* as "kolmikisa" and *nelljsiõrr* as "nelikisa." Toivo Immanuel Itkonen, *Koltan- ja Kuolanlapin sanakirja: Wörterbuch des Kolta- und Kolalappischen I* (Helsinki: Suomalais-ugrilainen Seura, 1958), 278, 493.
[2]Rausmaa, "Kolttien tanssiperinteet," 120.
[3]Viola Malmi, *Karjalaisen kansantanssin lähteillä* (Helsinki: Vapaan Sivistystoiminnan Liitto, 1993), 56.
[4]Dances called *Shestjorkka* and *Vosmerkka* have also been known among the Veps in Eastern Russian Karelia, but their choreographies differ completely from the respective Skolt Saami dances. Ollikainen, *Karjalaisia leikkejä ja kansantanhuja*, 59–63; Мальми, *Народные танцы Карелии*, 113–16.

hää'sǩ-e-bõžžân vie'ss-e-lõbbân	in a more fun and happy way.
Da vuäbb-i, vuäbb-i, vuäbb-i-žan a da	Sisters, sisters
Di ve't leä'ped siõrr-â-men de.	let's dance.
Šestjårkka tõt-i la siõrr-e.	*Šestjårkka*, that is our dance.
Njui'ǩkest-njui'ǩk-e-sâ'sttep-e,	Let's jump, let's jump,
di-di-di, di-di-di,	di-di-di, di-di-di,
di-di-di, di-di-di.	di-di-di, di-di-di.
Mij ve't siõrr-e-sâ'sttep di	We dance
nuõrr-â-hää'sǩ-poodd-i-žan â'tte	the happy times of our youth.
tij-e viillj-e ǩiičč-i-sâ'stted-e,	Brothers, you watch,
mij-e vuäbba siõrr-i-sâ'sttep-e.	we sisters, we dance.
Täk lie mij siõr	This is our dance
hää'sǩ viillj-i-laid.	for our merry brothers.
Tie puhtt-o-maž â'tte	We are brought here,
Lää'dd-e-jânnam hiârvv-a pääikaž	a pleasant place in Finland
Täk lie puhtt-o-maž â'tte	These are brought here,
Šâdd-i siidi viillja-žan-a da	the brothers from our birth villages.
di-di-diid-di, di-ed-de.	da di-di, di-di, di-di, da-da.
Mij lie hiârvv-a šuur-a da	We have a great joy and
mij lie hiârvv-a vuäbba.	We have merry sisters.

The performance of *Šestjårkka* differs from Skolt Saami songs and especially *leu'dds* in that the vocal register is much higher than the singer's own speaking voice and appears to imitate the nasal sound of an accordion. This feature, which appears in many dance songs, is probably related to the Russian and Karelian dance song tradition, where the dance also has its origins (Music Example 9).

Couple Dances

The documented couple dances originate from the late nineteenth and early twentieth centuries. Like the *ka'drel*, these dances came from Russia, and many of them were known in Karelia, Finland, and Northern Scandinavia. The fact that the dances were a common northern cultural heritage also means that they did not necessarily always originate from the Russians but could have arrived through various routes. All information about these dances is from the 1970s or later. Obviously, unlike the *ka'drel*, early-twentieth-century

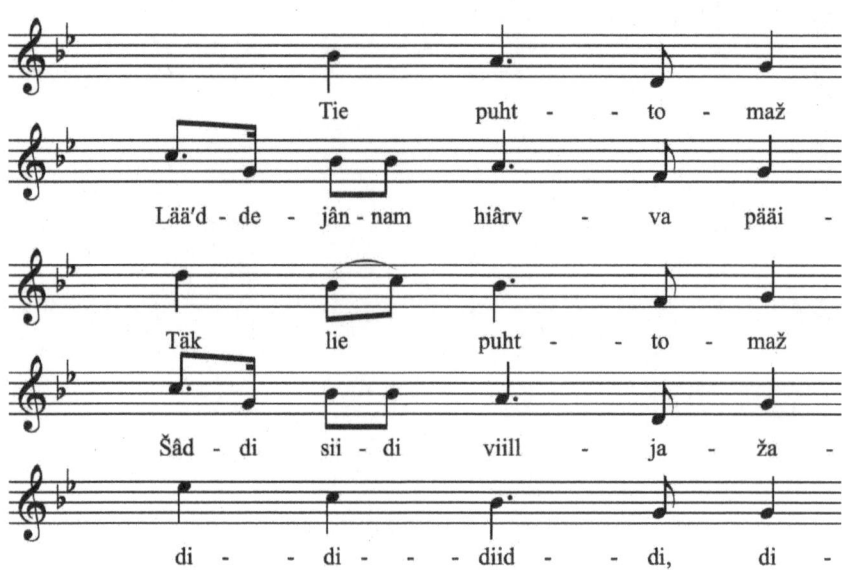
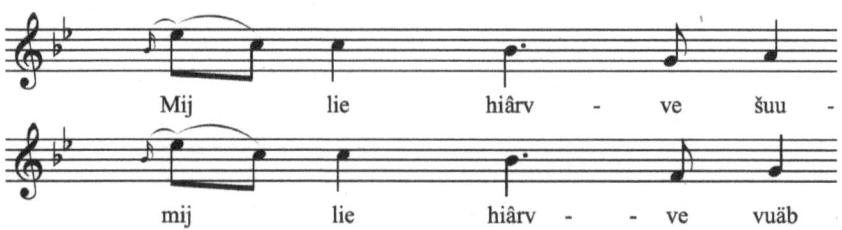

MUSIC EXAMPLE 9. *Šestjårkka.* Dä'rjj Jefremoff, interview by Erkki Ala-Könni. Transcription by Marko Jouste.

Source: The Folklife Archives in University of Tampere, AK/0865.

ethnographers likely did not regard them as authentic Skolt folk dances but rather as modern trends that were seen everywhere at that time, and therefore not worth documenting.

Most of the dances can be categorized as two-steps or polkas. It is difficult to make a clear difference between these two as their rhythmic structure (2/4) is similar, and both have either moderate or quick tempo. The steps are also close to each other, and two-steps and polka steps have been used alternatively in many of these dances.

Korobushka, *Oira*, and *Kuu loistaa* are typical Russian two-steps with popular melodies as their music. Among Skolt Saami couple dances, these are the ones that are least known in the Nordic countries. *Korobushka* (Russian: a small basket) was a common dance in Russia in different forms and was also known in Estonia (*Karoobuska*).[5] *Kuu loistaa* (Russian Светит месяц, "The Moon Is Shining") is better known as *Läpytystanssi* ("Clapping Dance") among Skolt Saami today.[6] A version of the dance has been documented from Russian Karelia, and there is a lot of information about it from other parts of Russia as well.[7] *Oira*[8] has also been danced among Finns in Salmijärvi and in Estonia (*Oirah*), and it has also been widely known in Russia.[9]

A special case among Skolt Saami couple dances is *Kerenski*, since. as a dance and especially song, it is connected to revolutionary society of the early twentieth century.[10] The name of the dance comes after a Russian politician at the time of the Russian Revolution, Alexander Kerensky. *Kerenski* was a very popular dance in Finland and Karelia for a brief period in the late 1910s and early 1920s; the dance was also known in Finnmark, Norway, where it had been taught by Finns from Salmijärvi village, formerly Finnish Pechenga.[11] It is not clear if the dance originally was introduced to Skolt Saami by the Russians or Karelians before the revolution—when it would have likely been called "Tuusteppi" and renamed to

---

[5]Rausmaa, "Kolttien tanssiperinteet," 130; Heino Aassalu, Pill Luht, and Kristjan Torop, *Vanad seltskonnatantsud* (Tallinn: Rahvakultuuri Keskus, 1997), 23–4.
[6]Rausmaa, "Kolttien tanssiperinteet," 129.
[7]Malmi, *Karjalaisen kansantanssin lähteillä*, 67; Е. Н. Эйхольц, "Освоение традиционных танцев Алтайского края как эффективное средство оздоровления детей и здоровьесберегающая технология," *Культурное наследие Сибири* 32, no. 2 (2021): 121-7 (124); В. Н. Нилов, "Экспедиционный материал русской традиционной хореографии Муромского края," *Учитель музыки* 59, no. 4 (2022): 15–23 (18).
[8]Rausmaa, "Kolttien tanssiperinteet," 126.
[9]Egil Bakka and Arne Wikan, *Dansetradisjoner fra Finnmark* (Bø i Telemark and Trondheim: Finnmark Ungdomslag and Rådet for folkemusikk og folkedans, 1996), 90; Aassalu et al., *Vanad seltskonnatantsud*, 63–4; Нилов, "Экспедиционный материал русской традиционной хореографии Муромского края," 18.
[10]Rausmaa, "Kolttien tanssiperinteet," 124.
[11]Pirkko-Liisa Rausmaa and Esko Rausmaa, "Tanssiselosteet," in *Tanhuvakka. Suuri suomalainen kansantanssikirja*, ed. Pirkko-Liisa Rausmaa and Esko Rausmaa (Helsinki: Suomalaisen Kansantanssin Ystävät, 1997), 74; Malmi, *Karjalaisen kansantanssin lähteillä*, 71; Bakka and Wikan, *Dansetradisjoner fra Finnmark*, 88–90.

Kerenski—or if it was learnt from the Finns after the revolution, while the name remained unchanged throughout.[12]

Patespa (Pas d'Espagne), *Vintjarkka* (Vengerka, from Russian Венгерская, Hungarian), and *Krakoviak* differ from the other couple dances, as they were known as high society ballroom dances in early-twentieth-century Russia and Finland, and their names refer to other European countries: Spain, Hungary, and Poland.[13]

Patespa was known by different names throughout Finland, Karelia, Torne River Valley in Sweden, Estonia, Norway, and Russia.[14] Unlike the other Skolt Saami couple dances, *Patespa* is a waltz in 3/4 rhythm. The name and music of *Krakoviak* is derived from a Polish national dance with the same name, but the dance itself is a lot simpler than the Polish one. There is a lot of information about *Krakoviak* and *Vintjårkka* from different parts of Finland as well as from Russia and Torne River Valley.[15]

The couple dances illustrate that, at the beginning of the twentieth century, Pechenga was a meeting place for various nationalities. They belonged to the Skolt Saami's own dance culture; at the same time, they were part of global trends, of which the Skolt Saami were clearly aware. Pechenga was not peripheral, but the Skolt Saami met many other ethnic groups also through dances. Apparently, couple dances were popular in Paččjokk and Peäccam *sijdd*s, but not in Suõ'nn'jel where the *ka'drel* and other set dances from the late nineteenth century dominated dance events until the Second World War.

---

[12]In the Russian Empire, *Kerenski* had different names: for example, Karapyet in Ukraine, Aissa or Tuustepp (<-two-step) in Estonia, and Tuusteppi in Olenets-Karelia. In Finland, it was renamed after the Russian Revolution. Kerensky was an important political leader after the First Russian Revolution in February 1917. After the second revolution in November, however, he had to flee Russia. In Finland, someone wrote a satirical song with a two-step melody about his fate soon after his defeat, and this song gave the name to the dance as well. Originally, *Kerenski* was apparently a Georgian dance, which, after being combined with a gypsy romance in Ukraine, spread like wildfire in the Russian Empire in the 1910s. Rausmaa and Rausmaa, "Tanssiselosteet," 74; Aassalu et al., *Vanad seltskonnatantsud*, 118–24; *Suomalaisen Kansantanssin Ystävät*, "Seuratanssit." Available online: https://www.kansantanssinyst.fi/kansantanssi/tanssit/seuratanssit/ (accessed June 10, 2024).

[13]The Finnish standard forms of Pas d'Espagne, Vengerka, and Krakoviak belong to the contemporary repertoire of academic festivities and high school proms. They were probably composed by Russian dancing masters.

[14]Rausmaa, "Kolttien tanssiperinteet," 125; Rausmaa and Rausmaa, "Tanssiselosteet," 23; Malmi, *Karjalaisen kansantanssin lähteillä*, 69–70; Bengt Martinsson, *Danser från Norr- och Västerbotten samt Finland* (Luleå: Svenska Ungdomsringen för Bygdekultur, Övre Norrlands distrikt, 1978), 33; Aassalu et al., *Vanad seltskonnatantsud*, 70–80; Bakka and Wikan, *Dansetradisjoner fra Finnmark*, 94; Нилов, "Экспедиционный материал русской традиционной хореографии Муромского края," 18.

[15]Rausmaa, "Kolttien tanssiperinteet," 127–8; Rausmaa and Rausmaa, "Tanssiselosteet," 23; Эйхольц, "Освоение традиционных танцев Алтайского," 124; Нилов, "Экспедиционный материал русской традиционной хореографии Муромского края," 18; Martinsson, *Danser från Norr- och Västerbotten samt Finland*, 34.

MUSIC EXAMPLE 10. *Vintjårkka*-melody (*Rom krenitsa*) performed by Grigori Koputoff with the harmonica. Interview by Irja Häkämies. Transcription by Marko Jouste.

Source: The Folklife Archives in University of Tampere, Y11312a.

As part of the revitalization of Skolt Saami dancing in the Njeä'llem area, various instruments began to be used as accompaniment. One of the musicians in Njeä'llem, Grigori Koputoff performed in 1974 various dance melodies on harmonica. These include *Rom krenitsa*, *Korobushka*, *Oira*, and *Ripaska* (Music Examples 10, 11, 12 and 13).

Dances in Different Formations

Obsikruugg is a circle dance that ends in a longways formation (gentlemen and ladies in two opposite lines).[16] The Skolt Saami word *kruugg*—"circle"—refers to the Russian word круг having the same meaning. In Karelia, several dances called *kruuga* or *ruha* were known until the twentieth century.[17]

---

[16] Rausmaa, "Kolttien tanssiperinteet," 131–3.
[17] E.g., Rausmaa and Rausmaa, "Tanssiselosteet," 356.

MUSIC EXAMPLE 11. *Oira* performed by Grigori Koputoff with the harmonica. Interview by Irja Häkämies. Transcription by Marko Jouste.
Source: The Folklife Archives in University of Tampere, Y11312a.

One Skolt Saami interviewee described a dance where men and women stand in two opposite rows, and one couple at a time dances through the formation from one end to the other. The name of the dance is not known, but similar dances have been documented in Rautu on the Karelian Isthmus (Finland) in 1908 and in Southern Ingria in 1939.[18] The name of the former is *Rikurilla* and the latter *Kasatškah*. Both dances contain squat movements, and their names refer to Russian-style improvisational dance as well. *Rikurilla* likely originates from the Russian word припляска, meaning "dance improvisation," and *Kasatškah* means "Cossack dance," which has been known in various, typically improvisational forms.

From the word припляска also comes the Finnish word *ripaska*, which means squat movements and a dance with these movements; the Skolt Saami use the same term. There is some information about *ripaska* as an improvised and sometimes even acrobatic men's dance among the Skolt Saami. According to some

---

[18]Ibid., 333; Juha-Matti Aronen, "Viron Inkerin tanssit – Kadrelia, kasatškahia ja Viron veräjää," *Elore* 21, no. 1 (2014): 1–30 (15–16). Available online: https://doi.org/10.30666/elore.79122 (accessed June 10, 2024).

MUSIC EXAMPLE 12. *Korobushka* performed by Grigori Koputoff with the harmonica. Interview by Irja Häkämies. Transcription by Marko Jouste.

Source: The Folklife Archives in University of Tampere, Y11312a.

MUSIC EXAMPLE 13. *Ripaska* performed by Grigori Koputoff with the harmonica. Interview by Irja Häkämies. Transcription by Marko Jouste.
Source: The Folklife Archives in University of Tampere, Y11312a.

interviewees, Skolt men could dance it as late as after the Second World War while they were, for example, participating in reindeer roundups.

A dance called *risttsiõrr*[19]—"cross dance" or "cross game"—might refer to "ristikontra"—a square dance resembling the quadrille known in Karelia—or "tikkuristi"—a solo dance known in Karelia and Finland as well as in Scandinavia. A third possible explanation is that it is connected to religious feasts, since the word *rist* means cross. Since only the name of the dance is known, it is not possible to track how it was performed.

Games

Until the twentieth century, it was typical that the lyrics of the Skolt Saami singing games were in Russian, even if many participants did not know Russian. There are two singing games ontained from historical sources.

The first singing game called *Ainamilaadu* is the oldest and best-known among singing games of the Skolt Saami. The game originates from Russia ("Sowing of Millet," А мы просо сеяли), and according to Finnish folklorist Viljo J. Mansikka, it was widely known in Russia at the end of the nineteenth and early twentieth centuries.[20] "Ay nam ladan" is the starting line of the song, and its

---

[19]Itkonen has a spelling *ristsierra*—"some kind of dance"—in his dictionary, but his source is Paulaharju, who has a spelling *ristisiirre* without any further description. Itkonen, *Koltan- ja Kuolanlapin sanakirja*, 443, 493; Paulaharju, *Kolttain mailta*, 41.
[20]Viljo J. Mansikka, "Laulu Hirssin kylvöstä," *Virittäjä* 14, no. 8 (1910), 137–9 (138).

FIGURE 9.2. *Ainamilaadu* (Sowing of Buckwheat) Antti Hämäläinen 1937.
Source: Museovirasto, Suomalais-ugrilainen kuvakokoelma (SUK529:456).

origin is in the respective Russian song's refrain: Ой дид, ладо, [сеяли, сеяли], which has become Ай нам Ладан выкупим, "We redeem [girl] Lada," in the Skolt Saami version. The Skolt song was originally performed with Russian text; it was later translated to Skolt Saami language and named *Tattarkâ'lvvmõš*, "Sowing of Buckwheat' or Tattarpeäldd 'Buckwheat field'. The same game was commonly known in both Russian and Finnish Karelia by the names *Prossan kylvö* ("Sowing of Millet") and *Tsuurun kylvö* ("Sowing of Sand") and with Karelian lyrics.[21] The song probably traveled north with the Russian and Karelian settlers who immigrated in the nineteenth century, or, at the latest, with the Skolt Saami who served in the Russian army during the First World War.

Antti Hämäläinen described *Ainamilaadu* in his book *Koltta-Lappia sanoin ja kuvin* [Skolt-Lapland in Words and Pictures].[22] He recalls that the term "Sowing of Buckwheat" was used at that occasion in 1938:

> Then the "village head" interrupted the chatter and immediately asked some bearded men into another room for a meeting. After a while, they entered the party again and announced that now the caller can rest. "Let's show the guest how we sow buckwheat!"

---

[21] Pirkko-Liisa Rausmaa, *Ilokerä. Laulutansseja ja piirileikkejä* (Helsinki: SKS, 1984), 133.
[22] Hämäläinen, *Koltta-Lappia sanoin ja kuvin*, 106–10; see also Rausmaa, "Kolttien tanssiperinteet," 119–20.

FIGURE 9.3A AND B. The start figure of *Ainamilaadu*. As the dance progresses, women go through men's gate. An excerpt from the video recording in Če'vetjäu'rr in 1979.

Source: Finnish Folk Music Institute, kik 44.

I already decided from the name of the game that it was a borrowed item because the Skolt Saami would know more about sowing than about buckwheat. On the other side of the wall, as many men went together as they could ever fit. Almost twenty! Similarly, women also gathered on the opposite wall. When the rows were ready, the men, in a tight front, grabbed each other's hands and rushed towards the women, stamping hard with their feet. The monotonous song was accompanied by all who were in good spirits, men, and women alternately, even those who did not take part in the game. and many had no more idea of the words than of the tune. Men stamping their feet:

"We sow the buckwheat field, we sow."

And as they retreated, they repeated the verse. The women rush towards the men, also holding each other's hands:

"We trample that seed, we trample it."

The men promise to catch the evildoers, which the women, in turn, promise to redeem.

"What do you pay them with, do you pay?" "We pay with gold and silver." "We don't care about gold, silver." "Then what do we leave as a pledge?"

That's when the men threaten to take the most beautiful one as a hostage!

After hearing this, the women turn from their chests into a row and, still holding each other's hands, start running behind the men's row.

I was already thinking sad thoughts to myself, how do the most beautiful people choose and what do other women say about that? But the men solved it in a very nice way. The last two men raised their hands and formed a gate through which the whole female stream would pass. Then the gate closed in front of the last woman, so the puzzling question was solved. The women now less organized again on their wall and the men in full numbers started their rush from the beginning. And so the game continued until the last "most beautiful of the bunch" was taken as a pawn."[23]

Ainamilaadu begins with men making a row on one side of the room and, likewise, women gathering on the opposite side.

The lyrics of the song explain the dance figures. At the beginning, a girl is bought with a dowry gift and drawn into the group. The number of buyers increases, while the number of others decreases. Buyers are wondering what to pay in dowry. They don't want to give the horse as a dowry, and it is locked away in the barn. Others want to buy a horse and let it out of the barn. In the end, they say "Yesterday we jumped, yesterday we cried."

---

[23]Hämäläinen, *Koltta-Lappia sanoin ja kuvin*, 106–10.

Näskk Mosnikoff performed the song in 1955:

Ai nam[y] Ladon[y] výkypim vykupím, da	We are redeeming "Ladon" (and)
Ai nam[y] Ladon[y] výsjaim vysjaím,	We are redeeming "Ladon" (and)
Ai nam[y] Ladon[y] výkypim vykupím, da	We are redeeming "Ladon" (and)
Ai nam[y] Ladon[y]	We are redeeming "Ladon" (and)
Nasha polka pribyla, pribyla, da	Our group has grown (and)
Nasha polka ubyla ubyla.	and our number is diminished.
Ai nam[y] Ladon[y] výkypim vykupím, da	We are redeeming "Ladon" (and)
My konjato v hlév zabrjum, v hlév zabrjóm,	We lock the horse in the stable
Ai nam[y] Ladon[y] výkypim vykupím, da	We are redeeming "Ladon" (and)
Chemto bednym vit' vykupit' vykupit'?	But with what is the poor girl redeemed?
My kunjato v hlev zabrjum v hlev zabrjom, da	The horse is locked in the stable (and).
My konjato ótkupim otkupím,	Our horse is redeemed
ne nada vasha sto rublej, sto rublej, da	We don't need your 100 rubles (and).
Chto zho vamto nádubnoj nadubnój?	What do you want from me?
Namto nadobnoj, nadubnoj, da	We want, we want (and)
iz kraja krajnaja, krasnaja devitsa.	beauty from a beautiful place the end of the queue'
Mytu konja výkypim vykupím, da	We will buy a horse (and)
Myto konja ótkroim otkroím.	and let out of the stable (open the doors).
Nasha polka se príbyla pribylá, da	Our group has grown (and)
Nasha polka ubýla ubylá, da	and our number is diminished (and)
My vcherato skákali skakalí, da	Yesterday we jumped (and)
My vcherato plakali, plakali.	Yesterday we cried
My kunjato v hlev zaprjom v hlev zaprjom, da	The horse is locked in the stable (and)
Chto zho vamto nadobnoj, nadobnoj, da	What do you need from me? (and)
namto ved' nadobnoj, nadobnoj, da	We need (and)

iz krajne krasnaja krasnaja devitsa.	beauty from a beautiful place. ('the end of the queue')
Otkroite shiroki voroty, da	Open the big gates (and)
otkrojte shiroki voroty, da	Open the big gates (and)
nasha polka s´ ubyla ubyla, da	Our group has grown (and)
i nasha polka pírbyla pribylá, da	and our number is diminished (and)
My vcherasja skákali, skakalí, da	Yesterday we jumped (and)
My vtsherato plákali plakalí.	Yesterday we cried.
"Vse ushli…"	"Everyone left…"

MUSIC EXAMPLE 14. *Ainamilaadu*. Näskk Moshnikoff in 1955, interview by Erkki Ala-Könni. Transcription by Marko Jouste.
Source: The Folklife Archives in University of Tampere, AK/0866.

MUSIC EXAMPLE 15. *Okldu'na* performed by Skolt Saami dancers in 1979. Transcription by Marko Jouste.
Source: The Finnish Folk Music Institute, kik 44.

The melody consists of two phrases (A and B), which are repeated throughout the dance. There is some rhythmic variation according to the different word structures in the lines of the lyrics (Music Example 14).

Another singing game is called *Okldu'na*; it is accompanied by singing of women dancers. The vocal timbre is rather nasal, thereby sounding like an imitation of an accordion sound. *Okldu'na* begins with one female dancer. She has a handkerchief in her hand, which she waves in the air while dancing. After a while, she asks another dancer with her, and this one asks a third one, and so on, until there is a long chain moving in a circle on the floor. The first dancer begins to go through other dancers' gates so that everybody's arms are crossed. Then she does the same in the opposite direction, straightening the arms. In the end, the chain moves in a circle and dancers leave it one at a time. The lyrics are in Russian in this game, as well.[24] The name of the singing game, *Okldu'na*, refers to a Russian girl's name. According to Häkämies, *Okldu'na* imitates reindeer tracks.[25]

The song used to accompany *Okldu'na* has Russian text, which is repeated until the dance is over.[26] The melody has a long pattern, which is also repeated (Music Example 15).

There was also a great variety of games that did not include dancing. One of the most often photpgraphed is *nue'rrsiõrr*—"rope game—in which players hold a long rope forming a circle. One player is inside it and tries to catch those standing around. The player who was chased was allowed to release the rope, but when caught, they had to enetr the ring as a new catcher. *Pällsiõrr*—"ball game"—was

---

[24]Rausmaa, "Kolttien tanssiperinteet," 121.
[25]Häkämies, "Kolttasaamelainen musiikkiperinne."
[26]The song *Okldu'na* was performed by Domna Sanila in 1973 and recorded by Heikki Laitinen. The first part of the lyrics contain words and sentences in pidgin Russian: *Okldu'na*, a young man looking for a bride walks on the edge of the village. There is Katerina, a young girl, who is interested in the young man. Saami Culture Archive of the University of Oulu, Finland.

played with a ball made of reindeer leather. In *põ'ttepiâčkklemsiõrr*—"a slap on the butt game"—one player is blindfolded and positioned against the wall while the others strike the player's backside with a stick made of a scarf; the blindfolded player must then guess who the hitter is.

The first half of the twentieth century can be regarded as the time when the Skolt Saami dance culture took form in a manner that can be considered traditional from today's perspective. From the perspective of this research, the 1920s and 1930s are the most relevant periods in the Finnish Skolt Saami areas, as conditions stabilized after the First World War. There are also contemporary sources related to dance from this period, based on which we have outlined the description of dance culture in this chapter. However, the Second World War and the territorial cession of the Pechenga region to the Soviet Union in 1944 tragically altered the lives of the Skolt Saami, having a significant impact on their flourishing dance culture.

PART THREE

RECESSION AND RECOVERY

The period after the Second World War was difficult for Skolt Saami culture, and conditions for dancing also declined, as the Skolt Saami were unable to follow their traditional annual cycle in the new places of residence. However, even though their dance culture faded for a long time, it did not disappear altogether. With the rise of the Saami movement in the 1970s, Skolt Saami culture—along with its traditional dances—experienced a revival. However, the contexts of dance had changed, with the performance of dance taking a central role.

10 OBMUTESCENCE

The Second World War was a challenging period for the Skolt Saami. During the Winter War (1939–40), the Soviet Union occupied the Pechenga area, and the entire population had to be evacuated. People could return to Pechenga, but during the War of Lapland in the winter of 1944–5, Skolt Saami were re-evacuated in Kalajoki, Haukipudas, and along the Oulujoki in Maikkula. After the war, the Finnish part of the Skolt region was ceded to the Soviet Union, and the entire population had to move out of the area. Skolt Saami were evacuated to the neighboring municipality of Inari in Northern Finland. The resettlement did not start until May 1949, and it proceeded during the period, when Skolt Saami lived in impermanent settlements, mainly in Inari municipality. People mainly from Suõ'nn'jel moved to Če'vetjäu'rr in northeastern Inari. The population of the Paččjokk and Peäccam siijds settled in Njeä'llem and the Keväjärvi area. However, no new winter village was built on Če'vetjäu'rr. This affected the culture of Suõ'nn'jel considerably because the winter village had been the central place for the common life of the entire population of the village and for the dance tradition.[1]

Dancing in New Settlements (1940s–50s)

The re-settlement in Če'vetjäu'rr had devastating consequences to Skolt Saami dance culture. According to various accounts from the 1950s and 1960s, the *ka'drel* just about disappeared for several decades before being revived as part of the Saami cultural revival in the 1970s. However, there is substantial evidence that in the 1950s, when Skolt Saami lived a rather closed life with their own group, there was dancing even in Če'vetjäu'rr, but when connections to other places opened, there were Finnish influences as well as the beginning of Skolt Saami

---

[1]Lehtola, *Saamelaiset suomalaiset*, 389, 396–401.

"emigration", and the old ways started to fall out of use.[2] The 1960s was a period of such a major revolution in the modern world, with many new cultural influences constantly shaping it, that it is understandable that the old dances fell out of practice. According to Pertti J. Pelto (1927–2024):

> In the prewar Suonjel [Suõ'nn'jel] village there was much dancing, games and drinking, during which it was possible for young men and women to become acquainted—When the Skolt Saami first moved to Sevettijärvi [Če'vetjäu'rr] (where there is no concentrated winter village), there were dances held frequently at one of the large houses. These dances were attended by both Skolt Saami and non-Skolt Saami.[3]

Pelto, who spent the winter of 1958–9 in Če'vetjäu'rr, argues that during the 1950s, many Skolt Saami women moved away from Če'vetjäu'rr since it was considered a place with only few "career" possibilities for women, in contrast to men, who could work as reindeer herders.[4] The social role and significance of traditional dancing as a meeting place for different genders diminished, which very likely led to a decline in interest within the community. This shift may have signaled the beginning of a transition toward Finnish dance hall events, which were organized for broader audiences.

Many elder residents of Če'vetjäu'rr recall that Finnish dances were once highly significant social events. These were frequently organized in neighboring Finnish villages such as Ivalo and Inari; a dance hall was also built to Če'vetjäu'rr, and Finnish dance hall dances began to compete with Skolt Saami dances.[5] Since it was likely that only the Skolt Saami knew how to dance *ka'drel*, the Finnish dance hall dances provided an opportunity to meet non-Skolt Saami partners, as dances were still valued as spaces for meeting future spouses. This fact could have diminished at least some of the interest in organizing dances with *ka'drel* as the only dance genre.

---

[2]Eeva Nykänen and Tanja Telkkälä, interview by Marko Jouste, Petri Hoppu, Markus Juutinen, and Kia Olin in Inari, Če'vetjäu'rr, March 19, 2023. Saami Culture Archive, The Giellagas Institute for Saami Studies, University of Oulu, SKA A1.2023, 4a–b; Lati Feodoroff and Paula Feodoroff, interview by Markus Juutinen, Kia Olin, and Marko Jouste in Inari, Keväjärvi, March 21, 2023. Saami Culture Archive, The Giellagas Institute for Saami Studies, University of Oulu, SKA A1.2023, 11.
[3]Pertti J. Pelto, *Individualism in Skolt Lapp Society* (Helsinki: Suomen Muinaismuistoyhdistys, 1962), 147.
[4]Ibid., 147–9.
[5]Hanna-Maaria Kiprianoff, Terhi Harju, Anna-Katariina Feodoroff and Heini Weslin. Interview by Marko Jouste and Petri Hoppu in Inari, Če'vetjäu'rr, March 18, 2023. Saami Culture Archive, The Giellagas Institute for Saami Studies, University of Oulu, SKA A1.2023, 2a–b.

Challenge of Modern Culture (1950–60s)

The Skolt Saami have always lived in harmony with their surroundings, making use of opportunities and fostering relationships with neighboring peoples, all while preserving the foundations of their own culture. However, the 1960s would seem to have been different, because during that period, social change began in Finland and eroded the Skolt culture more forcefully than before. This was common in Saami cultures during this time, which included generations of dormitories, the loss of language, and new forms of culture that were no longer structured in the context of Saami culture.

However, while there were challenges with cultural changes, the traditions of performing *leu'dd*s and telling stories continued. This is also shown by the fact that vast collections of traditional knowledge was recorded during the same period. Eeva Nykänen, a member of the Če'vetjäu'rr *ka'drel* group, recalls this phenomenon in her childhood during early 1960s:

> [The older generation] were performing leu'dds everywhere. Whatever they did, there were leu'dds. Sometimes they just talked to each other, talked and then they leu'dd. They came to visit and had their handicrafts with them and kept on asking advice for the handicrafts and taught each other. ...But children did not leu'dd, they were just playing [in the house] and listening the stories and leu'dds. Older people sit and tell stories. All day until the meal, then they eat. In the meantime, they collect the plates away and the tea starts to boil. Then they drink tea, have a dessert. And they tell stories and talk, and they talk and talk, who knows if the stories recalled something which brought some leu'dds to their minds. They began to leu'dd a bit. After a while they continue with talking and collect teacups away. In the meantime, a dinner is getting ready. Then they start eating.[6]

Thus, it is only natural that from time to time, people began to dance *ka'drel*, as the following story illustrates.

Crottet and the *Ka'drel* at a Wedding Party

One of the most interesting postwar *ka'drel* descriptions is written by Swiss writer Robert Crottet (1908–1987), who lived with the Skolt Saami first in Pechenga in the late 1930s and then in Inari after the war. As a young man, Crottet contracted tuberculosis during which he dreamed of small bright-eyed creatures that seemed to belong to the "Saami folk tribe." Having recovered, he traveled to Helsinki

---

[6]Nykänen and Telkkälä, interview by Jouste et al.

and met the geographer Väinö Tanner. From him, Crottet received hints about the Skolt Saami, who, according to Tanner, had preserved their ancient beliefs, practices, and stories, which the writer Crottet was particularly interested in. Crottet befriended Kaisa Gauriloff, a reindeer owner in her fifties in Suõ′nn'jel. From her, he heard stories from which he then wrote several of his books. Like the older generations of the Skolt Saami, Crottet knew Russian, which helped him to communicate with them.[7]

Crottet left Suõ′nn'jel before the Finnish Winter War (1939–40), and he spent the war years in London. After the war, he organized a fundraiser to collect money for purchasing reindeer for Skolt Saami, replacing those left in the Suõ′nn'jel forests at the beginning of the war. He also visited the Skolt Saami in Če′vetjäu′rr in the 1950s. In the book *Lapplands andra ansikte* published in 1966—based on a series of articles in a French journal from 1965—Crottet gives a lively description of the Skolt Saami's *ka′drel* danced at a wedding in Če′vetjäu′rr in 1955. One of the dancers is Jääkk Sverloff, whom Crottet got to know during his visit to Lapland and whom he calls the Skolt Saami' "king":

> After finishing the meal, we go out on the hill. The sky is cloudless, but it is not very hot, and no mosquito can be detected. The smell of pine comes from the forest. There are about thirty of us, and we stand quietly and watch big butterflies fluttering close over the calm waters of the lake. A young Skolt with a kind of balalaika in his arms. It starts wistfully but gradually turns into a dance rhythm. And the memories lift me back in time to the happy days in Suõ′nn'jel where I sat a couple of times a week, fascinated by the Skolt Saami' national dance? Now they all have the radio. Are they not helplessly affected?
>
> No. The Skolt Saami do not let go of their traditions. In Ivalo, where there is a dance hall, they dance rumba and foxtrot. But here at home they only accept their old ka′drel.
>
> The "king" bows to the bride's mother and opens the dance. I have tried many times, but never managed to learn it. It is far too difficult, or far too easy. You must be a Skolt. I sit under a tree and listen and watch, with my eyes half closed.
>
> Every Skolt, beautiful or not, well-dressed, or not, suddenly becomes a princely person. It is much more than a dance, it is a picture of life, its joys, and storms, and towards the end the calm that precedes death.
>
> The Saami believe that their dead dance in the northern lights. It must be the Skolt Saami' ka′drel they dance. No dance could be more dignified.

---

[7] Jorma Lehtola, "Kirjailija löysi unelmiensa kansan," *Apu*, 23 June 2016. Available online: https://www.apu.fi/artikkelit/kirjailija-loysi-uniensa-kansan (accessed June 20, 2024); Paula Alajärvi, "Kulttuurien kohtaaminen," *Jänkä* 12, nos. 2–3 (2016). Available online: https://janka.fi/arkistot/613 (accessed June 20, 2024).

It is also a drama in several acts. The first act is light in tone, slightly tentative, like man's first step in life. The second act is the youth, enthusiastic, overconfident, and sometimes full of pain. The third act is the mature age, more self-aware, prouder, but still unsure of having found the right path. And so on. But what the Skolt Saami' ka'drel really wants to portray means nothing. The essential thing is the graceful movements, the fantastic rhythm that breathes tenderness and suffering and sometimes becomes wild like the advance of the storm in the forest. There is no doubt, the dance is an expression of nature itself, just as nature still inspires the Skolt Saami in so much. But it is also an expression of their attraction to mysticism.

It's already midnight. The sunlight above the dancers takes on a deeper god tone. I dream of the time before the earth was born, when the gods danced like this to decide what kind of life they would bestow on our planet. It is possible that I see more in the Skolt Saami' dance than it contains. Few Finns or foreigners have seen it and no ethnologist has studied it.

"It's beautiful," says Raimo, "but completely different from our Finnish dances."

The "King" is the first to get tired. The dance stops. Slowly everyone pulls away. The young people get into the boat to go to Kiurelli's island. We hear a bear roaring in the distance and Raimo claims that it is the dance that attracted it.[8]

The excerpt reflects Crottet's attitude toward the Skolt Saami whose community, culture, and traditions he admired. For him, the Skolt community represented the ideal harmony of humanity. Similarly, the *ka'drel* was an expression of cosmic balance he thought the Skolt Saami had achieved. In the text, one finds several references to Northern nature, the smell of pine, northern lights, and the roar of a bear, which reflect Skolt Saami oral tradition and the mystical atmosphere of Lapland's "nightless night."

Crottet's description of the *ka'drel* is the most detailed written reference to it between the Second World War and the 1970s. It is the most concrete piece of evidence that the dance was still in use, although this was frequently denied in contemporary interviews. As discussed before, for many reasons, Skolt Saami might not have regarded occasional *ka'drel* dancing as proper dancing. It was different from the dance events in Suõ'nn'jel and those during the time of evacuation. On the other hand, it is also possible that they did not want to talk about it in their fragile situation. As Crottet states, they may have wanted to keep the dance only to themselves.

Moreover, Crottet had noticed that Skolt Saami attended dance events outside of their community and danced popular couple dances like the Rumba

---

[8]Crottet, *Lapplands andra ansikte*, 93–5.

and Foxtrot. Interviews conducted in the twenty-first century reinforce this observation. Compared to other ethnic groups in Inari, Skolt Saami see dance in a more positive light. Unlike people belonging to the Lutheran Church in Northern Finland, Skolt Saami have not been affected by the Laestadian pietistic revival movement that has a strong negative attitude toward dance. Crottet witnessed a change in Skolt dance culture, which still had preserved its old traditions although they were fading, while simultaneously embracing the Finnish ballroom dancing phenomenon that flourished during the decades after the Second World War. This shows how open they were to new cultural influences and especially dance, which unsettled the other inhabitants of the region.

Changes and Confusion

According to Pelto, there were signs of simplification of social events like weddings, funerals, and christenings during the 1950s. In particular, the weddings were shying away from old customs as the gatherings became smaller than those in Suõ'nn'jel and festivities were increasingly reduced to the basic elements of "official" Orthodox ceremony, formal banqueting, and ceremonial pledging of gifts. It is notable that Pelto attended two weddings that took place in 1958, and the dancing he observed was modern social dancing to the music of the gramophone, "though some of the old quadrilles and games were staged by the older participants."[9] It seems evident that the modern way of living and modern practices of Finnish social dancing were taking over the older prewar traditions.

Residents of Če'vetjäu'rr acknowledged the radical shift in the culture during the 1950s. Pelto points out many of the signs marking the change and how the "old style" way of life was Skolt Saami, but the "new style" is just a variety of "arctic Finnish life." The clothing is different, they no longer have the games and dances of the winter village, and they no longer migrate from winter to summer-fall dwelling places.[10]

It is no wonder that many Skolt Saami expressed that there has been a considerable rupture in the traditional dancing during the 1950s and 1960s. In *Saamelaisiltamat*, "The Saami Soiree," the *ka'drel* was announced with a claim that "this dance has not been performed in 32 years." A similar claim of a long break from dancing was made by Johannes Kiprianoff: he had not danced *ka'drel* since Suõ'nn'jel—forty years before he got a chance during a social event in 1974.[11] For

---

[9]Pelto, *Individualism in Skolt Lapp Society*, 172.
[10]Ibid., 177–80.
[11]Dancing the *ka'drel* can also come up in surprising situations. In 1974, a work camp was organized in Če'vetjäu'rr, which led to vivid discussions in the public department of newspapers. Apparently, a Finnish accordion player had been invited to the ecumenical camp's evening event and there had been dancing. The organizers explained the purpose of the event by offering an opportunity for dance, stating that "at the event, a Skolt Saami man (Johannes Kiprianoff) said that he had not danced ka'drel

the older generations, the cultural change must have felt heavy, and faith in the continuation of the Skolt Saami culture was not always strong. This is reflected on a more general level, as 74-year-old Liisa Feodoroff told researcher Heikki Laitinen in 1973: "Now it's the end of 'kolttaselämä' ['Skolt Saami life'] and it's already over."[12]

---

since Suõ'nn'jel, in forty years." Journalist Jorma Korhonen had written a critical story about the state's emergency aid measures and pointed out: "It is also a shame that the material impasse of the Skolt Saami impoverishes their cultural life so that the quadrille can only be danced when someone temporarily brings an accordion to the place. To remove temporary nature from the lives of the colts, the municipal councilors of Inari can also do more than currently" ("Työleirit eivät tulleet väkisin Sevettijärvelle," *Helsingin Sanomat*, 18 August 1974, 11).
[12]Laitinen, "Suonikylän laulut vuonna 1961," 17.

11 REVITALIZATION OF SKOLT SAAMI DANCE AND MUSIC

It seems likely that it was during the 1960s when traditional dances started to fall out of fashion for the younger generation. However, the idea of revitalizing traditional Skolt Saami dances emerged in the early 1970s, and it is possible to recognize some events in both Če'vetjäu'rr and Njeä'llem.

In general, the beginning of the 1970s marked an era of the building of a modern Saami society. The generation, which was born after the Second World War in the 1940s and 1950s, began to develop social, political, and cultural practices and principles of a modern Saami culture—a movement also called "the Sámi renaissance." Saami artists, for example, Nils Aslak Valkeapää (1943–2001), played a very significant role in this process. One of the key features, which has a clear connection with the revitalization of traditional Skolt Saami dances and music, is the idea of increasing the appreciation of Saami traditional culture. As seen in developments in the 1950s and 1960s, the modern Finnish and Western culture had such a strong impact that older traditions were fading away. This is seen especially in dance and music, as there were also Skolt Saami artists who performed modern music that were popular in Finnish dance hall dances. One of these musicians was Jaakko Gauriloff, a Skolt Saami singer, who performed as a soloist with Finnish dance musicians.

The main solution to the question of increasing the appreciation of Saami traditional culture by the Saami artists was to bring the tradition to various modern performing contexts (e.g., concerts, recordings, radio, television, film, etc.). Most evidently, this can be seen in the work of Valkeapää, who also described in detail the focus of his artistic work.[1] In fact, Valkeapää had already met Gauriloff in the

---

[1] See Jouste, "Áillohaš ja uuden joiun synty."

early 1960s while studying to become a schoolteacher in Kemijärvi; later, they also toured and recorded together.

Early Steps

It is most likely that at least some Skolt Saami tradition holders had already considered revitalizing dance before the revival actually began. Strong scholarly interest and appreciation of the Skolt Saami music and culture comes as no surprise after sixty years of audio recordings, filming, and linguistic and culture research. One of these tradition holders, Näskk Moshnikoff, had commented that she keeps on performing for researchers so that her tradition will remain in the archives for the coming Skolt Saami generations.[2]

However, at this moment of history in the early 1970s, one can also follow external events that might have sparked the revitalization of the Skolt Saami dance and music. In December 1972, Irja Häkämies travelled to the Skolt Saami area to conduct interviews specially on the Skolt Saami music and dance. What sets her work apart from the long line of researchers conducting interviews is that, soon after the first trip, Häkämies moved to Inari and began to organize a folklore group for Skolt Saami dances, thus utilizing the traditional knowledge she was gathering at the same time.

Soon after this, in April 1973, Heikki Laitinen, a Finnish ethnomusicologist and radio-journalist, executed a notable set of interviews focused on Skolt Saami traditional music and dance. One of his merits is that during the interviews, he organized a dance event at the Če'vetjäu'rr school, in which *ka'drel* was performed and explained in detail. His first encounter with the Skolt *ka'drel* took place in the spring of 1973, and a few years later, he recorded it on video together with his friends who were folk dance experts:

> It would be best to go to Če'vetjäu'rr again, they still know the old songs there. So then we went to Če'vetjäu'rr and traveled from house to house, learning leu'dds and Skolt ka'drel. It was unforgettable.
>
> I had read in the descriptions of the 1930s that the best thing in Suõ'nn'jel was the ka'drel. It was danced at night in winter villages, drinking and dancing. And so I started asking who could teach it. And then we danced in Ååjjaš (Oijjaš) Fofanoff's cabin into the night. Maa'ren (Marena) Gauriloff sings in a falsetto, with a shrill voice, I think she was trying to imitate accordion playing when the musician was not there. Ååjjaš Fofanoff and Å'll (Olli) Gauriloff are starting to show us the ka'drel figures. They must get another couple. Fortunately, we

---

[2] Moshnikoff, Satu. Interview by Marko Jouste and Markus Juutinen in Inari, Če'vetjäu'rr, 24 August 2017. Saami Culture Archive, The Giellagas Institute for Saami Studies, University of Oulu, SKA A1.2017, 2.

have a recording team of three people. Liisa Kautto records on Nagra and Aili Koverskoi and I try to follow the figures, but it's not going to turn out to be anything; it's too elaborate. I try to write down the figures, but it is difficult to make a dance out of the notes afterwards.

But the event made me want to return to ka'drel and made me into a passionate ka'drel dancer. In 1979, I videotaped Sevetti's ka'drel with Pirkko-Liisa and Esko Rausmaa. I studied the videos enthusiastically, used slow-motion and still image, wrote down the figures and the music. It was a completely different ka'drel than what I was used to in the Finnish folk-dance tradition. The accordion player starts and improvises his endless tune. It is impossible to determine whether the tune is duple or triple meter, a bit like with Karelian accordion players. Then the dancers start when they start, dance the first figure, and return to their places. Then the second figure starts when it starts, and so on for all six skillful figures.

The ka'drel had already come to Suõ'nn'jel a hundred years ago. I had always been taught that the Skolt Saami lived in the extreme periphery. Now, I began to understand that there was no point in this view. The village was no further from the new currents than the Finnish villages located several hundred kilometers further south. The only place where the Skolt Saami live on the periphery is the current Finnish society. Already in Pechenga, they knew about European dance trends, for example.

But, of course, the ka'drel had not remained the same as further south. It had become more improvisational, more communal. Nothing else could have been possible in such an improvisational world of singing.[3]

Laitinen's description of the dance is interesting in many ways, since it was the first time anyone attempted to analyze the *ka'drel*. Almost a decade earlier, Crottet wrote that no ethnographer had researched it, although several descriptions—still none in detail—had been documented since the early twentieth century. Since dance research in Finland was, in practice, nonexistent in the early 1970s, Laitinen was facing a very challenging task. He examined the *ka'drel* from the perspectives of dance and music and emphasized the relation between them. He considered them similar in character, with improvisation and free form as the basis for both.

Although there are many similarities between Crottet's and Laitinen's descriptions—both focused on the *ka'drel*'s elaborative and exclusive character as well as its difficulty—Laitinen did not want to merely observe the dance, which Crottet was satisfied with. In his own words, Laitinen became a *ka'drel* enthusiast, being interested in both dancing and analyzing it. He realized that it was not

---

[3]Laitinen, "Kokemuksia saamelaismusiikista viime vuosikymmeniltä," 91–3.

enough that he made written notes about the dance; a few years later, he organized a video-recording expedition to document the dance in detail.

In 1973, there was a third occasion for the *ka'drel* revival, when the Finnish Broadcasting Company (YLE) organized a television program called *Saamelaisiltamat*, "The Saami Soiree." It was a product of the new cultural awareness expressed by the producer Reino Paasilinna, who gave the organizing responsibility to young Saami, Matti Morottaja and Iisko Sara. The program, consisting of important social and cultural themes, was recorded in Inari. It aired on October 9, and all Saami were invited to participate. One part of the program was a performance of Skolt Saami *ka'drel*. For this event, a new accordion was acquired for Če'vetjäu'rr and a group of Skolt Saami were asked to prepare the dance performance on stage. This was the first-ever filming of the Skolt Saami *ka'drel*. Jaakko Gauriloff also performed his music in the program.[4] At the time that Laitinen saw the *ka'drel* for the first time, Skolt Saami had not performed in public. It is possible that Laitinen's positive attitude toward the *ka'drel* may have encouraged the Skolt Saami to attend the soiree with their dance.

"Dance-Boom" of Če'vetjäu'rr

These developments can be seen as events from which the dance began its "second life" as a form of modern culture, connecting to the new performing contexts, namely, on stage. In addition, revitalization efforts had an impact at the local level, since these convinced Skolt Saami of the importance of the traditional culture and encouraged people to create new ways of supporting the revitalization of dance culture.

People were needed to lead the effort. In 1975, Mari Fofanoff organized a *ka'drel* group, which began practicing dance in houses in Če'vetjäu'rr.[5] It brought togther not only those who wanted to dance or learn it but also those who could accompany dancing. Jä'ǩǩem Feodoroff, who had played accordion in *Saamelaisiltamat*, continued and remained active until the 1980s. More and more people were getting involved in the dancing as it provided social activities and ways to care for the elders in the community. Soon this work began to be supported by cultural institutions such as *Kolttien kannatusyhdistys*. One of the keypersons of the 1980s dance activities in Če'vetjäu'rr was Eeva Nykänen. She described this dimension of the work in detail in 2023:

---

[4]Lehtola, *Laulujen Lappi*,191–3.
[5]"Jiõnnäi'tt: Tuâl'jõžsääi'j taans, ouddoummu valljumuš, ǩiõtt-tuâjj tuåimmkä'dd sååbar," *YLE (The Finnish Broadcasting Company)*, Nuõrttsäämas, 12.12.1975. Available online: https://areena.yle.fi/podcastit/1-2597012 (accessed August 31, 2024).

First, we started in the early 1980s, with people walking around and dancing in the houses. Then we were young girls too. We were there. And this gave me the feeling that this could be learned. Then we went to houses in Supru, Saitajärvi. In Rautaperäjärvi, here in Če'vetjäu'rr. Did we ever pass by Kirakkajärvi? I don't think we did, I don't remember, we didn't. Then there was the old Nykänen shop, where the bar is today. Dances were held there. Sometimes we dance there. And later we started thinking that we could ask the civic college, that if they could give people trips, some, not all, needed them. Mostly traveled in their own cars, how they got there. We practiced two or three times a week, for many hours each time. There were a lot of people here then, there were people, otherwise dancing. Sometimes we danced the humppa-dance and then we continued with the ka'drel. The older people taught them how to dance the ka'drel. Marja, Elina, who were all there, told how it went, how it went. They said: it didn't go like this; it went like this. We learned together but the old teachers are not alive anymore, not one of them. Usually there were eight of us, four couples. A woman and a man were in pairs every time. Those houses in Če'vetjäu'rr weren't big, but we fit in just fine. And there were still people around. There were a lot of people who wanted to dance and liked to dance. Sometimes if there weren't enough people, a woman danced in the role of a man, but not often. That's how I learned both dance roles. We always danced inside the houses. I don't ever remember dancing outside. Later we danced here in the sports hall of Če'vetjäu'rr school. We had a good place to practice there. Some came and once danced and left, and again new people came along. Some were so enthusiastic that they danced for many hours. It could take four, five hours.[6]

Toini Hakkarainen wrote about her experiences in 1982 in Sää'mođđâz:

> We've been practicing the ka'drel all winter as a group of the civic college in the spring season. The group has had a few appearances: in the fall at the *Maaseudun Sivistysliitto* society's event in the multi-purpose hall, in the spring at Če'vetjäu'rr school when the committee for Free Cultural Work visited Saami and Skolt Saami areas. The most significant appearance of the spring was at the cultural evening organized by Sámi Siida [society] at Utsjoki. This must have been the first appearance of Skolt Saami at Utsjoki Saami events. The notable appearance was also because the indigenous president Jose Carlos Morales from Costa Rica was present. At first, we danced a ka'drel, after which our accordionist Jä'k̃kem Feodoroff played a beautiful folk tune. Va'ss Semenoja performed two leu'dds. At the end, we danced the ka'drel. The performance aroused a lot of appreciation and admiration. The director of the municipality

---

[6]Nykänen and Telkkälä, interview by Jouste et al.

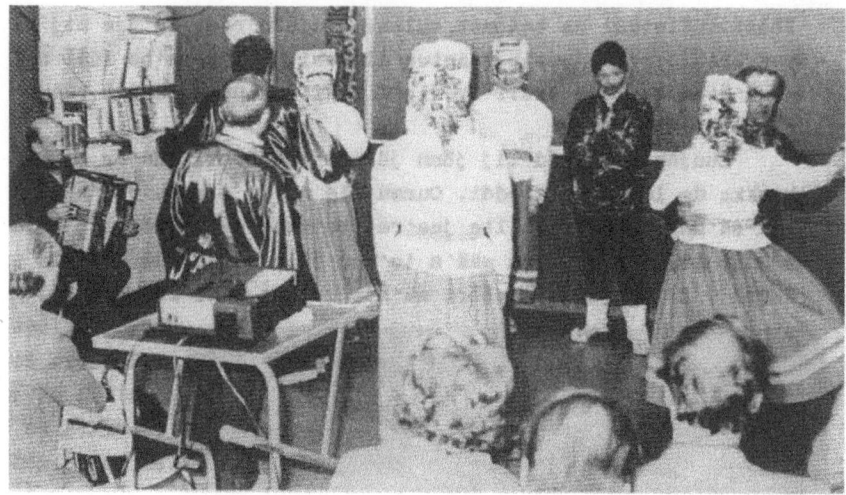

FIGURE 11.1. Čeʹvetjäuʹrr *kaʹdrel* group performing in Utsjoki in 1982. Jäʹǩǩem Feodoroff accompanies dancers with an accordion.

Source: *Sääʹmođđâz ǩiđđ - ǩiäʹss* (1982): 4–5.

of Utsjoki also came to thank our group. The representatives of Sámi Siida hoped that we would continue our hobby and come to them again. In the fall, we will have the opportunity to start the civic college again as a group. We hope to get more dancers involved. In addition to kaʹdrel, we could practice other traditional dances, e.g., "eight" = vošmerkka There are also accordion playing lessons planned in autumn. I think nurturing one's own dance tradition is a matter for the whole village.[7]

Although people were now committed to the task of reviving the dance, the rupture had created some challenges for the new generation.[8] According to Äʹnn (Anni) Feodoroff and Dåʹmnn (Tyyne) Fofanoff, the Skolt Saami have found reviving the old folk dances challenging because the young people have been reluctant to participate. For older people, however, dancing quadrilles has thrived in recent years, even in new places of residence. For more than twenty years, these skills were not considered appropriate to use. "We just don't know how to sing, because the words of the dances are originally in Russian. We don't know the language, and no one has ever translated them into Skolt Saami," they say.[9]

---

[7] Toini Hakkarainen, "Sevetin katrilliryhmä Saami siidan vieraana Utsjoella," *Sääʹmođđâz ǩiđđ - ǩiäʹss* (1982): 4–5.
[8] Häkämies, "Kolttasaamelainen musiikkiperinne," 19.
[9] "Vanhaa käsityötaitoa herätetään henkiin," *Helsingin Sanomat*, August 8, 1979. Available online: https://digi.kansalliskirjasto.fi/sanomalehti/binding/2679251?page=10 (accessed July 7, 2025).

Njeä'llem Folklore Group

Traditional dances were also actively revived in the village of Njeä'llem, but the activity there took a slightly different direction. In Njeä'llem, the Skolt Saami were never the majority; they always lived as a minority among Finns and other Saami. As mentioned, the initiator of the activity was Irja Jefremoff (née Häkämies), originally from Karelia, Finland; she married a Skolt Saami man and moved to Inari. During her studies and before her marriage, Irja Jefremoff participated in a research project, which investigated, among other things, the livelihood of the Skolt Saami. She conducted interviews with the Skolt Saami people in Inari. Since she studied folklore, especially folk music as a minor subject at the University of Tampere, she also inquired about music and dance. She was surprised by how often dance was mentioned in interviews. She was personally interested in dancing and folk dances, which motivated her to contribute to the revival of Skolt dances.[10]

Irja Jefremoff initiated revival activities in Njeä'llem after having gone there for ballroom dancing in the 1970s. The local sports club arranged dances every week, and they were extremely popular. She met Skolt Saami at these events and began to learn their old dances from Pechenga, which were not in the ballroom repertoire. One of her first informants was Julia Kytölä. A Skolt woman from Paččjokk, Pechenga. She taught her dances from her youth, such as *Vintjårkka, Šestjårkka, Kuu loistaa*, and *Oira*.[11]

Irja Jefremoff moved to Njeä'llem in 1973, and in the same year, a community college study group for folk dance was established. This group also belonged to the Njeä'llem sports club, and they rehearsed at the sports hall. There were several Skolt men and women who were good at dancing and remembered dances. Particularly important was the influence of the Jefremoff family whose five siblings actively reminisced about dances. Their mother Feäddsi had been an expert in dance singing, and they were used to dancing by singing. The siblings were united by their mother's legacy of dancing and dance songs. They tried the dances together and corrected each other. Under their guidance and that of another Skolt Saami family—the Koputoffs—the group eventually had a repertoire of almost ten dances.[12]

Typically, in the 1970s, the *ka'drel* was almost the only dance that was considered a traditional Skolt dance, and the Njeä'llem Folklore Group was also expected to dance it. However, while the Skolt Saami in Če'vetjäu'rr almost exclusively performed the *ka'drel*, the Njeä'llem group danced different couple dances such as the above-mentioned ones. The group consciously decided not to dance the

---

[10] Irja Jefremoff, interview by Hoppu.
[11] Ibid.
[12] Ibid.; "Perinteitä ja nykyaikaa. Kolttasaamelaisten elämän punainen lanka," *Keskipohjanmaa*, July 20, 1978; Yrjö Kujala, "Karjalaistytön tie kolttien sukuun," *Keskipohjanmaa*, July 22, 1978.

ka'drel, although many Skolt Saami living in Njeä'llem knew it, and in their home villages in Pechenga, it had been danced. At joint events with the Skolt Saami of Če'vetjäu'rr, they danced the *ka'drel* together, but it was never performed.[13]

The group set out to construct a repertoire of their own. There were several Skolt Saami musicians—Simo and U'cc-Åttaž (Antti) Jefremoff, Grigori Koputoff, and Vaa'ssel (Vasili) Titoff—in the village, so it was easy for the group to have accompaniment for the dance. Their instruments were harmonica, accordion, and even a comb. However, there were difficulties in the beginning, as the small village did not have enough Skolt Saami for the group. For this reason, everyone was allowed to join the group, including Finns and Inari Saami. They did not want to exclude anyone from the group, nor could they have, since everyone was free to join a civic college study group. As a result, their actions faced criticism, but they continued tenaciously for over twenty-five years. Gradually, the number of participants began to decrease. The school in the village of Njeä'llem was closed, and the young families moved elsewhere. Eventually, the group laid down its activities in the late 1990s.[14]

Impact of the Russian Saami

One can see that when revitalization processes begin to work, there are various activities, and possibly some unexpected events, which are all intricately intertwined. In this case, it was the process of reconnecting with the Skolt Saami living in the Soviet Union; such a development was least expected to have taken place after fifty years of closed borders behind the Iron Curtain. The most surprising fact is that this already took place in 1976, fifteen years before the collapse of the Soviet Union and opening of the borders for the next three decades, until the "Putin-wars" during the 2020s.

In 1976, Matti Sverloff, village head of the Finnish Skolt Saami, organized the first trip to Murmansk in the Soviet Union. The trips continued in 1981 and 1990 to Luujäu'rr (Lovozero), which is the center of the Russian Saami. Russian Saami with their folklore groups also had the opportunity to visit Finland in 1986 and 1990. Finnish journalist Jorma Korhonen wrote about the first trip in *Helsingin Sanomat*:

> During the history of the last few decades of the little Skolt Saami people, which has experienced hardships, there has hardly been a more joyful incident than

---

[13]Katri Jefremoff, Interview by Petri Hoppu in Inari, 2014. Saami Culture Archive, The Giellagas Institute for Saami Studies, University of Oulu, SKA A1.2014, 26.
[14]Ibid.; "Perinteitä ja nykyaikaa."

FIGURE 11.2A AND B. Two articles describing Irja Jefremoff's work on revitalizing Skolt Saami dance.

Source: *Ilta-Sanomat*, July 20, 1978.

FIGURE 11.3. Grigori Koputoff with his accordion in Njeä'llem.
Source: Photograph by Jorma Puranen.

FIGURE 11.4. Grigori Koputoff accompanying dance in Njeä'llem.
Source: Photograph by Jorma Puranen.

FIGURE 11.5. Vaa'ssel (Vasili) Titoff plays a harmonica in a bus in the 1970s.
Source: Photograph by Jorma Puranen.

FIGURE 11.6. Grigori Koputoff playing the mandolin with Martta Orttonen.
Source: Photograph by Jorma Puranen.

a recent trip to meet relatives living in Kola, Soviet Union, and at the same time to look at former living areas in old Pechenga. A bus full of Če'vetjäu'rr residents and members of the Skolt Saami tribe living elsewhere in Finland got a tourist trip to Murmansk and at the same time the opportunity to search for their relatives who live behind few and non-existent connections. There has been no communication between the parts of the Skolt Saami tribe that was divided to pieces, until now, when Matti Sverloff, village head of the Finnish Skolt Saami, went on this trip to the Murmansk and Tuloma regions.

There are several newspaper articles and radio programs,[15] in which the trip is described but most likely the contacts between musicians and dancers were not realized yet. Korhonen describes dancing only briefly in Murmansk:

> The national dress and naturally immediate Skolt Saami expedition gained the popularity of Murmansk people when the ka'drel music was played in the hotel's restaurant disco and the grandmothers danced happily.[16]

The newly acquired connections to Russian Saami had a significant impact on dance, especially on the music used to accompany dance, because in Finland, dance had not been accompanied by instruments since the Second World War. Among the Russian Saami, this tradition had remained unbroken, and the folklore groups typical of the Soviet era had also developed dance performances led by local professionals. However, it is likely that Russian musical influences were only introduced to the group Če'vetjäu'rr in the 1980s, as they are not included in the earlier recordings. The trip to Murmansk and Luujäu'rr in 1981 was organized by The Finnish Saami delegation, focusing mainly on reindeer herding and education.

Film Recordings of the *Ka'drel* and Other Dances

The 1973 performance at *Saamelaisiltamat* marked the first time the Skolt Saami ka'drel was captured on film. The stage featured eight dancers accompanied by a

---

[15]Radio programs (YLE, The Finnish Broadcasting Company): September 10, 1976: Če'vetjääu'r da Njeä'llem sää'm jie'lle Murmanskist, kuulât mä'tǩǩ-maainâs. Mie'ldd jm. Domna Sanila, Tyyne da Illeppi Fofonoff. Tuåimteei: Elli Rantala; October 29, 1976: Če'vetjääu'r da Njeä'llem sää'm jie'lle Murmanskist, mä'tǩǩ-maainâs nu'bb vuä'ss. Mie'ldd jm. Domna Jagolovna, Jukka Kalinin, Niina Taskinen de Olli Gauriloff. Tuåimteei: Elli Rantala.

[16]Jorma Korhonen, "Terveisiä Petsamosta," *Helsingin Sanomat*, September 12, 1976, 20. Available online: https://digi.kansalliskirjasto.fi/sanomalehti/binding/2654802?page=20 (accessed September 3, 2024).

single musician on a newly acquired two-row accordion. The soiree host Matti Morottaja presented the group with the following words:

> Then a group of Skolt Saami from Če'vetjäu'rr will perform. They perform Sevetti's ka'drel. This dance has not been danced for 32 years due to the unavailability of an accordion. Now they have an accordion, and we see and hear this ka'drel.

Interestingly, the host stated that the *ka'drel* had not been danced after the war due to the lack of accordions. Although it was true that accordions had been left in Pechenga, various sources presented in this book earlier indicate that the Skolt Saami had danced the *ka'drel* occasionally during the decades following the war.

As mentioned earlier in this chapter, Skolt Saami dances were recorded on video in the late 1970s, at the initiative of Heikki Laitinen. In July 1978, Njeä'llem Folklore Group performed at the Kaustinen Folk Music Festival; there, Laitinen recorded the Skolt Saami couple dances performed by the group together with folklorist and folk dance researcher Pirkko-Liisa Rausmaa and her husband PE teacher Esko Rausmaa.[17] The Rausmaas were keen folk dancers, and they belonged to the rare group that recorded folk dances in Finland at the end of the twentieth century.

In August 1979, Laitinen and the Rausmaas traveled to Inari, where they recorded dances in two places in Če'vetjäu'rr: the Supru area and the center of Če'vetjäu'rr. Most of the dancers in the Supru group had only learned to dance in Če'vetjäu'rr—some having been born there—while all the dancers in the latter group were born in Pechenga and danced traditional dances even before the war. All the women wore traditional dresses. In Supru, the men wore stylized Russian-style satin shirts, which belonged to their performance outfit then, while in the center of Če'vetjäu'rr, the male dancers were in their casual clothes. In Supru, dancing was accompanied by Jä'ǩǩem Feodoroff with his two-row accordion, while in the center of Če'vetjäu'rr, dancing was accompanied by singing. *Ka'drel*, *Šestjårkka*, and *Okldu'na* were recorded from both groups, and *Ainamilaadu* from the dancers of the center of Če'vetjäu'rr.[18]

The recordings by Laitinen and the Rausmaa were stored in The Finnish Folk Music Institute archive, and they were mostly forgotten for decades. At the beginning of the twenty-first century, very few Skolt Saami, if any, were aware of their existence. Therefore, they have not had any significance in the revitalization of Skolt Saami dances. Instead, a recording of the *ka'drel* by Pertti Tuisku, Juhani

---

[17]Rausmaa, "Kolttien tanssiperinteet," 123–35.
[18]Ibid., 111–22.

Kekkonen, and Erkki Lilja in Inari in 1992 achieved the status of a certain ideal form of dance. In this recording, men wore Saami kaftan (*määccaǩ*), which had now become their performance outfit. Only one of the dancers, Då'mnn (Tyyne) Fofanoff, had participated in the recording session in 1979.[19]

Although the basic form of the dance in the 1992 recording resembles those made in 1979, the most remarkable difference is that there are no breaks between the figures of the dance. The importance of the 1992 recording can be seen in the fact that this practice has completely fallen into oblivion, unknown for decades. The most likely reason for the disappearance of the breaks was that the *ka'drel* turned into a performance. Finnish folk dancers have had the same practice of dropping the breaks between the figures while performing their quadrilles since the emergence of regular folk dance activities in the early twentieth century; when the Skolt Saami began to perform their dances in the 1970s, Finnish folk dance was the most natural example for them to draw from. As early as in the performance at the Saami Soiree in 1973, the breaks were missing, which is conceivable since the time was probably limited. Still, it is obvious that the breaks belonged to the original *ka'drel*: that was also the practice in the French quadrille and folk quadrilles in the Russian Empire.

---

[19]Skolt ka'drell from Če'vetjäu'rr 1992. Folklife archives, Tampere University. KPL V A 118.

12 TAKING DANCES TO THE STAGE

One of the main parts of the dance activities was that Skolt Saami dance and music tradition began to gain growing interest coming from outside the community. It was realized in the emergence of new performance opportunities both in Finland and abroad. Besides the work inside the community, the work for preparing for various performances was the main part of the activities of the Če'vetjäu'rr dance group and Njeä'llem Folklore Group.

Performing dances for the public was a new kind of activity that required different practices from before. The 1970s and the beginning of the 1980s were clearly a period of exploration in this regard, and the establishment of the forms of performance did not happen overnight. The Skolt Saami dance performances were influenced by Finnish folk-dance performances, especially when Skolt Saami went to perform their dances outside their home region.

However, it should be noted that the development work took place almost entirely within the community. The Finnish folk-dance teachers had no visible influence at least on how the Skolt Saami put together their performances, what kind of music was used in them and what the dancers' clothings were like. Already at this stage they themselves were able to take advantage of the structures of the dominant culture to promote and preserve their own cultural activities.

Performances Home and Abroad

The *ka'drel* performance at the Saami Soiree was in many ways significant for the future of Skolt Saami dances. There is no information that the Skolt Saami *ka'drel* or other dances had been performed before on stage, so the dance moved almost unnoticed to a new environment. Although, for example, Eeva Nykänen recalls that in the 1970s old dances were revived for common use in Če'vetjäu'rr, they gradually turned into performances almost entirely for decades. In the same context, in Če'vetjäu'rr, only the *ka'drel*—and, to some extent, also *Ainamilaadu*—remained in use, while the rest of the dance traditions sank into near oblivion.[1]

Njeä'llem Folklore Group had a larger repertoire although it primarily consisted of small couple dances, not dances with several complicated figures like the *ka'drel*. Moreover, the group staged a play about courtship and engagement traditions in 1980, thus expanding their repertoire beyond dancing. Despite facing challenges such as losing key members—musician Grigori Koputoff and performer Raimo Jefremoff—during its early years, the group continued to grow and evolve throughout the 1970s and 1980s.[2]

Both the Če'vetjäu'rr and Njeä'llem groups performed several times at the Kaustinen Folk Music Festival in the 1970s and 1980s. The first time they attended the festival was in 1978. The Če'vetjäu'rr group danced the *ka'drel* and the Njeä'llem group Korobushka couple dance at the opening of the festival.[3] Since this was the first time the Skolt Saami performed their dance and music, they received a lot of positive attention in the press:

> The special theme of the week, the presentation of Saami music, got into full swing on Wednesday, when rare guests, the Skolt Saami people of Če'vetjäu'rr and Njeä'llem, took to the stage to talk about their own rich tradition. For the first time, the Skolt Saami group that had traveled this far south had recorded their own yoik or le'udd tradition, e.g., from Jääkk (Jaakko) Sverloff, who died last winter. The people in Kaustinen also heard the rare sheep call and lullaby of the elder Skolt Saami. Russian dance tunes from Pechenga were performed as live music samples, performed with harmonica by Simo and U'cc-Åttaž (Antti) Jefremoff, Vaa'ssel (Vasili) Titoff born in 1915, and Grigori Koputoff. All of them have behind them a typical Skolt life pattern: evacuee's journey here and there, finally settling in Njeä'llem.[4]

In 1979, Njeä'llem Folklore Group embarked on a trip to Northern Sweden, where they were guests of the *Same-Ätnam Club* and performed for the club's culture days in Arjeplog, a Saami village. Here, they explored the village's Saami museum and were particularly intrigued by the beautiful tinsel embroidery on the dresses. Their performance, which included old *leu'dd*s, folk dances, music, and spinning on a spindle, was enthusiastically received by the Saami people of

---

[1] Nykänen and Telkkälä, interview by Jouste et al.
[2] Irja Jefremoff, "Njeä'llem kaddrellneekk 5-ekksaž," *Sää'moddâz* čöhčč (1979): 2–4.
[3] Markku Huotari, "Lapinmies joikasi, noitarumpu kumisi," *Pohjolan Sanomat*, July 18, 1978.
[4] "Kolttien katrilli ja joiut elpymässä," *Helsingin Sanomat*, July 20, 1978. Translation by Marko Jouste. Available online: https://digi.kansalliskirjasto.fi/sanomalehti/binding/2666996?page=14 (accessed September 2, 2024).

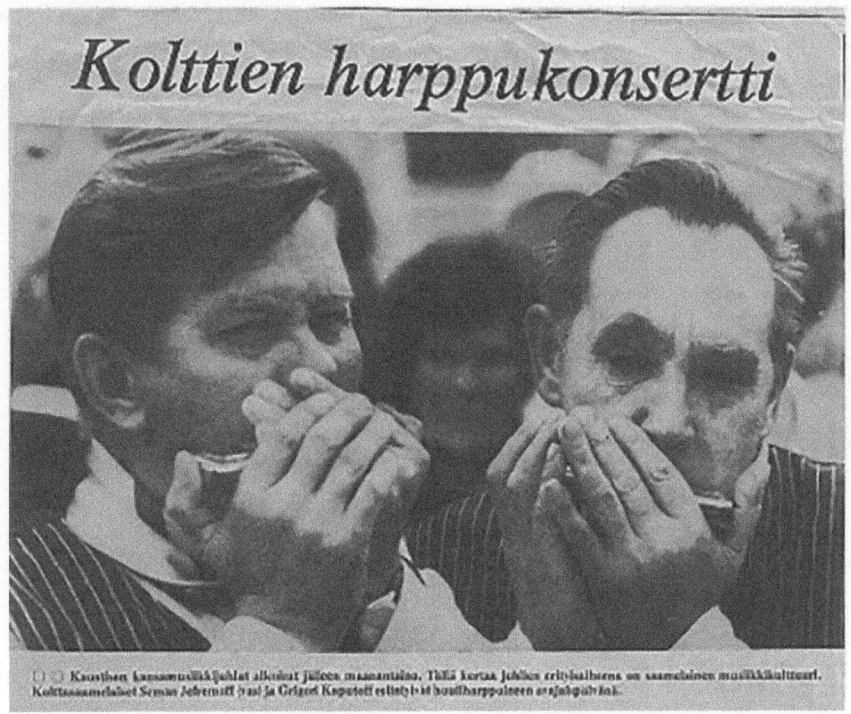

FIGURE 12.1. Seman Jeffremoff and Grigori Koputoff playing harmonicas in Kaustinen Folk Music Festival in 1978.

Sweden and Norway. Following this, the group produced a television program with the Norwegian Broadcasting Company about the music tradition of the Skolt Saami, filmed in Njeä'llem, in U'cc-Åttaž Jefremoff's yard. This program was also broadcast on Finnish television.[5]

In July 1982, Njeä'llem Folklore Group participated in the international folklore festival *Jeux Santos* in France, where they had the opportunity to present the Skolt Saami tradition of song, music, and dance. The group was completed by Helena Semenoff from Kirakkajärvi, allowing them to showcase a variety of Skolt Saami traditions as well as *leu'dd*s.[6]

During the festival, the group performed in a city full of historical monuments. They participated in a Catholic mass dedicated to world peace at Saint Pierre Cathedral and spent a day as guests of French families. Despite the language barrier, they were able to communicate through hand gestures and knitting. The group's performance was well-received, with the French elderly recognizing many of their

---

[5]Ibid.; Bertil Sundkvist, "Skoltsamer bjöd på sång, dans och musik i Arjeplog," *Norra Västerbotten*, June 2, 1980.
[6]Irja Jefremoff, "Matkakuvia Ranskasta - ystäviä maailman ääriltä," *Sää'moďďâz čõhčč* (1982): 2–5.

dances as the long-forgotten ballroom dances of their childhood and youth. The festivals were attended by groups from various countries all over the world.[7]

The Če'vetjäu'rr group also performed quite frequently during the first decades of its activities. A member of the group recalled they had approximately six performances annually during the early phase. Many performances took place in their home village or places nearby, but they travelled elsewhere in Finland and abroad as well: Moscow, Stockholm, and Norway. They also performed on five trips to Saami in Luujäu'rr and Murmansk on the Kola Peninsula. They were even asked to travel to Japan, but since most of the group were older people, they did not dare to go on such a long and strenuous journey. During their tours, they performed the *ka'drel* as often as they could. The leader of the group during the 1980s and 1990s, Eeva Nykänen, stated that they once performed the *ka'drel* at a night bar in Helsinki where a local orchestra was playing. When the orchestra was going to have a break, she asked if they could dance their *ka'drel* on the stage, which they were allowed to do. They rarely had a musician with them, but they had a *ka'drel* music recording that they used for dance.[8]

The activity of the Če'vetjäu'rr group declined in the late 1990s, but it never completely ceased as it happened in Njeä'llem. For various occasions, such as the fiftieth anniversary of the Skolt Saami resettlement in Če'vetjäu'rr in 1999, dancers gathered together for a performance, as it had happened ten and twenty years earlier; the tradition thus remained alive into the twenty-first century.[9] Moreover, the performance in 1999 was significant in that, for the first time, both children and adults were involved. In a certain sense, the occasion was a turning point for the Skolt Saami dance tradition in the same way as the Saami Soiree had been twenty-six years earlier.

New Music for the *Ka'drel*

During the 1980s, the Če'vetjäu'rr *ka'drel* group began to use new music called *Skolt ka'drel* or *Luujäu'rr ka'drel* in their performances. This melody became the most celebrated piece of *ka'drel* music and was used exclusively in performances from the late 1980s to the 2010s. When an accordionist was not able to participate, a recording of the melody was used instead. One of the leading persons in revitalizing the *ka'drel* in Če'vetjäu'rr was Då'mnn (Tyyne) Fofanoff. She offers some background of the dance and the music in a dance video titled *Skolt ka'drel from Če'vetjäu'rr*, recorded in 1992:

---

[7]Ibid.
[8]Skolt man from Če'vetjäu'rr, interview by Petri Hoppu, in Če'vetjäu'rr, Inari, Finland, August 17, 2014; Nykänen and Telkkälä, interview by Jouste et al.
[9]Minna Moshnikoff, interview by Petri Hoppu, in Kirkkonummi, Finland, April 14, 2016.

This ka'drel has been an old cultural tradition for us, and it came to us from Russia. Our fathers' fathers, they have brought us this and we have continued this ka'drel in Če'vetjäu'rr, which has still survived for us. It's a Saami play or Saami siõrr. This music has come with us from the Russian side, ka'drel music. Of course, we can't say what kind of background music it is, but it has [come on the journey of this dance]. And of course, we also have leu'dd as a [accompanying] material.[10]

According to Finnish accordionist Ahti Similä, Elias Moshnikoff from Če'vetjäu'rr had learned and recorded this dance melody while visiting Russia in the 1970s. By the late 1980s, Similä worked as an accordion player of the Če'vetjäu'rr *ka'drel* group, and he learned the melody from Moshnikoff.[11] On the same video, Similä talks about his involvement in developing the accompaniment for Če'vetjäu'rr Skolt *ka'drel*:

> I heard a tape, brought from Murmansk. I heard how a Russian folk music player had performed [this melody] on the tape and then I made a Finnish arrangement on it, for accordion. Tyyne has sung to me a leu'dd-melody that I have also played [as an accompaniment] for ka'drel.[12]

Most often, the song was performed with accordions; a sung version with Russian lyrics can also be found from a C-cassette. The music played by the guests were recorded by several individuals on C-cassettes.[13]

Why, then, did the dancers choose music from Russia as their accompaniment? One reason could be the consequence of renewing contacts with Russian Skolt Saami. When the Saami obtained permission to travel across the border to Kola Peninsula during the 1970s, many Skolt Saami relatives were found again from Luujäu'rr, Murmansk, and Tuållâm. The contacts stayed vivid also in the 1980s and 1990s, organized mainly by the Finnish Sámi Parliament. Russian Saami also came to Finland and visited Če'vetjäu'rr in 1982. In 1986, a folklore group "Lujavvr" visited Finland, performing in the Skolt Saami area of Njeä'llem and attending two Finnish folk music festivals: Jutajaiset in Sodankylä and Kaustinen Folk Music Festival. This visit is an important event for introducing a particular melody to dancers of the Če'vetjäu'rr *ka'drel* group besides Elias Moshnikoff's recording. This music was probably special as it had been developed by Russian Saami especially for the *ka'drel*.

Furthermore, one can argue that warm feelings and love for relatives and shared Skolt Saami traditions also played a role. These feelings are shown in the following

---

[10] "Skolt ka'drell from Če'vetjäu'rr 1992," Folklife archives, Tampere University. KPL V A 118.
[11] Ahti Similä, interview by Marko Jouste in Ivalo, Finland, August 27, 2023.
[12] Ibid.
[13] The collection of C-cassettes recorded by Elias Moshnikoff. Saami Culture Archive, The Giellagas Institute for Saami Studies, University of Oulu.

FIGURE 12.2. A musical notation of Če'vetjäu'rr Skolt *ka'drel* or Luujäu'rr *ka'drel* was published in *Sevettjärven kolttakatrilli*.

quote by Russian Saami Aleksandra Antonova, a cousin of the village head Matti Sverloff:

> When cousin Sandra sits among women from Če'vetjäu'rr and dances the traditional ka'drel, she is one of them: the same national attire, the same music, the same blood heritage, almost the same language. Relatives have been separated from each other for decades. Only last spring, a group of people from Če'vetjäu'rr visited Antonova's home village, Luujäu'rr (Lovozero), 150

FIGURE 12.3. The wedding festivities in Čeʹvetjäuʹrr in the 1960s.
Source: Irja Jefremoff's private collection.

kilometers east of Murmansk. "This is exactly glasnost, that Gorbachev sent me here to meet my brothers and my sisters", says Aleksandra.[14]

Costumes Used on Stage

As mentioned earlier in this book, Skolt women paid special attention to how they dressed at dances in their home villages in Pechenga. The practices in the use of costumes in dancing, especially on stage, vary from time to time and reflect the changes in the dance culture. There exist a variety of both historical and present-day sources of Skolt Saami clothing. These include photographs, descriptions, and costumes already from the early twentieth century. While women continued to use traditional outfits until the 1970s, men's clothing followed Finnish customs, especially while celebrating events like weddings and funerals.

The costumes worn on stage also represent a gradual change in esteem of dance as the "insiders" dance became one of the main symbols of Skolt Saami culture.

---

[14]"Glasnostin lähettiläät," *Suomen Kuvalehti*, October 27, 1989, 64.

The most remarkable changes have occurred in men's costumes, while the changes have been moderate for women's costumes.

At the Saami Soiree in 1973, the men wore dark suits, which had long been their formal wear. The women had their traditional Skolt dresses, each unique.

Notably, Matti Morottaja, the host of the Saami Soiree, did not use any words to mean folk dance in Finnish—for example, "kansantanssi," "tanhu," or "kansantanhu"—while introducing the group; isntead; he referred to the *ka'drel* as a dance ("tanssi"). One might interpret this as the *ka'drel* dancing at the soiree was seen less as a folk-dance performance and more as a demonstration of Skolt traditions. Against this background, it is conceivable that the dancers wore ordinary party clothing and not specially designed performance costumes.

Later in the 1970s, Če'vetjäu'rr Skolt Saami started to perform the *ka'drel* on different occasions, and with that came the need for special performance outfits. The women still wore their traditional clothing, but the men wore Russian-styled satin shirts at performances as the men of the group from Supru did during the recording session in 1979. It is possible that the inspiration to use these shirts came from Kola Saami whose performances the Skolt Saami had probably seen during their visit to the Soviet Union in 1976. It is also possible that the shirts, or at

FIGURE 12.4. Dancers at the Saami Soiree in 1973. An excerpt from the film *Saamelaisiltamat 1973*.

Source: Finnish Broadcasting Company.

FIGURE 12.5. Markus and Elina Moshnikoff dancing the quadrille and Sari Saxholm playing the accordion at the restaurant Peuralammen Paari in Če'vetjäu'rr, Inari, June 2018. Source: Photograph by Minna Moshnikoff.

least the fabrics, had been bought there. Apparently, this practice did not last long, and men soon started to wear men's Saami kaftan (*määccaǩ*), which is the case in the video from 1992 and is still common practice. The performance outfit has not changed over the past few decades. Each dancer has a personal attire, which nevertheless follows the Skolt Saami tradition and contemporary practices and fashion.

Njeä'llem Folklore Group also discussed the issue of costume for a while in the 1970s; at first, they could wear costumes with different backgrounds in their performance. However, they soon ended up with a solution where women had a traditional Skolt clothing and men wore a striped or dark vest, white shirt, black trousers, and scarf tied with a ring. These outfits were worn if the group was active.[15]

Contemporarily, the Skolt Saami often have discussions about their clothing, and views on proper dance attire are closely related to this discussion. It is considered particularly important that Skolt Saami wear their own traditional attire, in the form known today, when they perform the *ka'drel*. Although there

---

[15]Irja Häkämies, "Kolttasaamelaista perinnettä," *Perhonjokilaakso*, July 13, 1978; Irja Jefremoff, interview by Marko Jouste and Petri Hoppu in Njeä'llem, Inari, Finland, March 20, 2023. SKA.

FIGURE 12.6. Njeä'llem Folklore Group dances *Korobushka* in Njeä'llem, Inari, 1983. Source: Photograph by Urho Pietilä.

are also people other than Skolt Saami in the performances, the use of Skolt Saami clothing is exclusive to the Skolt Saami. For example, Finns typically wear their own national costumes when performing the *ka'drel* with the Skolt Saami.

This shows that although the *ka'drel* and the Skolt Saami clothing are both strongly symbolic, their symbolic meaning differs from each other. Today, the *ka'drel* is seen more as an inclusive cultural feature, which will be discussed later, while the Skolt attire is clearly exclusive, worn solely by the Skolt Saami.

13 SKOLT SAAMI DANCE CULTURE IN THE 2000s

Today, together with language and crafts, the *ka'drel* is considered one of the three distinct identity features of the Skolt Saami. The dance continues to be performed occasionally, but, more importantly, it has regained popularity as a social practice. This chapter examines contemporary practices and contexts of the Skolt Saami *ka'drel* dancing, the occasions in which it is danced, and the meanings contemporary Skolt Saami give to the dance.

Contemporary Contexts of the *Ka'drel*

Entering the twenty-first century has allowed for new contexts and meanings for the *ka'drel*, as new generations have rediscovered the dance in fresh ways. Younger Skolt Saami are searching for new perspectives to their dance history and, in a broader sense, to their cultural history. *Ka'drel* dancing is not limited to folklore performances anymore, but in addition to the fact that it is taught to Skolt children at Če'vetjäu'rr elementary school, it is also taught at occasional courses, not necessarily for Skolt Saami alone but for anyone willing to learn it. For example, the *Ka'drel* was one of the themes in the workshops of the international Skolt Saami language and culture conference in Inari in June 2012; moreover, it has been rehearsed in courses that have been arranged by Skolt Saami living outside of Inari.[1]

A completely new step in *ka'drel* dancing took place in the fall of 2016, when some Skolt Saami living in the capital region reached out to the Finnish folkdance association Helsingin Kansantanssin Ystävät, inviting them to rehearse

---

[1] Petri Hoppu, "Dancing Agency. Skolt Saami Identities in Transition," *Puls* 5 (2020): 26–44 (37).

and perform the *ka'drel* together. The performance took place at Savoy Theatre in Helsinki on November 12 of the same year. The challenge with folk costumes was resolved in such a way that the Skolt Saami wore their own attire and the Finns their national costumes, reflecting the idea that clothing was an exclusive element and the *ka'drel* an inclusive element of Skolt culture.[2]

Since the performance at Savoy Theatre, similar events featuring both Skolt Saami and non-Skolt Saami participants in the *ka'drel* have occurred frequently. These have been both performances and occasions for social dancing. For example, in February 2019, one of the authors of this book, Petri Hoppu, was invited to join a quadrille with two Skolt Saami and another Finn at a Saami national day celebration in Oulu, while the other author, Marko Jouste, played in the accompanying music group that consisted of Skolt Saami and Finns as well.

Although the *ka'drel* is evidently the only traditional Skolt dance still actively practiced today, awareness of other dances is steadily increasing. After a long hiatus, Irja Jefremoff, former leader of the Njeä'llem Folklore Group, organized a Skolt Saami couple dance course in the village of Njeä'llem in 2016. The participants included both older and younger Skolt Saami, and the success of the dance course highlights a strong interest toward couple dances as well.[3]

Ka'drel book

Although the contexts and forms of the *ka'drel* have evolved over the past few decades, this has not entailed a loss of connection to history and tradition. Even the young Skolt Saami believe that the *ka'drel* must be performed in an appropriate manner. Since the dance tradition is fading and many Skolt Saami are uncertain of how the *ka'drel* should be performed, precise instructions in written form are needed.

In 2022, Sari Saxholm, Minna Moshnikoff, and Mari Gauriloff published an instruction book for the Skolt *ka'drel*.[4] The book contains dance instructions, step patterns, and four *ka'drel* melodies. It also covers the history of the dance and contains information about *ka'drel* dancing. The *ka'drel* melodies serve as a significant enabler of the dance since this marks their first publication. All the authors are Skolt Saami.

Writing the book was a demanding task because, the terminology related to *ka'drel* was almost completely missing. For example, the figures of the *ka'drel* did not have names, probably because there was no need for that. As stated earlier,

---

[2] Ibid., 37–8.
[3] Ibid., 38.
[4] Saxholm, Moshnikoff, and Gauriloff, *Sevettijärven kolttakatrilli*.

the original French terms were not used in folk quadrilles, and the same was true of the *ka'drel*. The authors needed to create them for the instruction book. For inspiration, they drew from Finnish folk-dance vocabulary and names that reflect the cultural heritage of Če'vetjäu'rr, while also incorporating purely descriptive names.[5] For example, the names of the second *Kukkotappelu* ("cockfight") and the last figure *Loppukirnu* ("final churn") describe their character: in the background of the former is the bravado between the gentlemen that is part of the figure; the latter, on the other hand, describes the nonstop (*stretto*) nature of the figure.[6]

The authors wanted to name the parts to make remembering the dance order easier. However, they did not have to start entirely from scratch, as the figures had already been documented by Marja-Liisa Sanila, a teacher at Če'vetjäu'rr school, in the 1980s. This set of instructions, often referred to as "the paper," was commonly used for decades.[7]

The authors wanted to preserve the character of the *ka'drel* as a social form of dancing and, for this reason, decided not to specify the exact steps or counts in the instructions. It has been a common practice that when the dancers move on the floor, they take as many steps as necessary in each figure. The authors emphasize that unnecessary regularity does not suit the Skolt *ka'drel*'s character. The quality of the steps is also left open, letting the dancers decide whether they use walking or running steps or something in between. Typically, the tempo of the music may vary, which affects the steps as well.[8]

When referring to couples, the Finnish terms for girl (*tyttö*) and boy (*poika*) are used in the book. There are two reasons for this: (1) using these terms, the authors want to encourage young people to dance the *ka'drel*, and (2) this is a common practice in Finnish folk dance. The authors also use several pictures of dancing children to emphasize the significance of children's learning of the dance. They point out that despite the usage of the dichotomy of girl-boy, they see no reason why there cannot be girl-girl or boy-boy couples in the dance, since the joy of dancing should not depend on not finding the formally "right" partner.[9]

The publication of the book was of great importance in terms of Skolt dance culture, because it was the first publication about Skolt Saami dance produced by the Skolt Saami themselves. Although the authors used outside help during the process, they retained the right to make the final decisions about how the instructions were formulated. For this reason, the book strongly reflects the world of experience related to the dance of the current Skolt Saami and, by no means, the views constructed by Finnish scholars or folk-dance experts.

---

[5]Ibid., 47.
[6]Ibid., 60, 70.
[7]Hoppu, 'Dancing Agency', 37; Saxholm, Moshnikoff, and Gauriloff, *Sevettijärven kolttakatrilli*, 47.
[8]Saxholm, Moshnikoff, and Gauriloff, *Sevettijärven kolttakatrilli*, 46–8.
[9]Ibid., 50.

FIGURE 13.1. The cover of *Sevettijärven kolttakatrilli. Če'vetjääu'r ka'dre'l*, an instruction book for the Skolt *ka'drel* by Sari Saxholm, Minna Moshnikoff, and Mari Gauriloff.

PART FOUR

MEANINGS AND TURNING POINTS

Affected by a myriad of cultural and historical processes since the late nineteenth century, the *ka'drel* has been able to survive despite the extremely oppressive conditions the Skolt Saami have faced as a minority within a minority. By exploring the development and interaction of discourses and practices surrounding the Skolt Saami *ka'drel*, this chapter outlines the dramatic turning points in Skolt history and how, in their wake, the *ka'drel* has emerged as a feature drawing the community together.

14 INNOVATIVE AND INCLUSIVE CULTURE

The dances of the Skolt Saami, particularly the *ka'drel*, play a significant role in shaping their sense of identity and agency. The *ka'drel* has evolved from being a traditional practice to an emblem of contemporary Skolt culture. This shift is particularly evident among the younger generation of Skolt Saami, who view these dances not just as a link to their past, but also to negotiate their present and future identities. The significance of the *ka'drel* is so remarkable that it is today often seen as one of the main symbols of Skolt culture, the other ones being language and handicrafts. For example, the headmaster of Če'vetjäu'rr elementary school stated in 2009 that no pupil will leave the school without basic knowledge of all three.[1] Naturally, these elements of Skolt culture are not isolated, but they interact and reinforce each other. The dance, language, and handicrafts each play a role in preserving and revitalizing the Skolt Saami identity and culture. They serve as a means of expressing their unique identity, connecting with their history, and passing on their cultural heritage to future generations.

The *ka'drel* is nowadays referred to as the "Sevetin katrilli," that is, *Ka'drel* of Sevetti[järvi] (Če'vetjäu'rr), implying that the new generations connect it to the current Skolt region in Inari and not anymore to Pechenga and Suõ'nn'jel. However, it must be added that as early as at the Saami Soirée in 1973, the host presented Skolt Saami performance similarly as Sevetin katrilli, so it has been used for more than fifty years now.

---

[1] Anja Harju, "Kolttien koltuissa on asennetta," *Kaleva*, March 29, 2009. Available online: https://www.kaleva.fi/kolttien-koltuissa-on-asennetta/2464317 (accessed August 19, 2024).

Emerging Agency

In addition, it must be noted that not only *ka'drel*, language, and handicrafts are forms of Skolt Saami cultural expression, but also music, both traditional *le'udd*s and popular music, belongs firmly to contemporary Skolt culture, as well as films, especially those made by Katja Gauriloff, a Skolt Saami filmmaker. The difference between them is that active participants in the latter activities are significantly fewer that in the previous ones. This does not mean that music and films would be culturally less significant, but they are often the ones that gain the most visibility.

For example, films made by Skolt Saami in Finland, such as the recent *Je'vida*, have a profound impact on the Skolt Saami awareness of their own culture. These films explore themes related to the forced loss of language and the rediscovery of ethnic identity profoundly. *Je'vida*, the first full-length fictional movie filmed in the Skolt Saami language, is a poignant exploration of cultural loss, identity, and the enduring effects of historical trauma within the Skolt community. Directed by Gauriloff, it sheds light on the meaning of culture, language, memories, and, above all, on the community of the Skolt Saami in the era of forced assimilation. The film portrays the life journey of the fictional Je'vida, or Iida, from her childhood to adulthood, delving into the profound meaning of one's language, community, and the rupturing of roots. It addresses the crossroads of two cultures and the deep trauma inflicted by forced Finnishization after the war, a period during which Saami children were sent to distant schools, subjected to harsh dormitory conditions, and stripped of their language and culture.[2]

The film also features the new generation of Skolt Saami, who have learned the language—which is now supported—with the old who have been able to retain this. This screening of the film in the cinemas is also made possible by the renewed interest in the Saami culture at large, and, at times, the politicization of their struggle and representations of the Saami identity. Films like *Je'vida* play a crucial role in raising awareness about the Skolt Saami culture, their struggles, and their identity. They provide a platform for the Skolt Saami to tell their stories,

---

[2] Marta Balaga, "Katja Gauriloff Makes History with 'Je'vida,' the First Feature Shot in the Skolt Sámi Language: 'My Mother Never Let Me Forget,'" *Variety*, September 11, 2023. Available online: https://www.aol.com/katja-gauriloff-makes-history-je-132500682.html?guccounter=1&guce_r eferrer=aHR0cHM6Ly93d3cuZ29vZ2xlLmNvbS8&guce_referrer_sig=AQAAAEL_1uIKzryvBNB IpN1YT4-Jk_ZQaNBU2kvrU_Ev_yahhC8l1mLSUVJE8oYf7aq9sPYVzgLeEqMhutVwpi12MU 04J05_Vt1ygDtE1QUAjGkWFSfyw0_JDB0WjhhxjHn4MqmkhgUGPGfiQYmQr_yQb5BP_DJDj AQ5Cb69-ntD6pLh (accessed July 15, 2024); HEPP 2023, "Screening Je'Vida, First Film in the Skolt Sámi Language, with Its Director," *Helsinki Hub on Emotions, Populism and Polarisation*, University of Helsinki (2023). Available online: https://www.helsinki.fi/en/researchgroups/emotions-populism-and-polarisation/screening-jevida-first-film-in-the-skolt-sami-language-with-its-director (accessed July 15, 2024).

explore their history, and express their cultural identity, thereby contributing to the preservation and revitalization of their culture.[3]

Regarding dance, there has been a change in attitudes in recent decades, so that it is not considered an activity that belongs only to the Skolt Saami. On the other hand, there is already information from the beginning of the twentieth century that outsiders also participated in the *ka'drel*, and, as mentioned, Heikki Laitinen danced it in 1973, so it is not a totally new phenomenon. Today, the *ka'drel* is taught in various workshops in different parts of Finland, and the participants of the workshops are not only Skolt Saami but also other people interested in the dance. This inclusive approach to the dance has allowed it to transcend its traditional boundaries and become a shared cultural practice within the Skolt Saami community. Besides dance workshops, the dancing of *ka'drel* has been incorporated into concerts of Skolt Saami music groups such as *Suõmmkar*—which has been active since 2016—or performances by the Karjalasta Kolttien maille-project.

Moreover, the publications of the *ka'drel* book shows how younger Skolt Saami want to ensure that the dance is performed correctly. They feel the written instructions link their performance to that of their ancestors. This connection to the past provides a sense of continuity and authenticity, even as the dance evolves and adapts to contemporary contexts. Interestingly, the dance has also become a platform for Skolt Saami to assert their cultural distinctiveness. The insistence on wearing Skolt Saami clothing during performances, for instance, underscores the dance's connection to Skolt Saami culture. At the same time, the willingness to perform the dance with non-Skolt Saami, albeit on Skolt Saami's terms, indicates a recognition of the dance as an inclusive cultural marker.

Skolt Saami Identities

To understand the complicated reality where the Skolt Saami live today, one needs to investigate identities from the perspective of a process. This implies seeing identity as being created and recreated constantly, changing through time and history. Saami researcher Rauna Kuokkanen points out that what characterizes the Saami is that their identities are migrating.[4] This resembles the writing of Stuart Hall, who emphasizes people's routes and the different points by which they have come to be now while examining their identities.[5] These routes hold people in places, but not in the same place. According to Hall, identities are questions of

---

[3]Balaga, "Katja Gauriloff Makes History with 'Je'vida'"; HEPP, "Screening Je'Vida."
[4]Lehtola, *The Saami People*, 86.
[5]Stuart Hall, "Who Needs 'Identity,'" in *Questions of Cultural Identity*, ed. Stuart Hall and Paul du Gay (London: Sage, 1996), 4.

using the resources of history, language, and culture in the process of becoming rather than being.

Consequently, the contemporary Skolt Saami identities can be seen as a process reflecting these people's historical and cultural roots. There has and has not been one Skolt identity; rather, the Skolt Saami identities are meeting points where subjective and collective histories and experiences mingle. Their identities have been migrating in concrete ways: in their original homeland, they migrated throughout the year from winter villages to spring, summer, and autumn villages, and finally back to winter villages. Moreover, a profound migration process occurred during and after the war, when they finally had to leave their original homeland.

Critical theorist Homi Bhabha has stated that authorized power in a hybrid culture "does not depend on the persistence of tradition; it is resourced by the power of tradition to be re-inscribed through conditions of contingency and contradictoriness."[6] This view of culture is aligned with concepts of flux and transition. The Skolt Saami's hybrid cultural identity is created as time progresses. The boundaries of their culture are constantly negotiated in relation to their history and contemporary Finnish society. Hybrid cultures can absorb diverse cultural influences: borders are active sites of intersection and overlap, which support the creation of in-between identities, which is characteristic of the Skolt Saami today.

The current study emphasizes the significance of dancing in constructing and expressing Skolt Saami identity amid historical and cultural changes. Dancing, particularly the *ka'drel*, has transitioned from a hidden tradition to a key element in identity construction and cultural agency. It has become a crucial practice for Skolt Saami to assert their cultural identity and resist assimilation into Finnish society. Contemporary Skolt Saami use dancing to foster a sense of belonging and community, whether they live in traditional Skolt areas or in urban settings like Helsinki. Dance serves as an embodied expression of their cultural identity and a way to maintain agency over their traditions. However, they are also adapting their dance traditions to fit modern contexts, negotiating between historical authenticity and contemporary relevance. This includes creating new cultural symbols and practices that resonate with their current realities.

The ongoing migration, including the movement of young Skolt Saami to southern Finland, influences their identity formation. Dance and other cultural practices help them connect with their heritage and navigate their dual identities. The Skolt Saami dance culture reflects broader processes of cultural negotiation, blending historical traditions with contemporary influences. This dynamic process allows them to assert their cultural identity and agency in a changing world.

---

[6]Homi K. Bhabha, *The Location of Culture* (London: Routledge, 1994), 2.

Interestingly, in the Antilleans, the cultural significance of the quadrille dance, in many respects, resembles that of the *ka'drel*. The rise of Creole culture awareness in the 1980s led to the rediscovery of this shared dance form. Like the *ka'drel* among the Skolt Saami, Creole quadrille became a symbol of the Creole language and Caribbean experience, with entire festivals dedicated to it. Today, performers from the Creole continuum use quadrille to unify their community, transcending countries, social groups, and ethnic groups. The dance allows them to express their shared history and identity. Festivals celebrating their Creoleness provide a platform for them to engage in conversations in the Creole language, further erasing political borders. By performing quadrille together, they create a sense of community that transcends the geographic and political boundaries of their respective island nations, challenging colonial narratives of subordination and dispersion.[7] Similarly, the Skolt Saami have challenged the national borders that have divided their homeland and the dominant culture's narratives that have invalidated the originality and significance of their dance. The *ka'drel* is strongly attached to their identity, which is manifested both in discourses about Skolt culture and in their community activities. The *ka'drel* not only connects Skolt Saami from Inari to the Finnish capital region but has also served as a link with the Kola Saami, although this connection has been broken due to the current political situation.

Cultural Appropriation and Stereotypes

In Finnish and Scandinavian literature and popular culture, the Saami have been presented through repressing or idealizing stereotypes, and these representations have also been used in, for example, tourist business. Apparently, the question of representation is a delicate one since the Saami feel that the dominating culture continues to use stereotypes that depict them as naïve and retarded.[8] This picture was created as early as the nineteenth century when Finnish author Zacharias Topelius described a Saami as "slow, heavy-minded, and silent." Still, he also praised his "hospitality, pureness in the soul, and innocent behaviour." According to Rauna Kuokkanen, a Saami researcher of indigenous peoples, this reflects the Rousseaun idea of a "noble savage," which has characterized the Saami stereotypes.[9]

---

[7]Dominique O. Cyrille, "Creole Quadrilles of Guadeloupe, Dominica, Martinique, and St. Lucia," in *Creolizing Contradance in the Caribbean*, ed. Peter Manuel (Philadelphia: Temple University Press, 2009), 206.
[8]Vesa Puuronen, *Rasistinen Suomi* (Helsinki: Gaudeamus, 2011), 148.
[9]Rauna Kuokkanen, "Etnostressistä sillanrakennukseen. Saamelaisen nykykirjallisuuden minäkuvat," in *Pohjoiset identiteetit ja mentaliteetit, osa I: Outamaalta tunturiin*, ed. Marja Tuominen, Seija Tuulentie, Veli-Pekka Lehtola, and Mervi Autti (Rovaniemi: University of Lapland, 1999), 95.

FIGURE 14.1. *Ka'drel* dancing in Njeä'llem during the 75-year anniversary of resettlement of Skolt Saami, August 25, 2024.

Source: Marko Jouste. Saami Culture Archive, University of Oulu.

Negative portrayals or lack of representation of the Saami people in mainstream media have reinforced stereotypes and prejudices. Media plays a powerful role in shaping public perceptions, and when indigenous voices and perspectives are absent or misrepresented, it can perpetuate biases. An example of this is presented by the Finnish rap artist Uniikki, who composed a rap tune called "Nunnuka lailaa" (2015), which repeated racist stereotypes of the Saami and whose title referred to belittling and mocking of Saami luohti culture, both themes that were popular in the late 1980s and early 1990s Finnish television comedy series.[10] However, the artist removed the video from YouTube six years later, stating that he no longer performs the tune, and that he would no longer make this type of music. According to him, the criticism the tune received was of the right kind, and it had awakened him to find out more about the reality of the Saami people.[11] Moreover, there has been a lot of discussion about the Saami attire in Finland after a few

---

[10] Elina Westinen, "Suomiräpin ja suomalaisuuden moninaisuudesta," *Ilmiö*, June 15, 2023. Available online: https://ilmiomedia.fi/artikkelit/suomirapin-moninaisuudesta/ (accessed July 20, 2024).

[11] Ville Vedenpää, "Räp-artisti Uniikki poisti saamelaisia halventaneen musiikkivideon Youtubesta: 'Se oli aikansa elänyt,'" *YLE (The Finnish Broadcasting Company)*, May 4, 2021. Available online: https://yle.fi/a/3-11913751 (accessed July 20, 2024).

FIGURE 14.2. *Ka'drel* dancers in Inari, 2014.
Source: Photograph by Petri Hoppu.

Finnish, non-Saami celebrities have worn or intended to wear modified versions of them, which has been regarded as a form of appropriation of Saami culture.[12]

As Kuokkanen has stated, Saami representations have been largely produced by others, and, characteristically, they have been distorted and influenced by ethnocentric views. She points out that the Saami identities are diverse and multidimensional and are not without contradictions.[13]

The discussion on the use of the Skolt Saami traditions and the question of cultural appropriation has been also present in the Skolt Saami dance. During the 1970s, there seems to have been strict principles in Čeʹvetjäuʹrr that only Skolt Saami were allowed to take part in the forms of dancing that were considered

---

[12]Bikka Puoskari, "Tanja Poutiaisen pukuvalintaa kritisoidaan voimakkaasti," *YLE (The Finnish Broadcasting Company)*, March 17, 2014. Available online: https://yle.fi/a/3-7140720 (accessed August 2, 2024); Anne Aikio, "Suomen Miss Maailma -kilpailija edustaa pilailupuodin lapinpuvussa," *YLE (The Finnish Broadcasting Company)*, December 1, 2015. Available online: https://yle.fi/a/3-8493787 (accessed August 2, 2024).
[13]Kuokkanen, 'Etnostressistä sillanrakennukseen', 97–8; Rauna Kuokkanen, "Let's Vote Who Is Most Authentic! Politics of Identity in Contemporary Sami Literature," in (*Ad)Dressing Our Words. Aboriginal Perspectives on Aboriginal Literatures*, ed. Armand Garnet Ruffo (Penticton: Theytus, 2001), 96–8.

traditional.[14] However, the information of this is somewhat contradictory, since Heikki Laitinen was offered a chance to learn the *ka'drel* in 1973, and, before him, Robert Crottet had tried it but—according to him—never learnt. Moreover—as it was mentioned—as early as in the 1930s, two American ladies were invited to *ka'drel* dancing, so the *ka'drel* had not had any exclusive character.

The idea of keeping the *ka'drel* merely to the Skolt Saami probably reflected a fear of cultural appropriation on the part of the Finnish folk dancers.[15] This fear was real, since folk dance performances are used in many countries to create an image of national culture and authentic people for tourists. This can be considered as one manifestation of tourism art, that is, folk dance is, at least in some countries, an art form whose development is closely linked to the tourism industry and its changes. Tourism art can offer opportunities for local cultures to maintain their vitality and bring work opportunities to practitioners of traditional crafts and local performers; on the other hand, it can also mean cultural exploitation and covering up the oppression of minorities.[16] As an example of the latter, dance scholar Anthony Shay described how Mexico's national folk dance troupe (*Ballet Folklórico Nacional de México*) performed the dance of the Chiapas Indians in the 1990s. The performers were dressed in Native American costumes, and in the dance, the life of this group was presented as harmonious and happy. However, the reality was more atrocious: at the same time as this performance, the army troops bloodily defeated the rebellion of the Chiapas Indians as they demanded the rights to a livelihood and their own culture.[17]

Skolt Saami had every reason to fear that some degree of appropriation would happen to them as well. In the 1980s and 1990s, Finnish folk dance groups could use performance costumes resembling Saami clothing, which also raised criticism. However, it should be noted that the criticism was aimed at the fact that the costumes were not authentic. Defenders of the use of costumes, on the other hand, emphasized their aesthetic and artistic significance. The discussions did not ask for the opinion of the Saami themselves, and the use of Saami clothing by Finnish folk dancers was not questioned per se.[18]

Finnish folk dancers have also long been interested in the Skolt Saami *ka'drel*. The dance is reminiscent of Karelian quadrilles, which are very popular in folk dance circles, but the background was probably the same admiration of exoticism

---

[14]Katri Jefremoff, interview by Hoppu; Sari Saxholm, interview by Petri Hoppu in Helsinki 2016. Saami Culture Archive, The Giellagas Institute for Saami Studies, University of Oulu, SKA A1.2016, 67.
[15]Hoppu, "Dancing Agency," 34.
[16]Jari Kupiainen, "Antropologinen taiteentutkimus," in *Kulttuurintutkimus. Johdanto*, ed. Jari Kupiainen and Erkki Sevänen (Helsinki: SKS, 1994), 167–71.
[17]Anthony Shay, *Choreographic Politics: State Folk Dance Companies, Representation and Power* (Middletown: Wesleyan Unversity Press, 2002), 1–2.
[18]Irma Vienola-Lindfors, "Tanhu ei saa pysähtyä," *Helsingin Sanomat*, July 30, 1981; Päivyt Niemeläinen, "Aito kansantanssi ja luovuuden rajat," *Helsingin Sanomat*, August 17, 1981.

as in the case of Saami national clothing. The Finnish folk dancers wanted to create their own dance narratives about the Skolt Saami, because they thought they would arouse the public's interest. Since the dance descriptions recorded in the archives had been prohibited from being used in folklore performances, the folk dance group Rimpparemmi directly approached the Če'vetjäu'rr and the Njeä'llem Skolt Saami communities in 1988. Both had a negative stance on the use of Skolt Saami costumes in the performances. The people of Njeä'llem did not see an obstacle to Rimpparemmi performing the *ka'drel*, but they did not see the dance as exactly in the tradition of their own village. The stance of the people of Če'vetjäu'rr was that the dance should remain exclusively in the possession of the Skolt Saami communities.[19] In the end, the ka'drel did not end up in the repertoire of any Finnish folk dance group, even though there was interest in it later as well.

In relation to the struggle for cultural survival, the biggest questions in the 1970s were and are even today: How can the Skolt Saami avoid a complete assimilation to the dominant Finnish culture? How can such a small but distinct ethnic group survive in modern society?

Cultural Survival

For indigenous peoples, it is essential to create strategies to actively resist cultural assimilation. Guillermo Bonfil Batalla refers to three modes of indigenous struggle that has taken place in Mexico. First of these modes is resistance, through which the subaltern aim at preserving their decision-making capacity and their cultural patrimony. The second is constant and selective appropriation of foreign cultural elements that he sees as useful in surviving domination. The third, innovation, refers to creativity, which allows the forging of new elements and the modification of older ones, enabling subtle cultural adjustments to changes in the framework of oppression and aggression within which the minorities live.[20]

Resistance was the most apparent mode of the Skolt Saami survival strategy in relation to their dance culture at the end of the twentieth century, and it exists even today, though the other modes have become more visible. Commenting on the mode of resistance, Ernesto Colín notes that "dynamic cultural conservation

---

[19]"Nellim antaisi kolttakatrillin Rimpparemmille," *Lapin Kansa*, 1988:
The Skolt Saami village council of the Njeä'llem area does not object to the Tervola-based dance group Rimpparemmi adding the kolttakatrilli to its repertoire. The meeting considered that the ka'drel [as a dance form] is not related to the tribal tradition of the Njeä'llem area. However, the people of Njeä'llem do not consider it desirable for people outside the tribe to wear the Skolt Saami traditional costume. Here, they take the same position as the Skolt Saami of Če'vetjäu'rr, who want to keep the ka'drel in the community's possession.

[20]Guillermo Bonfil Batalla, *Mexico Profundo: Reclaiming a Civilization*, trans. Philip A. Dennis (Austin: University of Texas Press, 1996), 132–9.

is not simply resisting change but ensuring survival."[21] The resistance against the dominant culture has most clearly taken place in the form of already mentioned prohibitions against the use of Skolt Saami documented folklore material that is preserved in the Archive of the Finnish Literature Society, the most prominent Finnish tradition archive in Helsinki, and the archive of Finnish Folk Music Institute in Kaustinen. When the Skolt Saami traditional dances were documented and stored in archives, it was stated that it was not to be used for folklorist purposes—stage performances, for example. This prohibition exists even today.

This ideological position that can be characterized with literary theorist Gayatri Spivak's notion of "strategic essentialism"[22] was supported by many Skolt Saami and Finnish scholars who feared that the cultural products of the Skolt Saami would be abused by, for example, Finnish folklore groups, which was, as indicated before, a realistic threat. The resistance to outsiders using the Skolt Saami folklore material is still apparent today, though the essentialist stance has weakened significantly. Nevertheless, as mentioned earlier, the Skolt Saami still find it awkward that, for example, Finnish folklore groups with no Skolt Saami members would perform the quadrille because the dance is seen as strongly connected to Skolt Saami culture, especially when performed in traditional clothing.[23]

The formation of folk dance groups in the 1970s was already a form of appropriation, since the Skolt Saami incorporated folklorist dance activities of the Finnish culture to revitalize their own dances whose original contexts had disappeared. At the end of the 1990s, school children at the elementary school of Čeʹvetjäuʹrr started to learn the *kaʹdrel*. This implicated a change in the educational system, as Skolt children were no longer expected to be raised as Finns: their rights to their own culture were acknowledged. Thus, while once being the major fortress of the dominant Finnish culture, the local school became a source of cultural learning for the Skolt Saami, who could now use the educational system in a way they had never done before.

As it has been addressed earlier, quadrille dancing is not limited to folklorist performances anymore today, but it is taught at courses, not necessarily only for Skolt Saami but for anyone willing to learn it, which would have been unthinkable thirty years ago. All these cases witness the contemporary Skolt Saami ability to promote their dances, using institutions and practices of the dominant Finnish society. Thus, appropriation does not mean that minorities merely copy elements from dominant culture, but "communities may acquire the ability to produce,

---

[21]Ernesto Colín, *Indigenous Education through Dance and Ceremony: A Mexica Palimpsest* (New York: Palgrave Macmillan, 2014), 266.
[22]Gayatri Chakravorty Spivak, "Subaltern Studies: Deconstructing Historiography," in *Selected Subaltern Studies*, ed. Ranajit Guha and Gayatri Chakravorty Spivak (New York and Oxford: Oxford University Press, 1988).
[23]Hoppu, "Dancing Agency," 34–5.

reproduce, and maintain items that were once foreign to them and now cease to be so."[24]

When it comes to innovation, one can see that contemporary Skolt Saami develop new hybrid forms of culture, fusing, for example, traditional forms of Skolt Saami singing and rock music.[25] The quadrille is now danced in more versatile contexts than earlier, and it may be done in different compositions such as with two couples. Moreover, to accompany the dance, modern Skolt music may be used, not only with accordion or mouth organ—the traditional dance instruments—but bands with violins, electric guitars, vocalists, and so on. Music and dance can be combined in forms that have never been seen before. As it has been the case for centuries, Skolt culture is dynamic and adaptive, which is crucial for cultural survival.[26]

It can thus be seen that there is potential for indigenous dissent through the Skolt Saami dance culture, which can be facilitated by the modes of resistance, appropriation, and innovation. The struggle is not exclusionary or isolating, but an essential part of it is the search for a new kind of relationship with the dominant culture. Also, scholars from the dominant culture can have a role in it, for example, by providing resources to revive Skolt dance traditions. However, any development must respect the Skolt Saami conditions and give voice to the previously silenced Skolt Saami community. Importantly, there must exist a continuous dialogue between the Skolt Saami and scholars, acknowledging the Skolt Saami as the primary agents and experts of their dance culture. The recently opened Skolt Saami dance exhibition provides an example of such reciprocity.

Pleässjeei meer "Dancing People" Exhibition 2024

A Skolt Saami dance exhibition *Pleässjeei meer* "Dancing People" opened on March 13, 2024, in Ä'vv-museum in Neiden, Norway. It was the first exhibition dedicated solely on Skolt Saami dance, and the main idea was to exhibit Skolt Saami dance culture and its history for everyone interested. A year earlier, Jouste and Hoppu made a trip in Če'vetjäu'rr and Njeä'llem for interviews concerning Skolt Saami dance culture. The purpose of the interviews was to gather material for a new book, *Skolt Saami Dancing, Cultural Survival and the Arctic Ka'drel*. Soon after the trip, Hanna-Maaria Kiprianoff, who had just begun to work at the Ä'vv-museum,

---

[24]Colín, *Indigenous Education through Dance and Ceremony*, 267.
[25]Taru Oksanen, "Tiina Sanila – Sää'mjannam rocks!," *Pop-lehti* 6, no. 5 (2005): 12.
[26]See Colín, *Indigenous Education through Dance and Ceremony*, 266.

FIGURE 14.3A AND B. An overall view and dance costumes from the Skolt Saami dance exhibition Pleässjeei meer "Dancing People," March 13, 2024.

Source: Marko Jouste. Saami Culture Archive, University of Oulu.

suggested Jouste and Hoppu for planning an exhibition on Skolt Saami dance. The plan was agreed, and Christina Mathissen joined the workgroup.

The planning was based on two principles. First, dance is and always has been a form of a living culture expressed by Skolt Saami, and through dance, it is possible to understand not only dance—as an artform and its practices—but also more widely the Skolt Saami society. As members of different generations have contributed their own ideas, practices, and values to dancing, it also represents the changes in Skolt Saami's history, art, society, and politics. Second, the narrative presented in the exhibition is based on the Skolt Saami traditional knowledge, experiences, and practices of the Skolt Saami dance culture. The data was gathered both from the historical material of the earlier generations found from archives and from the interviews of the present-day Skolt Saami. Thus, this information clearly highlighted that one can define "two lives" for dancing—first, the traditional dance in Skolt Saami society, and, second, the modern dance on stage, expressing a "cultural symbol" of the Skolt Saami. Overall, the exhibition was meant to highlight the importance of dance in the Skolt Saami's efforts to preserve and redefine their cultural identity, emphasizing the role of embodied practices in these processes.

15 CONCLUSION: REVITALIZED AND RETAKEN DANCE CULTURE IN THE 2020s

This book concludes by reflecting on the resilience, adaptability, and enduring cultural significance of Skolt Saami dance within a history shaped by colonization, marginalization, and cultural revitalization. As the "Dancing People," the Skolt Saami have demonstrated a remarkable ability to sustain and adapt their dance traditions, which serve as a vital connection between past and present, cultural heritage and contemporary expression. Dance, and particularly the *ka'drel*, remains central to Skolt Saami identity, offering insights into the complex processes of cultural survival and resistance.

The history of Skolt Saami dance is inseparable from the broader sociopolitical challenges they have faced. After the Second World War, during which the Soviet Union was the main adversary, Russian culture was widely viewed negatively in Finland. This hostile perception significantly affected the Skolt Saami dance tradition, as its connections to Russian cultural elements were seen as suspect and were often disparaged by the dominant Finnish society. Given the strong historical connections between Skolt Saami dances and those of Northwest Russia and Karelia, such stigmatization rendered their dance practices vulnerable to marginalization. Within this context, many Skolt Saami refrained from openly sharing or teaching their dances, as parents feared exposing their children to practices associated with Russian culture—which was viewed with suspicion and disdain by the dominant Finnish society.

This climate contributed to a significant interruption in the intergenerational transmission of Skolt Saami dance during the 1950s and 1960s. The absence of formal documentation further exacerbated this loss, as early ethnographers often dismissed Saami dances as "borrowed cultural features," failing to recognize their role in shaping identity and community. These attitudes reflected a narrow understanding of cultural authenticity, which prioritized perceived "pure" traditions over dynamic and hybrid cultural practices. This lack of validation in research marginalized not only the dances themselves but also the Skolt Saami as cultural agents.

The historical experiences of the Skolt Saami stand in sharp contrast to other displaced populations, such as the Karelians evacuated to Finland after the war. Unlike the Skolt Saami, whose dances endured, Karelian traditional dance largely vanished in Finland, highlighting the precariousness of cultural continuity in the face of dislocation and societal pressure. That the Skolt Saami succeeded in preserving elements of their dance culture—despite similar challenges—underscores the remarkable adaptability and resilience of their traditions.

The revitalization of Skolt Saami dance from the 1970s onward represents a pivotal moment in their cultural history. This period marked not only a renewed interest in traditional practices but also the forging of new connections with Skolt Saami communities in Russia. As Finnish society gradually shifted its perception of Saami cultures, dance emerged as a visible and celebrated medium for asserting Skolt Saami identity. The influence of Russian cultural frameworks, where dance enjoyed state support and widespread acceptance, played a crucial role in shaping this revival. Exchanges with Russian Skolt Saami communities introduced Finnish Skolt Saami to performance traditions, musicians, and costumes that enriched and diversified their dance culture.

Central to this revitalization was the *ka'drel*, which stands out as a symbol of cultural continuity and transformation. Introduced through Russian and Karelian influences, the *ka'drel* was adapted by the Skolt Saami into a uniquely local expression of identity. Far from being a passive reflection of external cultural forces, it became a dynamic tool for negotiating identity, resisting stigmatization, and asserting agency. As a social event, the *ka'drel* fosters connection and communication, embodying the shared history of the Skolt Saami while forging paths forward in a modern context.

Today, the *ka'drel* occupies a central place in Skolt Saami cultural life, serving not only as a medium for community bonding but also as a form of public cultural expression. Through performances on stage and digital platforms, Skolt Saami dance connects generations and reaches audiences beyond their immediate communities. This adaptability highlights the enduring relevance of Skolt Saami dance, not as a relic of the past but as a living, evolving practice that bridges tradition and modernity.

In broader terms, the survival of Skolt Saami dance challenges the notion of "authenticity" in cultural practices. It underscores the importance of recognizing hybrid and adaptive traditions as equally valid and significant expressions of identity. The Skolt Saami story illustrates how marginalized communities can use cultural expression to navigate historical traumas, resist assimilation, and assert their place in the modern world.

In conclusion, the Skolt Saami dance culture—particularly the *ka'drel*—stands as a testament to resilience and adaptability. It reflects the intersections of colonial history, cultural negotiation, and identity formation, offering a powerful example of how traditions can thrive amid adversity. For the Skolt Saami, dancing is not merely an act of preservation but a declaration of identity and pride, making their story one of the most compelling dance phenomena in the world.

APPENDICES

Appendix 1: Comparison of Folk Quadrilles

Most Russian folk quadrilles are structurally close to each other. This is seen in the following three quadrilles, popular in the northeastern part of the Russian Empire at the turn of the nineteenth and twentieth centuries.

The first one is a quadrille from the surroundings of Lake Ilmen, Novgorod region (Table A1.1). In this quadrille, as in the two following ones, the dancing couples are in two opposite lines facing each other and not in a square as in the original French quadrille. This was common in Russian folk quadrilles. The main parts of the dance occur between two opposite couples. The description is based on a video recording of a performance by a folklore group from the Novgorod region at the Kaustinen Folk Music Festival in the 1990s.

The second example describes a quadrille that was danced in Repola (Table A1.2.), Russian Karelia, near the Finnish border. Anni Homanen (1903–1981), who was born in Repola but later moved to Ilomantsi on the Finnish side of the border, taught the dance to folk dancers in Ilomantsi.

The last example is a quadrille danced in Southern (Western) Ingria (Table A1.3.), Russia. It was originally documented by one of the most famous Estonian folk dance teachers Ullo Toomi in 1939. Although most of historical Ingria, the region surrounding Saint Petersburg and inhabited by Baltic Finns, belonged to the Soviet Union then, its westernmost villages were part of Estonia that became independent in 1918, and Toomi conducted his fieldwork in those villages. The description is based on Toomi's handwritten notes, interpreted by a Finnish folk dance researcher Juha-Matti Aronen (2014).

The comparison of these quadrilles reveals that their first figures resemble each other and also the French quadrille's first figure *le pantalon*. The first part of *le pantalon, Chaine anglaise*, is found in all of them, although in slightly different forms. The complicated introductions of the figures in the French quadrille have dropped out in folk quadrilles. Still, it is possible that the starting part of the first figure in some of them, moving forward and back as a compliment toward the

Table A1.1. Quadrille from Novgorod region, Russia[a]

Figure	Description
1	Couples cross over and back, swing with a ballroom hold, and, finally, ladies cross over and back.
2	The figure begins with gentlemen dancing toward the opposite gentleman and turning back to their partners, swinging with a ballroom hold, after which gentlemen cross over and back.
3	The gentlemen from the one side and ladies from the other move to the center, take hand in hand behind their back, and swing clockwise in the middle of the formation, after which they return to their partners and swing with a ballroom hold with them. The other dancers repeat the same.
4	The couples face counterclockwise with their left hands joined and the gentlemen's right hands around the ladies' waist, and they dance in a circle one after the other until they reach their places where they swing with a ballroom hold.
5	Everybody moves to the center, where they take a ballroom hold with the opposite dancer and swing with them, moving to the gentlemen's original positions, which is repeated.
6	Giving the right hand to the partner, everybody starts the grand chain once round and finally swings with their partners. The gentlemen form a right-hand star and move around swinging with each lady. The dance ends with ladies crossing over and back.

[a] Esko Rausmaa, *Katrillia tanssimaan!* (Kaustinen: Kansanmusiikki-instituutti, 2000), 47–50.

opposite couple, is a remnant of it. In all cases, the couples cross over to the opposite side, with ladies moving through the opposite couple. The Le Pantalon's second part, *Balancez et Tour de main*, is replaced by couples swinging in a ballroom hold. *Chaine des Dames* is almost identical, but in these examples, ladies do not give right hands to each other. The last two parts of the French quadrille, *Demi-promenade à quatre* and *Demi-chaine anglaise*, are not present in these examples.

The second figures in the examples begin with gentlemen dancing toward each other, most often also crossing over, which is sometimes repeated by the ladies. This resembles the beginning of the French quadrille's figure *L'été*, which, however, is danced by a lady from one side and a gentleman from the other. *L'été* ends with couples turning clockwise with right hand in hand, usually replaced with couples swinging in a ballroom held in folk quadrilles.

In the examples, the third figures consist of two persons turning around in the middle of the formation. These can be opposite gentlemen, ladies, or a lady and a gentleman. Except for the first example, other dancers join these two, with or without holding the center dancers' hands. Especially with the last addition, this is close to the beginning of the French quadrille's figure *la poule*, which is danced by a lady from one side and a gentleman from the other. In *la poule*, the dancers turn around with right hand in hand and then left hand in hand returning to their places without releasing hands. They give their right hands to their own partners, and the two couples make one line, after which the couples take a crossed-hand hold sideways and move counterclockwise to their places. The latter parts of the figure are not found in folk quadrilles.

After the third figure, similarities between folk quadrilles and the French quadrille are harder to be found. However, one can still see traces of *la tréniz* and *la pastourelle* in some folk quadrilles. These figures were usually alternative, but sometimes they could be danced one after the other. Both contain parts where three dancers are joined one way or another. In *la tréniz*, this happens with a couple moving toward the opposite couple while the lady moves to the opposite gentleman's left side. Next, the first gentleman, standing alone on the opposite side, moves forward between two ladies, who move forward and pass each other behind the first gentleman, after which everybody returns to their places. A similar feature can be seen in the fourth figure of the quadrille from Repola (Table A1.2) and several other quadrilles from Russian Karelia.[1] Typically, one couple begins the figure moving toward the opposite couple whose gentleman or lady moves to the opposite side. While returning, the solo gentleman or lady moves through the first couple.

Figures resembling *la pastourelle* are less common, but in a quadrille from Suojärvi, a Karelian parish that belonged to Finland until 1944, and Ukhta (present-day Kalevala), Russian Karelia, there are figures close to both *la tréniz* and *la pastourelle*.[2] In the original *la pastourelle*, a couple moves toward the opposite couple while the lady moves to the opposite gentleman's left side, all three taking hand in hand and moving forward and back twice. The solo gentleman dances alone, after which two couples join hands in a circle, turn clockwise half turn and cross over to their places. The quadrilles from Suojärvi's and Ukhta's fifth figures consist of all these parts, although the details are different. Moreover, the solo gentleman's dance is pure improvisation, and its most important element is the squat movements (*ripaska*).

In the latter part of folk quadrilles, there could be several figures that did not originate from the French quadrille, but, as already mentioned, they were probably from other contradances, Lanciers, and potpourri as the most significant ones. Most typically, these figures consisted of various circles, either closed or open. Open circles were most often danced with couples side by side. Different closed circles could follow each other: for example, a simple circle, gentlemen's and ladies' nested circles, and a double circle with arms crossed front or behind. Grand

---

[1] Ollikainen, *Karjalaisia leikkejä ja kansantanhuja*, 43–53.
[2] Rausmaa and Rausmaa, "Tanssiselosteet," 169–72, 297–300.

Table A1.2. Quadrille from Repola, Russian Karelia[1]

Figure	Description
1	Couples move toward each other, retire, cross over and back, and swing with a ballroom hold.
2	Approximately equal to figure 2 in the previous description, but the ladies also dance the same figure.
3	The opposite gentlemen's elbows turn counterclockwise, take their ladies with them, and continue in the same direction, retreat with their ladies to the opposite places, and cross over to their places. The same is repeated so that ladies begin the figure.
4	Couples from one side with a ballroom hold move forward to the opposite couple while the opposite gentlemen simultaneously move to the opposite place. The couples swing and move back to their places, making an arch under which the opposite gentlemen move back to their ladies. The other couples repeat the figure.
5	Couples from one side with a ballroom hold move forward and retire, move forward again, and take the outer hands in hands with the opposite couples. These two couples move to the center of the formation, move back, and to the center again. Two couples make a circle with hands in hands and move clockwise and counterclockwise. The couples cross over and back and swing.
6	Couples with a ballroom hold change places, swing, return, and swing.
7	Figure 2 is repeated.
8	Grand chain, ending with couples swinging.
9	Each gentleman dances improvised moves, including squat movements (*ripaska* in Finnish), toward a lady of his choice, ending with the couple swinging.
10	All the dancers make a big circle that moves clockwise and counterclockwise.

[1] Rausmaa and Rausmaa, "Tanssiselosteet," 294–7.

chains were also known: couples split up and moved around in a circle in opposite directions, passing all other dancers and giving right and left hand to them.

At the end of folk quadrilles, elements from the second figure (opposite gentlemen dancing) are often repeated. This resembles the French quadrille's finale, within which the second figure, L'été, is repeated. Otherwise, there are no similarities between them. Folk quadrilles end in different manners, for example, with a circle or dancers greeting each other.

Table A1.3. Quadrille from Southern (Western) Ingria, Estonia[1]

Figure	Description
1	Couples move toward each other, retire, cross over and back. Ladies cross over and swing with crossed arms with the opposite gentleman. Ladies return and couples swing with a ballroom hold.
2	Gentlemen dance toward the opposite gentleman and turn back to their partners, swinging with a ballroom hold, after which ladies do the same.
3	The opposite ladies elbow-turn counterclockwise. Gentlemen join their ladies without holding hands and continue in the same direction. Ladies retire to their places while gentlemen elbow-turn counterclockwise and retire to their places where the couples swing.
4	Couples from one side with a ballroom hold a gallop toward the opposite couples, retire, move forward again, curve left, and swing counterclockwise. They release their hold and cross over and back while the opposite couples gallop between them to the opposite side and back. Couples swing with a ballroom hold. The figure is repeated while the opposite couples start.
5	Couples from one side with a ballroom hold a gallop toward the opposite couples, retire and move forward again. Two opposite couples make a circle with hands in hands and move half around clockwise. Gentlemen swing with opposite ladies, cross back to their places, and swing with their own ladies.
6	The couples face counterclockwise with an open ballroom hold and dance in a circle one after the other until they reach their places where they swing. The gentlemen form a circle and move around swinging with each lady.
7	Ladies cross over and gentlemen cross over after them. Couples cross back to their places. Gentlemen from one side move toward opposite ladies and improvise with them, return to their ladies and swing. Gentlemen from the other side do the same. Finally, everybody moves to the center, two opposite couples make a circle and lift the joined hands up.

[1] Aronen, "Viron Inkerin tanssit," 16–21.

Comparison with the *Ka'drel*

The *ka'drel* follows the original structure of the French quadrille's first four figures relatively strictly, with similar variations that occur in Russian and Karelian quadrilles. The fifth figure of the *ka'drel* consists mostly of circles, which are formed with gentlemen facing outside and with their hands crossed in front of

APPENDICES   175

them, while ladies face inside and with hand in hand in a common way. This kind of a circle is relatively rare in folk quadrilles of Russian origin, whereas it was quite common in West Finnish quadrilles in the late nineteenth century. However, at least in the Russian Karelian contradance Humahus, it was used.[3]

The last figure of the *ka'drel* is interesting, since it does not follow the same kind of repetition between head and side couples as in the first four figures. The head couples cross over with a ballroom hold, gentlemen moving forward and ladies backward, and immediately after they have passed each other in the middle, sides do the same. Thus, unlike in the first figures of the quadrille, sides do not wait until head couples have finished all the parts of the figure but do the same movements with a few steps after them. In musical terms, this could be described as a *stretto* figure. The last figure of the *ka'drel* also includes the repetition of the second figure like many other folk quadrilles and the French quadrille.

At the time the *ka'drel* was recorded in the 1970s, there was a short pause between each figure while the musicians changed to another tune, which was, as mentioned, typical of folk quadrilles in the Russian Empire and the original French quadrille. However, one of the best-known recordings from 1992 shows that these breaks disappeared, and the *ka'drel* was danced non-stop with the same tune the whole time.

Appendix 2: Structures of Couple Dances

The structure of the couple dances is very similar. They consist of 2–3 parts ending with turning in couples or just moving forward in a circle. The following descriptions are derived from the documentation by Heikki Laitinen and Pirkko-Liisa and Esko Rausmaa at Kaustinen Folk Music Festival, July 1978.

Despite their different backgrounds and time signatures, *Korobushka* (Table A2.3) and *Patespa* (Table A2.2) share an almost identical structural pattern. Apart from the meter, the main difference is that, unlike in *Patespa*, there is no turning at the end of *Korobushka*. Additionally, *Korobushka* is danced in one row with couples one after another, whereas *Patespa* is performed in a circle. There are slight differences between this description of *Korobushka* and the 1995 video recording: in the video, partners do not release hands in Part a; instead, the ladies turn under joined arms, and the gentlemen take two two-steps and three walking steps instead of four slow steps.

Unlike other couple dances, *Vintjårkka* (Table A2.4.) begins with partners facing each other.

---

[3]Ibid., 271–4.

Table A2.1. *Kerenski*[a]

Part	Bars (2/4)	Dance
a.	1–8	Couples dance four side-steps in a ballroom hold counterclockwise and four side-steps back.
b.	9–16	Couples take hand in hand, face each other, take two step-swings, and turn around from each other, which is repeated.
c.	17–20	Couples take both hands in hand and move with four walking steps to the centre of the circle and four steps back.
	21–24	Couples turn around with two-steps in a ballroom hold.

[a] Rausmaa, "Kolttien tanssiperinteet," 124.

Table A2.2. *Patespa*[a]

Part	Bars (3/4)	Dance
a.	1–4	Couples dance four side-steps in a ballroom hold counterclockwise.
	5–8	Couples release the hold and move back, turning around with four waltz-steps.
	1–8	Part a. is repeated.
b.	9–10	Couples take two slow walking steps hand in hand counterclockwise, simultaneously turning their back towards the partner.
	11	Couples take a side-step back,
	12	and a step sideways to the same direction.
	13–14	Couples take two slow walking steps counterclockwise, gentlemen starting with right and ladies left foot, turning finally toward each other.
	15–16	Couples take two side-steps back.
c.	9–16	Couples take a ballroom hold and dance waltz.

[a] Ibid., 125.

Table A2.3. *Korobushka*[a]

Part	Bars (2/4)	Dance
a.	1–4	Couples dance four side-steps in a ballroom hold forward.
	5–8	Partners release hands while gentlemen take four slow walking steps sideways back and ladies also move back with four two-steps and turning simultaneously once around counterclockwise.
	9–16	Part a. is repeated.
b.	9–10	Couples take two slow walking steps hand in hand forward, simultaneously turning their back towards the partner and pushing the joint hands forward.
	11–12	Couples take three walking steps back.
	13–14	Couples take two slow walking steps forward gentlemen starting with right and ladies left foot, turning finally toward each other.
	15–16	Couples take three walking steps back.

[a] Ibid., 130.

Table A2.4. *Vintjårkka*[a]

Part	Bars (2/4)	Dance
a.	1–2	Couples holding right hands in hand and facing each other change places with four running steps.
	3–4	Everyone moves one's left toe across the right, then to the left side and finally joins the feet.
	5	A hop with right foot in front.
	6	A hop with left foot in front.
	7–8	Bars 3–4 are repeated.
	9–16	Part a. is repeated.
b.	17–24	Everyone moves counterclockwise while gentlemen take eight slow walking steps and ladies turn clockwise with two-steps under partners' joint right arms.

[a] Ibid., 127.

Table A2.5. *Oira*[a]

Part	Bars (2/4)	Dance
a.	1–2	Couples with a shoulder hold and facing counterclockwise in a circle move their left toe twice diagonally forward and back.
	3–4	The same is repeated with right toe.
	5–8	Part a. is repeated.
b.	17–24	Couples move forward in a circle with eight polka steps without a hop.

[a] Ibid., 126.

Table A2.6. *Krakoviak*[a]

Part	Bars (2/4)	Dance
a.	1–4	Couples, hand in hand and facing each other, take four step-swings.
	5–6	Couples dance three walking steps counterclockwise in a circle and swing their inside legs to the same direction.
	7–8	Keeping the hand hold, couples turn to the opposite direction and repeat the walking steps and swing.
b.	1–8	Couples take a ballroom hold and turn clockwise with eight two-steps.

[a] Ibid., 128.

A reminiscent dance is *Oira* (Table A2.5.), where couples dance the whole time with a shoulder hold and begin by moving their left and right toe twice diagonally forward and back. After that, they move forward with polka steps.

The documented couple dances include two additional polka dances: *Krakoviak* (Table A2.6.) and *Kuu loistaa* (Table A2.7.) (Russian Светит месяц, "The Moon Is Shining").

The melody of *Kuu loistaa* is actually a Russian song called Выйду ль я на реченьку ("When I Will Go to the River"), whereas Светит месяц is the name of another Russian folk song. It has been common for melodies to be used in connection with different dances, as a result of which the names of dances and tunes sometimes conflict with each other. Both melodies have also been used in folk quadrilles.

Table A2.7. *Kuu loistaa (Светит месяц)* or *Läpytystanssi*[a]

Part	Bars (2/4)	Dance
a.	1–4	Couples facing each other, clap their own hands, partners' hands, own hands, right hands, own hands, left hands, and finally three claps with their own hands, gentlemen simultaneously taking three stamps.
b.	5–8	Couples take a ballroom hold and turn clockwise with four two-steps.

[a] Ibid.,129.

Appendix 3: *Ainamilaadu* Structure

Ainamilaadu (Sowing of Buckwheat) starts with men making a row on one side of the room, and likewise, women gathering on the opposite side. The description in Table A3.1 is from the recording in 1979, and it resembles the earlier description by Antti Hämäläinen.

Table A3.1. *Ainamilaadu* (Sowing of Buckwheat)[a]

First, men rush in a tight line, hands in hand, toward the women. Men sing, stamping their feet: "We shall sow a buckwheat field." And while retreating, they repeat the verse.
Women rush toward the men hand in hand, as well: "We shall trample the sowing."
Men intend to catch the evildoers, while women intend to redeem them.
Finally, the men threaten to take "the most beautiful one" as pledge.
Having heard this, women run hand in hand as a chain behind the men's line. The last two men lift their hands as a gate through which the whole group of women must go. Then, in front of the last woman, the gate is closed, so the problem of the pledge is solved.
Women – with one less – make a new row by their wall, and the whole group of men begin their rush from the beginning.
The game is repeated as long as the last "most beautiful one" has been taken as pledge.

[a] Ibid., 119–20.

REFERENCES

Interviews

Feodoroff, Lati, and Paula Feodoroff. Interview by Markus Juutinen, Kia Olin and Marko Jouste in Inari, Keväjärvi, 21 March 2023. Saami Culture Archive, The Giellagas Institute for Saami Studies, University of Oulu, SKA A1.2023, 11.
Fofanoff, Åäjjaž. Interview by Erkki Ala-Könni. The Folklife Archives in University of Tampere, AK/0530.
Fofanoff, Åäjjaž, Marina Gavriloff, and Där'jj Jefremoff. Interview by Erkki Ala-Könni. The Folklife Archives in University of Tampere, AK/0531.
Jefremoff, Där'jj. Interview by Erkki Ala-Könni. The Folklife Archives in University of Tampere, AK/0865.
Jefremoff, Irja. Interview by Marko Jouste and Petri Hoppu, Nellim, Inari, Finland. 20 March 2023. SKA.
Jefremoff, Irja. Interview by Petri Hoppu in Keväjärvi, Inari, Finland. August 15, 2014.
Jefremoff, Katri. Interview by Petri Hoppu in Inari, 2014. Saami Culture Archive, The Giellagas Institute for Saami Studies, University of Oulu, SKA A1.2014, 26.
Kiprianoff, Hanna-Maaria, Terhi Harju, Anna-Katariina Feodoroff, and Heini Weslin. Interview by Marko Jouste and Petri Hoppu in Inari, Čeʹvetjäuʹrr, 18 March 2023. Saami Culture Archive, The Giellagas Institute for Saami Studies, University of Oulu, SKA A1.2023, 2a–b.
Moshnikoff, Minna. Interview by Petri Hoppu, in Kirkkonummi, Finland. 14 April 2016.
Mosnikoff, Elias. Interview by Marko Jouste in 2001. Saami Culture Archive, The Giellagas Institute for Saami Studies, University of Oulu, A1.2001, 1.
Moshnikoff, Satu. Interview by Marko Jouste and Markus Juutinen in Inari, Čeʹvetjäuʹrr, 24 August 2017. Saami Culture Archive, The Giellagas Institute for Saami Studies, University of Oulu, SKA A1.2017, 2.
Nykänen, Eeva, and Tanja Telkkälä. Interview by Marko Jouste, Petri Hoppu, Markus Juutinen and Kia Olin in Inari, Čeʹvetjäuʹrr 19 March 2023. Saami Culture Archive, The Giellagas Institute for Saami Studies, University of Oulu, SKA A1.2023, 4a–b.
Rausmaa, Pirkko-Liisa. "Kolttien tanssiperinteet." Manuscript. Finnish Literature Society, Traditional and Contemporary Culture Collection. KRA Pirkko-Liisa Rausmaa (1978/1979), 111–19.
Saxholm, Sari. Interview by Petri Hoppu in Helsinki, 2016. Saami Culture Archive, The Giellagas Institute for Saami Studies, University of Oulu, SKA A1.2016, 67.
Similä, Ahti. Interview by Marko Jouste in Ivalo, Finland, August 27, 2023. The Giellagas Institute for Saami Studies, University of Oulu, SKA A1.2023, 1–2.

Skolt man from Čeʹvetjäuʹrr. Interview by Petri Hoppu, in Čeʹvetjäuʹrr, Inari, Finland. Digital recording. 17 August 2014.

Sverloff, Jääkk. Interview by Erkki Ala-Könni. The Folklife Archives in University of Tampere, AK/0568.

Sverloff, Jääkk. Interview by Irja Häkämies, 1972. The Folklife Archives in University of Tampere, Y/04479.

Sverloff, Jääkk. Interview by Mikko Korhonen. The Institute for the Languages of Finland, Kotus 09842_a.

Sverloff, Jääkk. Interview by Mikko Korhonen. The Institute for the Languages of Finland, Kotus 00631_1a.

Sverloff, Paaʹvvel. "*Mäiddneäʹttel leuʹdd 'Laskiaislaulu'*." Interview by A. O. Väisänen in Suõʹnnʹjel, 1926, Finnish Literature Society (SKS), ph 4/192.

Radio programs

YLE *(The Finnish Broadcasting Company)*. 'Čeʹvetjääuʹr da Njeäʹllem sääʹm jieʹlle Murmanskist, kuulât mäʹtǩǩ-maainâsʹ. Mieʹldd jm. Domna Sanila, Tyyne da Illeppi Fofonoff. Tuåimteei: Elli Rantala, radio program, 10 September 1976

YLE *(The Finnish Broadcasting Company)*. 'Čeʹvetjääuʹr da Njeäʹllem sääʹm jieʹlle Murmanskist, mäʹtǩǩ-maainâs nuʹbb vuäʹssʹ. Mieʹldd jm. Domna Jagolovna, Jukka Kalinin, Niina Taskinen, and Olli Gauriloff. Tuåimteei: Elli Rantala, radio program, 29 October 1976.

YLE *(The Finnish Broadcasting Company)*. 'Jiõnnäiʹtt: Tuâlʹjõžsääiʹj taans, ouddoummu valljumuš, ǩiõtt-tuâjj tuâimmkåʹdd sååbarʹ, *Nuõrttsäämas*, 12.12.1975. Available online: https://areena.yle.fi/podcastit/1-2597012 (accessed 31 August, 2024).

Seminar paper

Wesslin, Heini. "Ajatuksia berliiniläisen MEK-museon tutkimusprojektista." Paper presented at the Sámi National Day Seminar in Oulu, February 6, 2024.

Video and audio recordings

Saamelaisiltamat 1973. The Saami Soiree 1973. Finnish Broadcasting Company.

Sevettijärven kolttakatrilli 1992. "Skolt kaʹdrell from Čeʹvetjäuʹrr 1992." The Folklife Archives, Tampere University. *KPL* V A 118.

Tanssi Sevettijärvellä 1979. Dance in Čeʹvetjäuʹrr in 1979. Dancers: Iida Feodoroff, Tyyne Fofanoff, Anni Feodoroff, Anton Feodoroff, Elias Fofanoff, Mari Fofanoff, Kauko Gauriloff, Reino Fofanoff and Jakkim Feodoroff (accordion player). The Finnish Folk Music Institute. Kik 44.

Terveiset Petsamon Lapinkylästä 1995. Nellim folklore group. Video.

The collection of C-cassettes recorded by Elias Moshnikoff. Saami Culture Archive, The Giellagas Institute for Saami Studies, University of Oulu.

Bibliography

Aassalu, Heino, Pill Luht, and Kristjan Torop. *Vanad seltskonnatantsud.* Tallinn: Rahvakultuuri Keskus, 1997.

Aikio-Puoskari, Ulla. "The Ethnic Revival, Language and Education of the Sámi, an Indigenous People, in Three Nordic Countries (Finland, Norway and Sweden)." In *Social Justice through Multilingual Education*, ed. Tove Skutnabb-Kangas, Robert Phillipson, Ajit Mohanty, and Minati Panda, 238–62. Bristol, Blue Ridge Summit: Multilingual Matters, 2009.

Aikio, Áile. "Gákti – sukujen puku." *Fáktalávvu* (2018). Available online: https://faktalavvu.net/2018/02/27/gakti-sukujen-puku/ (accessed August 15, 2024).

Aikio, Anne. "Suomen Miss Maailma -kilpailija edustaa pilailupuodin lapinpuvussa." *YLE (The Finnish Broadcasting Company)*, December 1, 2015. Available online: https://yle.fi/a/3-8493787 (accessed August 2, 2024).

Alajärvi, Paula. "Kulttuurien kohtaaminen." *Jänkä* 12, nos. 2–3 (2016). Available online: https://janka.fi/arkistot/613 (accessed June 20, 2024).

Alerby, Eva. "In School You Learn to Get on in Life: Sámi Children in Sweden." In *Voices from the Margins*, ed. Eva Alerby and Jill Brown, 31–41. Leiden: Brill, 2008.

Allemann, Lukas. *The Saami of the Kola Peninsula: About the Life of an Ethnic Minority in the Soviet Union*, Senter for samiske studier, Skriftserie nr. 19. Tromsø: University of Tromsø, 2013. Available online: http://dx.doi.org/10.7557/sss.2013.19 (accessed July 31, 2024).

Andersson, Gustaf Adolf. *Tietoja Sodankylän ja Kittilän pitäjien aikaisemmista ja myöhemmistä waiheista.* Kemi: Kemin uusi kirjapaino, 1914.

Arminen, Elina. "'Seikkailu Jäämerellä', Kaarlo Hännisen Jäämeren sankari ja suomalainen kolonialismi." *Historiallinen aikakauskirja* 118, no. 4 (2020): 481–93. Available online: https://erepo.uef.fi/handle/123456789/24083 (accessed July 20, 2024).

Aronen, Juha-Matti. "Viron Inkerin tanssit – Kadrelia, kasatškahia ja Viron veräjää." *Elore* 21, no. 1 (2014): 1–30. Available online: https://doi.org/10.30666/elore.79122 (accessed June 10, 2024).

Bakka, Egil, and Arne Wikan. *Dansetradisjoner fra Finnmark.* Bø i Telemark and Trondheim: Finnmark Ungdomslag and Rådet for folkemusikk og folkedans, 1996.

Balaga, Marta. "Katja Gauriloff Makes History with 'Je'vida,' the First Feature Shot in the Skolt Sámi Language: 'My Mother Never Let Me Forget.'" *Variety*, September 11, 2023. Available online: https://www.aol.com/katja-gauriloff-makes-history-je-132500682.html?guccounter=1&guce_referrer=aHR0cHM6Ly93d3cuZ29vZ2xlLmNvbS8&guce_referrer_sig=AQAAAEL_1uIKzryvBNBIpN1YT4-Jk_ZQaNBU2kvrU_Ev_yahhC8l1m LSUVJE8oYf7aq9sPYVzgLeEqMhutVwpi12MU04J05_Vt1ygDtE1QUAjGkWFSfyw0_JDB0WjhhxjHn4MqmkhgUGPGfiQYmQr_yQb5BP_DJDjAQ5Cb69-ntD6pLh (accessed July 15, 2024).

Berg-Nordlie, Mikkel, and Anna Andersen. "Cities in Sápmi, Sámi in the Cities: Indigenous Urbanization in the Nordic Countries and Russia." In *An Urban Future for Sápmi? Indigenous Urbanization in the Nordic States and Russia*, ed. Mikkel Berg-Nordlie, Astri Dankertsen, and Marte Winsvold, 54–106. New York and Oxford: Berghahn Books, 2022.

Bergholm, Kari. "Suomalaisen kansantanssin tyylipiirteitä." In *Tanhuvakka. Suuri suomalainen kansantanssikirja*, Pirkko-Liisa Rausmaa and Esko Rausmaa, 24–26. Helsinki: Suomalaisen Kansantanssin Ystävät, 1997.

Bhabha, Homi K. *The Location of Culture*. London: Routledge, 1994.

Bocking, Stephen. "Indigenous Knowledge and Perspectives." In *Handbook of the Historiography of the Earth and Environmental Sciences*, ed. Elena Aronova., David Sepkoski, and Marco Tamborini. Historiographies of Science, 1–24. Cham: Springer, 2023. Available online: https://doi.org/10.1007/978-3-030-92679-3_20-1 (accessed June 12, 2024).

Bonfil Batalla, Guillermo. *Mexico Profundo: Reclaiming a Civilization*. Translated by Philip A. Dennis. Austin: University of Texas Press, 1996.

Brablec, Dana, and Andrew Canessa. "Introduction: Indigenous Peoples in the Cities of the World." In *Urban Indigeneities: Being Indigenous in the Twenty-First Century*, ed. Dana Brablec and Andrew Canessa, 3–28. Tuczon: University of Arizona Press, 2023.

Bracknell, Clint. "Identity, Language and Collaboration in Indigenous Music." In *The Difference Identity Makes: Indigenous Cultural Capital in Australian Cultural Fields*, ed. Lawrence Bamblett, Fred Myers, and Tim Rowse, 99–123. Canberra, ACT: Aboriginal Studies Press, 2019. Available online: https://ro.ecu.edu.au/ecuworkspost2013/6643 (accessed June 15, 2024).

Cajigas-Rotundo, Juan Camilo. "Ontoepistemologías indígenas." *Tabula Rasa* 26 (2017): 123–39.

Carpelan, Christian. "Saamelaisten esihistoriaa ja saamelaisarkeologiaa." In *Lappi 4 – Saamelaisten ja suomalaisten maa*, ed. Martti Linkola, 99. Hämeenlinna: Karisto, 1985.

Climates to Travel. "Weather and Climate in Tromso (Norway)." *World Climate Guide*. Available online: https://www.climatestotravel.com/climate/norway/tromso (accessed July 31, 2024).

Colín, Ernesto. *Indigenous Education through Dance and Ceremony: A Mexica Palimpsest*. New York: Palgrave Macmillan, 2014.

Crottet, Robert. *Lapplands andra ansikte*. Translated from French to Swedish by Gun Hägglund. Stockholm: LTs förlag, 1966.

Cyrille, Dominique O. "Creole Quadrilles of Guadeloupe, Dominica, Martinique, and St. Lucia." In *Creolizing Contradance in the Caribbean*, ed. Peter Manuel, 188–208. Philadelphia: Temple University Press, 2009.

Cyrille, Dominique O. "The Politics of Quadrille Performance in Nineteenth-Century Martinique." *Dance Research Journal* 38, no. 1 (2006): 43–60.

Daniel, Yvonne. "An Ethnographic Comparison of Caribbean Quadrilles." *Black Music Research Journal* 30, no. 2 (2010): 215–40.

Desrosiers, Brigitte. "Ile de la Réunion: musiques et identité." *Canadian Folk Music Journal* 20 (1992): 47–54.

Dobrijevic, Daisy. "Midnight Sun: What It Is and How to See It." *Space.com* (2024). Available online: https://www.space.com/midnight-sun-facts-where-and-when-to-see (accessed July 31, 2024).

Dunseith, Michael Hamlyn. "Manifestations of 'Langarm': From Colonial Roots to Contemporary Practices." MA diss. thesis in Musicology. Stellenbosch University, 2017.

Eerola, Jari. *Vepsäläiset lühüdpajot: perusrakenteet, esityskäytännöt ja tyylillinen muutos*. Tampere: Tampere University Press, 2012.

Ervasti, August Wilhelm. *Suomalaiset jäämeren rannalla. Matkamuistelmia*. Oulu: Wickström, 1884.

Evans, Mike, Adrian Miller, Peter Hutchinson, and Carlene Dingwall. "Decolonizing Research Practice: Indigenous Methodologies, Aboriginal Methods and Knowledge/Knowing." In *Oxford Handbook of Qualitative Research*, ed. Patricia Leavy, 179–92. Oxford: Oxford University Press, 2014. Available online: https://doi.org/10.1093/oxfordhb/9780199811755.013.019 (accessed June 15, 2024).

Feuillet, Raoul Auger. *IIIIe Recueil de danses de bal pour l'année 1706*. Paris: 1705.

Firmino-Castillo, María Regina. "Dancing the Pluriverse." *Dance Research Journal* 48, no. 1, Special Issue: Indigenous Dance Today (April 2016): 55–73.

Friis, Jens Andreas. *En Sommer i Finmarken, Russisk Lapland og Nordkarelen*. Christiania: Cammermeyer, 1871.

Gareau Paul L., and Molly Swain. "Indigenous Knowledges." *Oxford Research Encyclopedia of Religion* (2024, January 30). Available online: https://oxfordre.com/religion/view/10.1093/acrefore/9780199340378.001.0001/acrefore-9780199340378-e-1178 (accessed June 15, 2024).

Gaski, Harald. "Indigenism and Cosmopolitanism: A PanSami View of the Indigenous Perspective in Sami Culture and Research." *AlterNative: An International Journal of Indigenous Peoples* 9, no. 2 (2013): 113–24. Available online: https://doi.org/10.1177/117718011300900201 (accessed June 15, 2024).

Genetz, Arvid. "Kuolan niemimaan asukkaiden oloja tutkimassa vuonna 1876." In *Kuolan niemimaalla kayneiden suomalaisten tiedemiesten matkakertomuksia*, ed. and trans. Leif Rantala, 19–66. Acta Lapponica Fenniae 20. Rovaniemi: Lapin Tutkimusseura, 2008.

Guilcher, Jean-Michel. *La Contredanse et les renouvellements de la danse française*. Paris: Walter de Gruyter, 1969.

Guttorm, Hanna."Becoming Earth: Rethinking and (Re-)Connecting with the Earth, Sámi Lands and Relations." In *Bridging Cultural Concepts of Nature: Indigenous People and Protected Spaces of Nature*, ed. Rani-Henrik Andersson, Boyd Cothran, and Saara Kekki, 229–58. Helsinki: Helsinki University Press, 2021. Available online: https://doi.org/10.33134/AHEAD-1-8 (accessed 15 August, 2024).

Häkämies, Irja. "Kolttasaamelainen musiikkiperinne." *Kansanmusiikki*, no. 2 (1978): 16–21.

Häkämies, Irja. "Kolttasaamelaista perinnettä." *Perhonjokilaakso*, July 13, 1978.

Hakkarainen, Toini. "Sevetin katrilliryhmä Saami siidan vieraana Utsjoella." *Sää'moddâz ǩiđđ - ǩiä'ss* (1982): 4–5.

Hämäläinen, Antti. *Koltta-Lappia sanoin ja kuvin. Uutta Lapin lääniä I*. Helsinki: WSOY, 1938.

Hall, Stuart. "Who Needs 'Identity?'" In *Questions of Cultural Identity*, ed. Stuart Hall and Paul du Gay, 1–17. London: Sage, 1996.

Hansen, Lars Ivar, and Bjørnar Olsen. *Hunters in Transition: An Outline of Early Saami History*. The Northern World Series Nr. 63. Leiden: Brill, 2014.

Harju, Anja. "Kolttien koltuissa on asennetta.", *Kaleva*, 29 March 2009. Available online: https://www.kaleva.fi/kolttien-koltuissa-on-asennetta/2464317 (accessed 19 August, 2024).

Harlin, Eeva-Kristiina, and Veli-Pekka Lehtola. "Skolt Sámi Heritage, Toivo Immanuel Itkonen (1891–1968), and the Sámi Collections at the National Museum of Finland." *Nordic Museology* 27, no. 3 (2019): 45–60.

Hart, Michael Anthony. "Indigenous Worldviews, Knowledge, and Research: The Development of an Indigenous Research Paradigm." *Journal of Indigenous Voices in*

Social Work 1, no. 1 (2010): 1–16. Available online: http://hdl.handle.net/10125/15117 (accessed June 12, 2024).

Heikkilä, Lydia, Rauna Kuokkanen, Veli-Pekka Lehtola, Päivi Magga, Sigga-Marja Magga, Janne Näkkäläjärvi, Sanna Valkonen, and Pirjo Kristiina Virtanen. *Ethical Guidelines for Research Involving the Sámi People in Finland*. Oulu: Oulun yliopisto, 2024. Available online: https://urn.fi/URN:NBN:fi:oulu-202405294076 (accessed June 15, 2024).

Heikkilä, Tuomas, and Antero Järvinen. "Saamelaisalueen luonto ja sen muutokset." In *Saamentutkimus tanaan*, ed. Irja Seurujärvi-Kari, Petri Halinen, and Risto Pulkkinen, 56–76. Helsinki: SKS, 2011.

Helsingin Sanomat. "Kolttien katrillit ja joiut elpymässä." *Helsingin Sanomat*, July 20, 1978. Available online: https://digi.kansalliskirjasto.fi/sanomalehti/binding/2666996?page=14 (accessed September 2, 2024).

Helsingin Sanomat. "Työleirit eivät tulleet väkisin Sevettijärvelle." *Helsingin Sanomat*, 18 August 1974, 11.

Helsingin Sanomat. "Vanhaa käsityötaitoa herätetään henkiin." *Helsingin Sanomat*, August 8, 1979. Available online: https://digi.kansalliskirjasto.fi/sanomalehti/binding/2679251?page=10 (accessed July 7, 2025).

HEPP 2023. "Screening Je'Vida, First Film in the Skolt Sámi Language, with Its Director." *Helsinki Hub on Emotions, Populism and Polarisation*, University of Helsinki (2023). Available online: https://www.helsinki.fi/en/researchgroups/emotions-populism-and-polarisation/screening-jevida-first-film-in-the-skolt-sami-language-with-its-director (accessed July 15, 2024).

Hilder, Thomas R. *Sámi Musical Performance and the Politics of Indigeneity in Northern Europe*. London: Rowman & Littlefield, 2015.

Hirvasvuopio-Laiti, Annukka. "Gárddi luhtte lávddi ala - Poroaidalta esiintymislavalle. Saamelaiset elementit tenonsaamelaisessa musiikissa kolmen sukupolven aikana." MA diss., Department of Music Anthropology, University of Tampere, 2008.

Holmberg, Uno. "Kolttain omistusoikeuksista ja -merkeistä." In *Kalevalaseuran vuosikirja* 7, 197–213. Helsinki: Kalevalaseura 1927.

Hoppu, Petri. "Dancing Agency. Skolt Saami Identities in Transition." *Puls* 5 (2020): 26–44.

Hoppu, Petri. "Från kotiljong till Röntyskä. Franska kontradanser i Finland, Karelen och Ingermanland." *Folkdansforskning i Norden* 44 (2021): 34–9.

Hoppu, Petri. "Introduction." In *The Nordic Minuet. Royal Fashion and Peasant Tradition*, ed. Petri Hoppu, Egil Bakka, and Anne Fiskvik, 5–18. Cambridge: Open Book, 2024.

Hoppu, Petri. "Jablochko: dans, musik och revolution." *Folkdansforskning i Norden* 43 (2020): 34–7.

Horsthemke, Kai. "Indigenous (African) Knowledge Systems, Science, and Technology." In *The Palgrave Handbook of African Philosophy*, ed. Adeshina Afolayan and Toyin Falola, 585–603. New York: Palgrave Macmilla, 2017. Available online: https://doi.org/10.1057/978-1-137-59291-0_38 (accessed June 15, 2024).

Hosia, Heikki. "Ryssän rajalla juhannusta viettämässä." *Helsingin Sanomat Viikkoliite*, July 14, 1929, 3.

Huotari, Markku. "Lapinmies joikasi, noitarumpu kumisi." *Pohjolan Sanomat*, July 18, 1978.

Ingold, Tim. *The Skolt Lapps Today*. Cambridge: Cambridge University Press, 1976.

Itkonen, Toivo Immanuel. *Koltan- ja Kuolanlapin sanakirja. Wörterbuch des Kolta- und Kolalappischen I*. Helsinki: Suomalais-ugrilainen Seura, 1958.

Itkonen, Toivo Immanuel. *Suomen lappalaiset vuoteen 1945 II*. Porvoo: WSOY, 1948.
Jefremoff, Irja. "Matkakuvia Ranskasta - ystäviä maailman ääriltä." *Sää'moďđâz čõhčč* (1982): 2–5.
Jefremoff, Irja. "Njeä'llem kaddrellneekk 5-ekksaž." *Sää'moďđâz čõhčč* (1979): 2–4.
Jones-Bamman, Richard Wiren. "As long as we continue to joik, we'll remember who we are: negotiating identity and the performance of culture: the Saami joik." PhD diss., Department of Music, University of Washington, 1993. Available online: https://digital.lib.washington.edu/researchworks/items/22ed0e8e-f525-41f5-b071-16c0c9f3e4d1 (accessed 6 August, 2024).
Jouste, Marko. "Suomen saamelaisten musiikkiperinteet." In *Suomen musiikin historia: Kansanmusiikki*, ed. Anneli Asplund, Petri Hoppu, Heikki Laitinen, Timo Leisiö, Hannu Saha, and Simo Westerholm, 272–307. Helsinki: WSOY, 2006.
Jouste, Marko. "'Maailman pienin kansa musiikissa rikkain'. A. O. Väisänen saamelaisten musiikkiperinteiden kerääjänä ja tutkijana." In *Kalevalaseuran vuosikirja* 90, 201–10. Helsinki: Kalevalaseura, 2011.
Jouste, Marko. "Áillohaš ja uuden joiun synty." In *Mina soin – Mun čuojan. Kirjoituksia Nils-Aslak Valkeapaan elamantyosta*, ed. Taarna Valtonen and Leena Valkeapää, 233–58. Rovaniemi: Lapland University Press, 2017.
Jouste, Marko. "Katsaus koltan- ja kuolansaamelaisiin musiikkiperinteisiin." In *Sommelon saikeita. Runolaulu-Akatemian seminaarijulkaisu 2009–2010*, ed. Pekka Huttu Hiltunen, Janne Seppänen, Frog, Eila Stepanova, and Riikka Nevalainen, 51–74. Juminkeon julkaisuja, no. 86. Kuhmo: Juminkeko, 2011.
Jouste, Marko. "Katsaus Venäjän saamelaisten musiikkiperinteiden keräykseen ja tutkimukseen." In *Song and Emergent Poetics*, ed. Pekka Huttu-Hiltunen, Frog, Karina Lukin and Eila Stepanova, 189–222. Runolauluakatemian julkaisuja, no. 18, Juminkeon julkaisuja, no. 119. Kuhmo: Juminkeko, 2014.
Jouste, Marko. "Katsaus Venäjän saamelaisten musiikkiperinteiden keräykseen ja tutkimukseen." In *Song and Emergent Poetics: Oral Traditions in Performance: Conference Proceedings*, ed. Pekka Huttu-Hiltunen, Frog, Karina Lukin, Sari Karikko, and Eila Stepanova, 21–4. Runolaulu-Akatemian julkaisuja 18. Kuhmo: Runolaulu-Akatemia & Juminkeko 2013.
Jouste, Marko. "Saamelaismusiikin tallennus Suomessa." In *Kohtaaminen – Gavnnadeapmi*, ed. Marko Jouste, 27–35. Inari: Sámi Museum – Saamelaismuseosäätiö & Yhteispohjoismainen joikuarkistoprojekti, 2007.
Jouste, Marko. "Skolt Saami Leu'dd: Tradition as a medium of individual and collective remembrance." In *The Sámi World*, ed. Sanna Valkonen, Áile Aikio, Saara Alakorva, and Sigga-Marja Magga, 53–71. London: Routledge, 2022.
Jouste, Marko. "The Historical Skolt Saami Music and the Two Types of Melodic Structures in Leu'dd-Tradition." *Folklore–Electronic Journal of Folklore* 68 (2017): 69–84.
Jouste, Marko. "Tullâčalmaaš kirdâččij – 'tulisilmillä lenteli'. 1900-luvun alun musiikkikulttuuri paikallisen perinteen ja ympäröivien kulttuurien vuorovaikutuksessa." PhD diss., School of Social Sciences and Humanities, University of Tampere, 2011. Available online: https://urn.fi/urn:isbn:978-951-44-8551-0 (accessed September 2, 2024).
Jouste, Marko. "Venäläisen bylinan ja kolttasaamelaisen leu'ddin välisestä yhteydestä." *Musiikin suunta* 30, nos. 3–4 (2008): 11–31.

Jouste, Marko, Elias Mosnikoff, and Seija Sivertsen. *Maaddaraajji leeu'd - Historiallisia kolttasaamelaisia leu'ddeja. The Leu'dds of the Ancestors. Historical Skolt Saami leu'dds*. Inari and Kaustinen: Saamelaismuseosäätiö & Kansanmusiikki-Instituutti & Kolttien kyläkokous, 2007

Jouste, Marko, Markus Juutinen, and Miika Lehtinen. "Isak Saba ja Paččjogas 1919:s čohkejuvvon nuortalaš leu'ddat. Isak Saba og de skoltesamiske leu'ddene som ble samlet inn i Paččjokk i 1919." In *Optegnelser. Isak Sabas folkeminnesamling. Čállosat. Isak Saba álbmotmuitočoakkáldat*, Norsk Folkeminnelags skrifter 173, 283–301. Oslo: Skandinavian Academic Press, 2019.

Jouste, Marko, Markus Juutinen, Miika Lehtinen, Anna Lumikivi, and Hanna-Maaria Kiprianoff. "Sää'mǩiõl da kulttuur jeälltummuš Skolt Sää'm mosttbaŋkk - ha'ŋǩǩõõzzâst." *Dutkansearvvi dieđalaš áigečála* 2, no. 1 (2018): 11–16. Available online: https://www.dutkansearvi.fi/volume-2-issue-1-fi/ (accessed August 6, 2024).

Kabir, Ananya Jahanara. "Creolization as Balancing Act in the Transoceanic Quadrille: Choreogenesis, Incorporation, Memory, Market." *Atlantic Studies: Global Currents* 17, no. 1 (2020): 135–57. Available online: https://doi.org/10.1080/14788 810.2019.1700739 (accessed June 5, 2024).

Kallio, Alexis Anja. "Decolonizing Music Education Research and the (Im)possibility of Methodological Responsibility." *Research Studies in Music Education* 42, no. 2 (2020): 177–91. Available online: https://doi.org/10.1177/1321103X19845690 (accessed June 30, 2024).

Keskinen, Suvi. "'Kolonialismin ja rasismin historiaa Suomesta käsin." In *Rasismi, valta ja vastarinta: Rodullistaminen, valkoisuus ja koloniaalisuus Suomessa*, ed. Suvi Keskinen, Minna Seikkula and Faith Mkwesha, 69–84. Helsinki: Gaudeamus, 2021.

Keskipohjanmaa. "Perinteitä ja nykyaikaa. Kolttasaamelaisten elämän punainen lanka." *Keskipohjanmaa*, July 20, 1978.

Khupe, Constance. "Indigenous Knowledge Systems." In *Science Education in Theory and Practice. An Introductory Guide to Learning Theory*, ed. Ben Akpan and Teresa J. Kennedy, 451–64. Cham: Springer, 2020. Available online: https://doi.org/10.1007/978-3-030-43620-9_30 (accessed June 15, 2024).

Korhonen, Jorma. "Terveisiä Petsamosta." *Helsingin Sanomat*, September 12, 1976, 20. Available online: https://digi.kansalliskirjasto.fi/sanomalehti/binding/2654 802?page=20 (accessed September 3, 2024).

Kozakand, Roman. "Overview of Saami Costume." *Blog: Folk Costume & Embroidery* (2013). Available online: http://folkcostume.blogspot.com/2013/05/overview-of-saami-costume.html (accessed July 28, 2024).

Kuhn, Gabriel. *Liberating Sápmi: Indigenous Resistance in Europe's Far North*. Oakland, CA: PM Press, 2020.

Kujala, Yrjö. "Karjalaistytön tie kolttien sukuun." *Keskipohjanmaa*, July 22, 1978.

Kuokkanen, Rauna. "Etnostressistä sillanrakennukseen. Saamelaisen nykykirjallisuuden minäkuvat." In *Pohjoiset identiteetit ja mentaliteetit, osa I: Outamaalta tunturiin*, ed. Marja Tuominen, Seija Tuulentie, Veli-Pekka Lehtola, and Mervi Autti, 95–112. Rovaniemi: University of Lapland, 1999.

Kuokkanen, Rauna. "Let's Vote Who Is Most Authentic! Politics of Identity in Contemporary Sami Literature." In *(Ad)Dressing Our Words. Aboriginal Perspectives on Aboriginal Literatures*, ed. Armand Garnet Ruffo, 79–100. Penticton: Theytus, 2001.

Kuokkanen, Rauna. "Sami Higher Education and Research: Toward Building a Vision for Future." In *Indigenous Peoples: Self-determination – Knowledge – Indigeneity*, ed. Henry Minde, 267–86. Utrecht: Eburon, 2008.

Kuokkanen, Rauna. "The Problem of Culturalizing Indigenous Self-determination: Sámi Cultural Autonomy in Finland." *Polar Journal* 14, no. 1 (2024): 148–66.

Kupiainen, Jari. "Antropologinen taiteentutkimus." In *Kulttuurintutkimus. Johdanto*, ed. Jari Kupiainen and Erkki Sevänen, 164–83. Helsinki: SKS, 1994.

Laitinen, Heikki. "Kokemuksia saamelaismusiikista viime vuosikymmeniltä." In *Kohtaaminen – Gavnnadeapmi*, ed. Marko Jouste, 86–93. Inari: Sámi Museum – Saamelaismuseosäätiö & Yhteispohjoismainen joikuarkistoprojekti, 2007.

Laitinen, Heikki. "Saamelaisten musiikki." In Kansanmusiikki, ed. Anneli Asplund and Matti Hako, 179–98. Suomalaisen Kirjallisuuden Seuran toimituksia 366. Helsinki: SKS, 1981.

Laitinen, Heikki. "Suonikylän laulut vuonna 1961: Tutkielma kolttasaamelaisten musiikkiperinteestä." MA diss., Department of Musicology, University of Helsinki, 1977.

Länsman, Anni-Siiri. "Kenelle saamentutkija tutkii?." In *Tutkijan kirja*, ed. Kirsti Lempiäinen, Olli Löytty, and Merja Kinnunen, 87–98. Tampere: Vastapaino, 2008.

Lapin ELY-keskus. "Luonnon monimuotoisuus turvaa elämän edellytykset maapallolla." *ymparisto.fi* (2023). Available online: https://www.ymparisto.fi/fi/luonto-vesis tot-ja-meri/luonnon-monimuotoisuus/luonnon-monimuotoisuus-lappi (accessed July 31, 2024).

Lapin Kansa. "Nellim antaisi kolttakatrillin Rimpparemmille." *Lapin Kansa*, 1988.

Launis, Armas. *Kaipaukseni maa. Lapinkävijän matkamuistoja.* Jyväskylä: Gummerus, 1922.

Lehtola, Jorma. "Kirjailija löysi unelmiensa kansan." *Apu*, 23 June 2016. Available online: https://www.apu.fi/artikkelit/kirjailija-loysi-uniensa-kansan (accessed June 20, 2024).

Lehtola, Jorma. *Laulujen Lappi*. Inari: Kustannus-Puntsi, 2007.

Lehtola, Veli-Pekka. "Aito saamelainen ei syö haarukalla ja veitsellä. Stereotypiat ja saamelainen kulttuurintutkimus." In *Pohjoiset identiteetit ja mentaliteetit. Osa 1: Outamaalta tunturiin*, ed. Marja Tuominen, Seija Tuulentie, Veli-Pekka Lehtola, and Mervi Autti. Lapin yliopiston taiteiden tiedekunnan julkaisuja C:16, 15–32. Rovaniemi: Lapin yliopisto, 1999.

Lehtola, Veli-Pekka. "Sámi Histories, Colonialism, and Finland." *ARCTIC ANTHROPOLOGY* 52 (2015): 22–36.

Lehtola, Veli-Pekka. *Saamelainen evakko*. Inari: Kustannus-Puntsi, 2004.

Lehtola, Veli-Pekka. *Saamelaiset – historia, yhteiskunta, taide*. Inari: Kustannus-Puntsi, 2015.

Lehtola, Veli-Pekka. *Saamelaiset suomalaiset – kohtaamisia 1896–1953*. Helsinki: SKS, 2012.

Lehtola, Veli-Pekka. *Saamelaisten parlamentti. Suomen saamelaisvaltuuskunta 1973–1995 ja Saamelaiskäräjät 1996–2003*. Inari: Saamelaiskäräjät, 2005.

Lehtola, Veli-Pekka. *The Saami People – Traditions in Transition*. Translated by L. Weber Müller-Wille. Inari: Kustannus-Puntsi, 2002.

Lehtola, Veli-Pekka. "Vanishing Lapps, Progress in Action. Finnish Lappology and Representations of the Sámi in Publicity in the Early 20th Century." *Arctic and North* 2, no. 27 (2017), 83–102.

Lindstrom, Gabrielle L. "Accountability, Relationality and Indigenous Epistemology: Advancing an Indigenous Perspective on Academic Integrity." In *Academic Integrity in Canada. An Enduring and Essential Challenge*, ed. Sarah Elaine

Eaton and Julia Christensen Hughes, 125–39. Cham: Springer, 2022. Available online: https://doi.org/10.1007/978-3-030-83255-1_6 (accessed June 15, 2024).

Linkola, Anni, and Martti Linkola, "Kolttasaamelaiset: Vähemmistön vähemmistö." In *Siiddastallan: Siidoista kyliin. Luontosidonnainen saamelaiskulttuuri ja sen muuttuminen*, ed. Jukka Pennanen and Klemetti Näkkäläjärvi, Inarin saamelaismuseon julkaisuja 3, 158–67. Jyväskylä: Pohjoinen, 2000.

Linkola, Martti, and Pekka Sammallahti. "Koltanmaa, osa Saamenmaata." In *Koltat, karjalaiset ja setukaiset. Pienet kansat maailmojen rajoilla*, ed. Tuija Saarinen and Seppo Suhonen, 39–57. Kuopio: Snellman-instituutti, 1995.

Linkola, Martti. "Jaakko Sverloff." In *Lappi 4 – Saamelaisten ja suomalaisten maa*, ed. Martti Linkola. Hämeenlinna: Karisto, 1985.

Luleå Guided Tours & Activities. "Swedish Lapland Climate." Available online: https://www.laplandtours.se/Lapland_climate.html (accessed July 31, 2024).

Lynch, Michael. "The Emancipation of the Russian Serfs, 1861." *History Review*, no. 47 (December 2003). Available online: https://www.historytoday.com/archive/emancipation-russian-serfs-1861 (accessed June 10, 2024).

Mabingo, Alfdaniels, Gerald Ssemaganda, Edward Sembatya, and Ronald Kibirige. "Decolonizing Dance Teacher Education: Reflections of Four Teachers of Indigenous Dances." *African Postcolonial Environments. Journal of Dance Education* 20, no. 3 (2020), 148–56. Available online: https://doi.org/10.1080/15290824.2020.1781866 (accessed June 30, 2024).

Magga, Sigga-Marja. 'Nurinpäin käännetty gákti saamelaisen vastarinnan muotona', *Politiikka* 60 (2018): 260–64.

Malmi, Viola. *Karjalaisen kansantanssin lähteillä*. Helsinki: Vapaan Sivistystoiminnan Liitto, 1993.

Mansikka, Viljo J. "Laulu Hirssin kylvöstä." *Virittäjä* 14, no. 8 (1910): 137–9.

Markkula, Inkeri, Minna Turunen, Taru Rikkonen, Sirpa Rasmus, Veina Koski, and Jeffrey M. Welker. "Climate Change, Cultural Continuity and Ecological Grief: Insights from the Sámi Homeland." *Ambio* 53 (2024): 1203–17. Available online: https://doi.org/10.1007/s13280-024-02012-9 (accessed August 3, 2024).

Martinsson, Bengt. *Danser från Norr- och Västerbotten samt Finland*. Luleå: Svenska Ungdomsringen för Bygdekultur, Övre Norrlands distrikt, 1978.

Minde, Henry. "Assimilation of the Sami - Implementation and Consequences." *Acta Borealia* 20, no. 2 (2003): 121–46.

Mustonen, Tero, and Kaisu Mustonen. *Eastern Saami Atlas*. Tampere: Snowchange, 2011.

Näkkäläjärvi, Klemetti. "Climate Change = Culture Change: What Happened to the Snow?." *The Circle: WWF magazine*, no. 1 (2019): 6-7. Available online: https://arcticwwf.org/site/assets/files/2127/thecircle0119_web_2.pdf (accessed July 31, 2024).

Naum, Magdalena, and Jonas Nordin. "Introduction: Situating Scandinavian Colonialism." In *Scandinavian Colonialism and the Rise of Modernity. Small Time Agents in a Global Arena*, ed. Magdalena Naum and Jonas Nordin. Contributions To Global Historical Archaeology, vol. 37, 3–16. New York: Springer, 2013.

Nickul, Karl. *The Skolt Lapp Community, Suenjelsijd, during the Year 1938*, Nordiska Museet: Acta Lapponica V. Stockholm: Hugo Gebers Förlag, 1948.

Niemeläinen, Päivyt. "Aito kansantanssi ja luovuuden rajat." *Helsingin Sanomat*, August 17, 1981.

Nylander, Eeva-Kristiina. *From Repatriation to Rematriation: Dismantling the Attitudes and Potentials Behind the Repatriation of Sámi Heritage*. Oulu: Giellagas Institute, University of Oulu, 2023.

Nyyssönen, Jukka. "Nation-Building and Colonialism: The Early Skolt Saami Research of Väinö Tanner." In *Finnish Colonial Encounters: From Anti-Imperialism to Cultural Colonialism and Complicity*, ed. Raita Merivirta, Leila Koivunen, and Timo Särkkä, 121–43. Cham: Palgrave Macmillan, 2021.

Nyyssönen, Jukka. "Väinö Tanner, saamentutkimus ja uudelleen herännyt kansainvälinen kritiikki." In *Saamenmaa. Kulttuuritieteellisia nakokulmia*, ed. Veli-Pekka Lehtola, Ulla Piela and Hanna Snellman, 244–53. Helsinki: SKS, 2012.

Ojala, Carl-Gösta. "East and West in Sápmi: – Borders and Identities in Sámi Historical Archaeology." *META – Historiskarkeologisk Tidskrift* (March 2021): 143–60. Available online: https://doi.org/10.59008/meta.vi.10924 (accessed August 19, 2024).

Oksanen, Taru. "Tiina Sanila – Sää'mjannam rocks!." *Pop-lehti* 6, no. 5 (2005): 12.

Oktavuohta. "Saamen puku kertoo monta asiaa." Available online: https://www.oktavuohta.com/gakti (accessed July 20, 2024).

Ollikainen, Meri. *Karjalaisia leikkejä ja kansantanhuja*. Porvoo: WSOY, 1947.

Olthuis, Marja-Liisa, Suvi Kivelä, and Tove Skutnabb-Kangas. *Revitalising Indigenous Languages: How to Recreate a Lost Generation*. Bristol, Buffalo, and Toronto: Multilingual Matters, 2013.

Össbo, Åsa. "Hydropower Company Sites: A Study of Swedish Settler Colonialism." *Settler Colonial Studies* 13, no. 1 (2023): 115–32.

Outakoski, Aslak. "Kolttakylää paastosta kevätmuuttoon." *Kaleva*, May 27, 1934, 6.

Paulaharju, Samuli. *Kolttain mailta*. Helsinki: Kustannusosakeyhtiö Kirja, 1921.

Pelto, Pertti J. *Individualism in Skolt Lapp Society*. Helsinki: Suomen Muinaismuistoyhdistys, 1962.

Pentikäinen, Juha. "Lappalaisten perinnealuejako." In *Vanhaa ja uutta Lappia*, ed. Hannes Sihvo, Kalevalaseuran Vuosikirja 51, 127–46. Porvoo & Helsinki: Söderström, 1971.

Pidgeon, Michelle, and Riley Tasha. "Understanding the Application and Use of Indigenous Research Methodologies in the Social Sciences by Indigenous and Non-Indigenous Scholars." *International Journal of Education Policy and Leadership* 17, no. 8 (2021): 1–17. Available online: https://doi.org/10.22230/ijepl.2021v17n8a1065 (accessed June 15, 2024).

Pit'k Randaane Pajod, Lyydiläisiä lauluja. Helsinki: Maailman musiikin keskus, 2008.

Pohjola, Jaakko. "Käynnillä Koltta-Lapissa, miesväen 'paratiisissa.'" *Turun ylioppilaslehti*, March 15, 1939, 15–16.

Porthan, Henrik Gabriel. "De Poësi Fennica." PhD diss., Regia Academia Aboensis [Royal Academy of Turku], 1766.

Puoskari, Bikka. "Tanja Poutiaisen pukuvalintaa kritisoidaan voimakkaasti." *YLE (The Finnish Broadcasting Company)*, March 17, 2014. Available online: https://yle.fi/a/3-7140720 (accessed August 2, 2024).

Puuronen, Vesa. *Rasistinen Suomi*. Helsinki: Gaudeamus, 2011.

Ramnarine, Tina K. "Aspirations, Global Futures, and Lessons from Sámi Popular Music for the Twenty-First Century." In *The Oxford Handbook of Popular Music in the Nordic Countries*, ed. Fabian Holt and Antti-Ville Kärjä, 277–92. Oxford: Oxford University Press, 2017. Available online: https://doi.org/10.1093/oxfordhb/9780190603908.013.0015 (accessed June 30, 2024).

Rausmaa, Esko. *Katrillia tanssimaan!*. Kaustinen: Kansanmusiikki-instituutti, 2000.

Rausmaa, Pirkko-Liisa, and Esko Rausmaa. "Tanssiselosteet." In *Tanhuvakka. Suuri suomalainen kansantanssikirja*, ed. Pirkko-Liisa Rausmaa and Esko Rausmaa, 57–361. Helsinki: Suomalaisen Kansantanssin Ystävät, 1997.

Rausmaa, Pirkko-Liisa. "Purpuri suomalaisessa tanssiperinteessä." In *Suomalainen purpuri*, ed. Kari Bergholm, 11–16. Helsinki: Suomalaisen Kansantanssin Ystävät, 2016.

Rausmaa, Pirkko-Liisa. *Ilokerä. Laulutansseja ja piirileikkejä*. Helsinki: SKS, 1984.

Rikkinen, Kalevi. *Suuri Kuolan retki 1887*. Helsinki: WSOY, 1980.

Ristaniemi, Helena. "Saamelaisnuoret ja historian läsnäolo." *Lähihistoria* 2, no. 1 (2023): 96–107. Available online: https://lahihistoria.journal.fi/article/view/131054 (accessed August 3, 2024).

Rogers, Ellis A. *The Quadrille: A Practical Guide to Its Origin, Development and Performance*. Orpington: C & E Rogers, 2003.

Saastamoinen, Ilpo. "Itäsaamelaisten musiikkiperinteestä." In *Beaivvi manat. Saamelaisten juuret ja nykyaika*, ed. Irja Seurujärvi-Kari, 83–122. Tietolipas 164. Helsinki: SKS, 2000.

Saastamoinen, Ilpo. "Laulu – puu – rumpu: Saamelaismusiikin alkulähteillä." Licentiate of Arts diss., Department of Musicology, University of Jyväskylä, 1998.

Salminen, Väinö. "Lappalaisten 'joikaus'-lauluista." *Valvoja* 27, no. 1 (1907): 1–9.

Sámi Duodji. "Kolttasaamelainen puku." Available online: https://www.samiduodji.com/16 (accessed July 20, 2024).

Sámi Duodji. "Puvut." Available online: https://www.samiduodji.com/puvut (accessed August 15, 2024).

Sammallahti, Pekka, 'Saamelaisten juuret." In *Ennen muinoin: Miten menneisyyttamme tutkitaan*. Tietolipas 180, ed. Riho Grünthal, 159–73. Helsinki: SKS, 2004.

Sammallahti, Pekka. *Vuõ'lǧǧe jåå'tted oouđâs*. Edited by Marko Jouste, Miika Lehtinen, and Markus Juutinen. Publications of the Giellagas Institute vol. 16. Oulu: University of Oulu, 2021.

Saxholm, Sari, Minna Moshnikoff, and Mari Gauriloff. *Sevettijärven kolttakatrilli. Če'vetjääu'r ka'dre'l*. Inari: Sámi Duodji, 2022.

Say It in Saami. "Quick Guide to Saami Culture". YLE *(The Finnish Broadcasting Company)* (2018). Available online: http://sayitinsaami.yle.fi/quick-guide-to-sami-culture/ (accessed August 15, 2024).

Scheller, Elisabeth. "The Sámi Language Situation in Russia." In *Ethnic and Linguistic Context of Identity: Finno-Ugric Minorities*, ed. Riho Grünthal, Magdolna Kovács. Uralica Helsingiensia 5, 79–95. Helsinki: Société Finno-Ougrienne, 2011.

Seurujärvi-Kari, Irja. "'We Are No Longer Prepared to Be Silent': The Making of Sámi Indigenous Identity in an International Context." *Suomen Antropologi: Journal of the Finnish Anthropological Society* 35, no. 4 (2010): 5–25.

Seurujärvi-Kari, Irja. "Alkuperäiskansatutkimus, alkuperäiskansaliike ja saamelaiset." In *Saamentutkimus tänään*, ed. Irja Seurujärvi-Kari, Petri Halinen, and Risto Pulkkinen, 10–55. Helsinki: SKS, 2011.

Shay, Anthony. *Choreographic Politics: State Folk Dance Companies, Representation and Power*. Middletown: Wesleyan Unversity Press, 2002.

Shea Murphy, Jacqueline. "Editor's Note." *Dance Research Journal* 48, no. 1, Special Issue: Indigenous Dance Today (April 2016): 1–8.

Shizha, Edward. "Indigenous Epistemologies and Decolonized Sustainable Livelihoods in Africa." In *The Palgrave Handbook on Critical Theories of Education*, ed. Ali A. Abdi and Greg William Misiaszek, 465–80. Cham: Palgrave Macmillan, 2022. Available online: https://doi.org/10.1007/978-3-030-86343-2_26 (accessed June 15, 2024).

Spivak, Gayatri Chakravorty. "Subaltern Studies: Deconstructing Historiography." In *Selected Subaltern Studies*, ed. Ranajit Guha and Gayatri Chakravorty Spivak, 3–32. New York and Oxford: Oxford University Press, 1988.

Sundkvist, Bertil. "Skoltsamer bjöd på sång, dans och musik i Arjeplog." *Norra Västerbotten*, June 2, 1980.

Suomalaisen Kansantanssin Ystävät, 'Seuratanssit'. Available online: https://www.kansantanssinyst.fi/kansantanssi/tanssit/seuratanssit/ (accessed 10 June, 2024).

Suomen Kuvalehti. "Glasnostin lähettiläät." *Suomen Kuvalehti*, October 27, 1989, 64.

Suomen Kuvalehti. "Lappiin joulu-ukkoa tapaamaan – Kaliforniasta asti." *Suomen Kuvalehti*, March 10, 1934, 330–1.

Szwed, John F., and Morton Marks. "The Afro-American Transformation of European Set Dances and Dance Suites." *Dance Research Journal* 20, no. 1 (1988): 29–36.

Tanhua, Sonja. "Kolttasaamelaisen kyläkokousjärjestelmän vaikuttamisen strategiat ja taktiikat 1920–1979." PhD diss., Faculty of Humanities, University of Oulu, 2023. Available online: https://urn.fi/URN:ISBN:9789526235745 (accessed August 15, 2025).

Tanner, Väinö. "Antropogeografiska studier inom Petsamo-området: 1 Skoltlapparna." *Fennia* 49, no. 4 (1929): 1–518.

Thauwon, Johan Fredrik. *Matka-muistelmia Wenäjän Lapista* (1870). Available online: https://urn.fi/URN:NBN:fi-fd2010-00001764 (accessed August 4, 2024).

Tulonen, Hannele. "Popmusiikki nousi pelimanni- ja tanhuperinteen rinnalle Sodankylän Jutajaisjuhlilla." *Helsingin Sanomat*, July 7, 1986, 11.

Valkeapää, Nils-Aslak. *Terveisiä Lapista*. Helsinki: Otava, 1971.

Valkonen, Jarno. *Lapin luontopolitiikka. Analyysi vuosien 1946–2000 julkisesta keskustelusta*. Tampere: University of Tampere, 2003. Available online: https://urn.fi/urn:isbn:951-44-5775-7 (accessed July 31, 2024).

Valkonen, Sanna. *Poliittinen saamelaisuus*. Tampere: Vastapaino, 2009.

Vanistendael, Cornelius. "Shaping Europe's First Dance Craze – The Role of Napoleon's Grande Armée in the Dissemination of the Quadrille (1795–1815)." *Dance Research* 36, no. 1 (2018): 91–111.

Vartiainen, Hilja. *Koulupaikan neitinä kolttain parissa*. Jyväskylä: Gummerus, 1929.

Vedenpää, Ville. "Räp-artisti Uniikki poisti saamelaisia halventaneen musiikkivideon Youtubesta: 'Se oli aikansa elänyt'." *YLE (The Finnish Broadcasting Company)*, May 4, 2021. Available online: https://yle.fi/a/3-11913751 (accessed July 20, 2024).

Vienola-Lindfors, Irma. "Tanhu ei saa pysähtyä." *Helsingin Sanomat*, July 30, 1981.

Virtanen, Pirjo Kristiina, and Irja Seurujärvi-Kari. "Introduction: Theorizing Indigenous Knowledge(s)." *Dutkansearvvi dieđalaš áigečála* 3, no. 2 (2019): 1–19. Available online: https://www.dutkansearvi.fi/volume-3-issue-2-en/pirjo-kristiina-virtanen-irja-seurujarvi-kari-introduction-theorizing-indigenous-knowledges-en/ (accessed June 12, 2024).

Vladimirova, Vladislava K. "'We are Reindeer People, We Come from Reindeer.' Reindeer Herding in Representations of the Sami in Russia." *Acta Borealia* 28, no. 1 (2011): 89–113. Available online: https://doi.org/10.1080/08003831.2011.575661 (accessed 15 August 2024).

Voionmaa, Väinö. *Suomi Jäämerellä*. Helsinki: Edistysseurojen Kustannusosakeyhtiö, 1918.

Westinen, Elina. "Suomiräpin ja suomalaisuuden moninaisuudesta." *Ilmiö*, June 15, 2023. Available online: https://ilmiomedia.fi/artikkelit/suomirapin-moninaisuudesta/ (accessed July 20, 2024).

Whitelocke, Bulstrode. *Bulstr. Whitelockes Dag-Bok öfver dess ambassade til Sverige åren 1653 och 1654.* Öfversatt ifrån engelskan. Uppsala: Johan Edman, 1777.

World Wildlife Fund. "Kola Peninsula Tundra." *WildWorld* (2001). Available online: https://web.archive.org/web/20100308074247/http://www.nationalgeographic.com/wildworld/profiles/terrestrial/pa/pa1106.html (accessed July 31, 2024).

WorldData.info. "Climate in Lapland (Finland)." Available online: https://www.worlddata.info/europe/finland/climate-lapland.php (accessed July 31, 2024).

Zemtsovsky, Izaly. "Russian Federation. II. Traditional Music. 1. Russian." In *The New Grove Dictionary of Music and Musicians,* ed. Stanley Sadie, 1–10. New York: Macmillan, 2001.

Захарова, О. А. *Русский бал XVIII — начала XX века. Танцы, костюмы, символика.* М.: ЛитРес, 2010.

Мальми, Виола. *Народные танцы Карелии.* Петрозаводск: Карелия, 1978.

Мирек, Альфред. "Череповка, черепашки обыкновенные." *Аккордеонист.Ру* (2017). Available online: http://www.akkordeonist.ru/history_view.php?id=24 (accessed August 3, 2024).

Нилов, В.Н. "Экспедиционный материал русской традиционной хореографии Муромского края." *Учитель музыки* 59, no. 4 (2022): 15–23.

Первушина, Е. В. "Французская кадриль 'на русские темы.'" *Культура и искусство,* no. 11 (2021). Available online: https://nbpublish.com/library_read_article.php?id=34939 (accessed June 10, 2024).

Эйхольц, Е. Н. "Освоение традиционных танцев Алтайского края как эффективное средство оздоровления детей и здоровьесберегающая технология." *Культурное наследие Сибири* 32, no. 2 (2021): 121–7.

INDEX

Aanaar Saami 15–18, 68
accompaniment 1, 9, 69, 73, 76, 87, 101, 130, 141
accordion 45, 50–2, 62, 64, 68, 75–9, 86–7, 90–1, 95, 110, 120–1, 124–8, 130, 132, 135, 140–1, 145, 163, 182
Ainamilaadu 104–7, 109, 135, 138, 180
   Prossan kylvö 105
   Tattarkâ'lvvmõš 105
   Tsuurun kylvö 105
Akkala Saami 14–15
archive 6–7, 9–10, 16, 30, 53, 67, 69–75, 90–2, 98, 101–4, 109–10, 116, 124, 130, 135–6, 141, 158, 160–2, 164–5, 181–2
assimilation 13, 15, 19–20, 154, 156, 161, 169, 190
authenticity 155–6, 168
Ä'vv, *see* Skolt Saami Museum Ä'vv

Bolshevik 5
Bonfil Batalla, Guillermo 161, 184

Če'vetjäu'rr 7, 29, 50, 64, 69, 78, 90, 94, 106, 115–18, 120, 123–4, 126–7, 129–30, 134–8, 140–5, 147, 149–50, 153, 159, 161–3, 181–2
Če'vetjäu'rr ka'drel group 7–8, 137–8, 140–1
Christmas 57, 59, 61–2
climate change 19, 21–3, 190–1
cockfight, *see* Kukkotappelu
Colín, Ernesto 161–3, 184
colonialism 19–22, 31, 33, 189–91, 194
contradance 82–3, 86, 157, 176, 184
   contredanse 81–3, 185

cotillion 81–3, 86
Crottet, Robert 89, 117–20, 125, 160, 184
cultural heritage 6–8, 23, 96, 149, 153, 167

dance song 69, 72, 95
dance tradition 52, 115, 125, 128, 140, 148, 167
Dancing People, *see* Pleässjeei meer
decolonialism 19
decolonization 20, 37, 43

Easter 62–4
Ee'lj pei'vv 64
emancipation reform 85
embroidery 17, 31, 54, 138, 188
ethical guidelines 8, 41–2, 186
ethnocentrism 20, 159
ethnomusicology 3
evacuation 28–9, 78, 119
exoticism 160
exploitation 19, 160

final churn, *see* Loppukirnu
finale, *see* French quadrille
Finnish Broadcasting Company, *see* YLE
Finnish Winter War 28, 53, 115, 118
Finnishization 154
First World War 52, 72, 74, 105, 111
Fofanoff, Då'mnn (Tyyne) 128, 136, 140–1
foxtrot 118, 120
French quadrille, *see* quadrille

gákti 17, 183, 190
Gauriloff, Katja 154–5, 183
Gauriloff, Mari 3, 148–50, 192

Genetz, Arvid 51–2, 65–6, 185
gramophone 76, 120

Häkämies, Irja, *see* Jefremoff, Irja
Hakkarainen, Toini 127–8, 185
Hämäläinen, Antti 34, 49, 63, 76, 78, 87, 105, 107, 180, 186
harmonica 64, 75–6, 78, 101–4, 130, 133, 138
Hoppu, Petri 9, 29, 68, 72, 81, 86, 116, 129–30, 140, 145, 147–9, 159–60, 162–3, 165, 181, 186–7

iigrâs-siõrr, *see* ka'drel
Inari 3, 6–9, 13, 15–16, 19, 25, 27–9, 44, 48, 64, 68, 89, 115–17, 120–1, 124, 126, 129–30, 134–6, 140, 145–7, 153, 157, 159, 181, 187–90, 192
indigenous knowledge systems 40, 188
indigenous onto-epistemologies 38–9
indigenous studies 11, 20, 37–9, 41, 43
instrument (music) 62, 66, 69, 75–6, 87, 101, 130, 134, 163
instrumental music 45, 68, 75, 78, 90
Itkonen, T. I. 27–8, 32–3, 43, 58, 66, 93, 95, 104, 185, 187
Ivalo 116, 118, 141, 181

Jefremoff, Irja 29, 68, 89–90, 101–4, 124, 128–9, 131, 138–9, 143, 145, 148, 181–2, 186–7
Jefremoff, Simo 130, 138
Jefremoff, U'cc-Åttaž (Antti) 130, 138
Jõnn lä'znpei'vv 49
Jouste, Marko 5–6, 9–10, 13, 15–16, 19, 25, 30, 33, 41, 44, 51, 64–5, 67–8, 71–5, 79, 89, 91–2, 98, 109–10, 116–17, 123, 127, 138, 140–1, 145, 148, 158, 163–5, 182, 187–9, 192

kaatrel, *see* quadrille
ka'drel, *see* quadrille
Kasatškah 102
Kerenski 99–100, 177
  Tuustepp 100
  Tuusteppi 99–100
Keväjärvi 29, 115–16, 181
Kildin Saami 14–15, 50, 68
Kiprianoff, Hanna-Maaria 16, 163, 181, 188

Kõllažjokk 52
Koputoff, Grigori 75, 101–4, 129–30, 132–3, 138–9
Korobushka 99, 101, 103, 138, 146, 176
Krakoviak 100, 179
Kukkotappelu, *see* ka'drel
Kuu loistaa 99, 129, 179–80

la pastourelle, *see* French quadrille
la polonaise, *see* French quadrille
la poule, *see* French quadrille
la tréniz, *see* French quadrille
Laestadism 48–9, 120
Laitinen, Heikki 30, 67–8, 75, 89, 110, 121, 124–6, 135, 155, 160, 176, 187, 189
lament 68
lappology 33, 189
Läpytystanssi, *see* Kuu loistaa
Launis, Armas 43, 74, 189
le pantalon, *see* French quadrille
Lehtola, Veli-Pekka 6–8, 13, 18–20, 27–8, 32–3, 40–1, 118, 157, 185–6, 188–9, 191
Lent 49, 57–9, 61–4
Les Lanciers 84, 86, 173
  lanssi 86
  lantsik 86
l'été, *see* French quadrille
leu'dd 5, 13, 60–1, 64–5, 67–9, 72–4, 90–1, 117, 127, 138–9, 141, 182, 187–8
livđe 16, 68
Loppukirnu, *see* ka'drel
Lovozero, *see* Luujäu'rr
Lulejan Saami 14–15
lullaby 68, 138
luohti 18, 48, 68, 158
Lutheran Church 15, 48, 120
Luujäu'rr 50–1, 130, 134, 140–2
luvvjt 68

määccaǩ 17, 136, 145
Magga, Sigga-Marja 5, 8, 17, 186–7, 190
Mäiddneä'ttel, *see* Mäiddpâ'sslašttâm
Mäiddpâ'sslašttâm 57–62, 64, 182
Midsummer, *see* Ee'lj pei'vv
Moshnikoff, E'llj (Elias) 64, 68, 74, 78–9, 141, 181–2, 188
Moshnikoff, Minna 3, 140, 145, 148–50, 181, 192

Mue'tǩk 25–6, 58
music tradition 49–50, 67–8, 70, 137, 139

Neiden, see Njauddâm
Nellim, see Njeä'llem
nelljsiõrr 95
Njauddâm 9, 25, 163
Njeä'llem 7, 28–9, 69, 75, 101, 115, 123,
    129–30, 132, 134–5, 137–41, 145–6,
    148, 158, 161, 163, 181–2, 189
Njeä'llem Folklore Group 7, 75, 129–30,
    135, 137–9, 145
Njuõ'ttjäu'rr 25–6
North Saami 14–18
nue'rrsiõrr 59–60, 110

Obsikruugg 101
Oira 99, 101–2, 129, 179
Okldu'na 66, 110, 135
oral history 64, 68
oral tradition 7, 68, 119
Orthodox Church 15, 30, 49, 68
Orthodox Old Believers 49–50

Paččjokk 25–7, 29, 52, 65–6, 100, 115,
    129, 188
pällsiõrr 110
Pas d'Espagne, see Patespa
Patespa 100, 177
Paulaharju, Samuli 34, 52, 58, 68, 104,
    191
Peäccam 25–6, 29, 75, 100, 115
Pechenga 5, 26–9, 31–2, 52, 61, 69–70, 75,
    99–100, 111, 115, 117, 125, 129–30,
    134–5, 138, 143, 153
Peeddar pei´vv 64
pee'rvesǩ 31, 54
pervest, see pee'rvesǩ
Peter's Day, see Peeddar pei´vv
Phinnoi 13
pihttâz 17
Pite Saami 14
Pleässjeei meer 163–4
polka 99, 179
pot-pourrée, see potpourri
pot-pourri, see potpourri
potpourri 82–3, 86, 173, 192
põ'ttepiåčkklemsiõrr 111
po'vdneǩ 31

prää'zneǩ 59, 64
Prossan kylvö, see Ainamilaadu
Purpuri, see potpourri

quadrille 1, 3, 81–9, 104, 121, 136, 145,
    157, 162–3, 171–6, 184, 188,
    192–3
  French quadrille 81, 83, 85–9, 136,
    171–3, 176
  finale 83, 174
  la pastourelle 83, 173
  la polonaise 83
  la poule 83, 88, 173
  la tréniz 83, 88, 173
  le pantalon 83, 88, 171–2
  l'été 83–4, 88, 172
kaatrel 52
ka'drel 1, 3–5, 7–10, 50, 52–3, 57, 61–6,
    72–3, 76, 78–9, 81, 87–91, 93, 95–6,
    100, 115–20, 124–30, 134–8, 140–2,
    144–51, 153–63, 167–9, 175–6, 182
  Kukkotappelu 149
  Loppukirnu 149

racism 34
radio 7, 76, 78, 118, 123–4, 134, 182
reindeer herding 16–17, 20, 22, 25, 33,
    134, 193
revitalization 7, 16, 20, 30, 101, 123–4, 126,
    130, 135, 155, 167–8
revival 20, 44, 48–9, 113, 115, 120, 124,
    126, 129, 168, 183
Rikurilla 102
Rimpparemmi 161
ripaska 101–2, 104, 173–4
ristsiõrr 104
Risttǩe'dd 28
Röntyskä 86, 186
rope-game, see nue'rrsiõrr
rumba 118–19

Saamelaisiltamat 120, 126, 134–7, 140, 144,
    153, 182
Saami parliament 13, 19, 21, 141
Saami Soirée, see Saamelaisiltamat
šaamšiǩ 31, 54
Säärves 25–6
Salminen, Väinö 43, 49, 192
samsäd, see šaamšiǩ

Saxholm, Sari 3, 145, 148–50, 160, 181, 192
Scrithifinoi 13
self-determination 18, 21, 40, 42
self-governance 20
Semenoja, Va'ss 73, 75, 127
Šestjårkka 73, 93–6, 98, 129, 135
Sevettijärvi, *see* Če'vetjäu'rr
Shestjorkka, *see* Šestjårkka
Shrove, *see* Mäiddpâ'sslašttâm
sijdd 25–8, 49, 51, 53, 57–8, 64, 75
Similä, Ahti 141, 181
singing 49, 65–6, 69, 110, 125, 129, 135, 163
singing game 66, 93, 104, 110
siõrr 49, 64, 141
Skolt Saami Museum Ä'vv 9, 163
snowmobile 17, 23
song
  Karelian 67–8, 72, 95
  Russian 67–8, 72, 95
  Skolt Saami 67, 72, 95
soroka 31
South Saami 14–15
Sowing of Buckwheat, *see* Tattarkå'lvvmõš
Sowing of Millet, *see* Prossan kylvö
Spivak, Gayatri 162, 192
St. Mary's Day, *see* Jõnn lä'znpei'vv
Suõmmkar 9–10, 155
Suõ'nn'jel 29, 49, 53, 58–63, 69, 78, 115–16, 118, 120–1, 124–5, 182
Supru 127, 135, 144
Sverloff, Jääkk 59–60, 64–5, 72, 74–5, 89–92, 118, 181–2

Tähtiherrat 49
Tanner, Väinö 33, 52, 118, 190–1, 193
Tattarkå'lvvmõš, *see* Ainamilaadu
Ter Saami 14–15, 154, 183
Titoff, Vaa'ssel (Vasili) 75, 130, 133, 138
Topelius, Zacharias 157
Tsuurun kylvö, *see* Ainamilaadu
Tuustepp, *see* Kerenski
Tuusteppi, *see* Kerenski
two-step 99–100, 177–80

Ume Saami 14
UN Declaration on the Rights of Indigenous Peoples 20
UNESCO 8, 15
Urrvuõnn 52
Utsjoki 29, 127–8
uu'rčeškuõ'đi 64

Valkeapää, Nils-Aslak 8, 19, 123, 187, 193
Vartiainen, Hilja 63–4, 76, 193
Vengerka, *see* Vintjårkka
Vintjårkka 100, 176, 178
Voionmaa, Väinö 32, 193
Vosmerkka 73, 93, 95

waltz 100, 177
wedding 65–6, 117–18, 143
Wesslin, Heini 8, 116, 181–2

Yabloko 72–4
YLE 7, 17, 126, 134–5, 158–9, 182–3, 191–3
yoik 18, 48, 68, 138